Taking the Red Pill
Science, Philosophy and Religion in The Matrix

Seven Seasons of Buffy
Science Fiction and Fantasy Writers Discuss Their Favorite Television Show

Five Seasons of Angel
Science Fiction and Fantasy Writers Discuss Their Favorite Vampire

What Would Sipowicz Do?
Race, Rights and Redemption in NYPD Blue

Stepping through the Stargate
Science, Archaeology and the Military in Stargate SG-1

The Anthology at the End of the Universe
Leading Science Fiction Authors on Douglas Adams' Hitchhiker's Guide to the Galaxy

Finding Serenity
Anti-heroes, Lost Shepherds and Space Hookers in Joss Whedon's Firefly

The War of the Worlds
Fresh Perspectives on the H. G. Wells Classic

Alias Assumed
Sex, Lies and SD-6

Navigating the Golden Compass
Religion, Science and Dæmonology in Philip Pullman's His Dark Materials

Farscape Forever!
Sex, Drugs and Killer Muppets

Flirting with Pride and Prejudice
Fresh Perspectives on the Original Chick-Lit Masterpiece

Revisiting Narnia
Fantasy, Myth and Religion in C. S. Lewis' Chronicles

Totally Charmed
Demons, Whitelighters and the Power of Three

King Kong Is Back!
An Unauthorized Look at One Humongous Ape

Mapping the World of Harry Potter
Science Fiction and Fantasy Authors Explore the Bestselling Fantasy Series of All Time

The Psychology of The Simpsons
D'oh

THE UNAUTHORIZED
X-MEN

SF and Comic Writers on Mutants, Prejudice and Adamantium

THE UNAUTHORIZED
X-MEN

EDITED BY
Len Wein
WITH Leah Wilson

BENBELLA BOOKS, INC.
Dallas, Texas

BenBella Books, Inc.
6440 N. Central Expressway, Suite 617
Dallas, TX 75206
www.benbellabooks.com
Send feedback to feedback@benbellabooks.com

Printed in the United States of America
10 9 8 7 6 5 4 3 2 1

Library of Congress Cataloging-in-Publication Data

The unauthorized X-men : SF and comic writers on mutants, prejudice, and adamantium / edited by Len Wein with Leah Wilson.
     p. cm.
   ISBN 1-932100-74-1
   1. X-men (Comic strip) 2. X-Men (Fictitious characters) I. Wein, Len. II. Wilson, Leah.
   PN6728.X2U52 2006
   741.5'973—dc22

                                                                          2005037139

Proofreading by Rebecca Green and Stacia Seaman
Cover design by Todd Michael Bushman
Text design and composition by John Reinhardt Book Design
Printed by Victor Graphics, Inc.

Distributed by Independent Publishers Group
To order call (800) 888-4741
www.ipgbook.com

For media inquiries and special sales contact Yara Abuata at yara@benbellabooks.com

Contents

It's Just Mutants

An Unauthorized Introduction to
The Unauthorized X-Men

THERE'S A WONDERFUL, almost certainly apocryphal story about a guy who went to a comic book convention some number of years ago, and started thumbing through a box of old Disney comics. One by one, he pulled the mylar-snugged books that caught his attention from the box and piled them beside him. Finally, satisfied with his choices, he presented the stack of books to the dealer.

"So, how much to I owe you for these?" he asked.

The dealer carefully went through the pile, added up the prices, then turned back to the potential buyer.

"That'll be three hundred fifty bucks," he said. "Plus tax."

The buyer's chin practically bounced off the floor. "Wh-wh-what?" he stammered. "B-b-but how...?"

So the dealer went through the musty stack book by book, trying to explain. "Well, this one here is *Uncle Scrooge #23*," he said. "It's worth forty bucks these days. That one there is *Disney's Comics and Stories #32*. It's $150 in near-mint." And so forth and so on. And with each price named, the buyer's jaw dropped lower and lower.

Finally, with what little verbal capacity he had left, the stunned buyer managed to mutter, "Th-th-three hundred fifty bucks for a bunch of comic books? B-b-b-but it's...it's just ducks!"

And that, gentle reader, is sort of how I feel about the X-Men.

After two successful animated series, two top-grossing live action features—with a third coming late this spring and a fourth already in development—and, frankly, more toys, games, action figures and ancillary merchandise than one can shake the average Wal-mart at—

1

I still often think to myself, "All this fuss about the X-Men? But it's...it's just mutants."

You have to understand, when the X-Men comic book was first created, it was pretty much a flop. Creators Stan Lee and Jack Kirby had a fairly impressive record at Marvel Comics up to that point. *Fantastic Four, The Incredible Hulk, The Mighty Thor, The Avengers, The Astonishing Ant-Man* (well, okay, so maybe not Ant-Man), *Sgt. Fury and his Howling Commandos*: all had quickly become hits and continue to be to this day. But the X-Men, not so much. Granted, the reason may have been that Stan and Jack left the title fairly early on, leaving it to other, lesser creative lights to chart the course for Charles Xavier's merry band of superpowered students. Or it may have been that people just weren't as interested in a group of teenage misfits in matching blue-and-yellow uniforms.

Oh, there were still a few highlights during the series' run, most notably a brief arc by writer/artist Jim Steranko and a still highly regarded run by writer Roy Thomas and artist Neal Adams, and the costumes kept changing almost every other week in an attempt to find something more pleasing to the eye, but the sales continued their slow decline until, with issue #67, as if finally throwing in the towel, *Uncanny X-Men* became a reprint title.

And thus it might well have remained.

But Roy Thomas, then editor-in-chief at Marvel, was never one to easily admit defeat. For many months, he batted around the idea of bringing back some version of the X-Men, possibly featuring an international team of heroes, not unlike DC Comics' long-running *Blackhawk* title. But, for a long time, that was all it remained: an idea.

Still, those rumors were the primary reason that, when artist Herb Trimpe and I introduced Marvel's first Canadian hero, a feisty little fella you may have heard of called Wolverine, in the pages of *Incredible Hulk* #181, I chose to make him a mutant as a way of explaining his superpowers. I figured, if Marvel ever did get around to reviving the X-Men, this would give them another non-American character to possibly cull for the new line-up. Little did I suspect at the time that the person who would one day have to make that choice would be me.

Truth to tell, I don't exactly recall how I came to be Roy Thomas' choice to write the X-Men revival. Right up until the week preceding, there was another writer everyone expected to get the gig. Nonetheless, the finger ultimately came to be pointed at me. So, with artist extraordinaire Dave Cockrum—who had just recently concluded a long and very successful run on DC's *Legion of Super-Heroes*—at my side, we set to work.

Dave had a notebook filled with sketches of characters he'd been just itching for a chance to use someplace. So the first thing we did was to sit down with that notebook and start looking for potential team members. In that notebook we found rough versions of characters who, with a few minor costume and character adjustments, would go on to become Nightcrawler, Colossus and Thunderbird. Storm was a tad more difficult to come by. In the end, she ended up as a combination of two other characters—one whose visual we liked, one whose powers we liked—neither of whom was working out of their own. Tossing Banshee and Sunfire, two of Marvel's few other international mutants—oh, and that Canadian guy I'd come up with earlier—into the mix, we had our new team of X-Men. We even kept in Cyclops, so the good old US of A would still be represented.

The all-new, all-different X-Men, as they were called, were introduced in the pages of something called *Giant-Size X-Men #1*, part of an enthusiastic—but brief—attempt by Marvel to introduce a new size and type of packaging to the comics market. (The line also included a book called *Giant-Size Man-Thing*, possibly one of the most unfortunate titles in comics history.) At any rate, our efforts were, he says with all due modesty, fairly well-received. By the time we'd finished plotting the second issue, however, the giant-sized experiment was over. We decided instead to resume the regular-sized *X-Men* comic with the old numbering. Thus, *Giant-Size X-Men* #2 instead became *X-Men* #94 and 95. Dave and I simply split our double-sized plot to spread over two normal-sized issues.

Now here, of course, is where things start to get interesting. Sometime between when I'd begun *Giant-Size X-Men* #1 and then finished it, I'd also suddenly become Marvel Comics' new editor-in-chief, replacing Roy, who happily went back to writing and editing his own titles. It became immediately apparent to me that I couldn't handle this sixteen-hour a day job and the various Marvel titles I was then writing every month as well. Something had to give and the writing was the obvious choice. I doled out my other assignments to other writers until I had only two titles left in hand. One was *The Incredible Hulk*, which I had been writing for several years then and was much enamored with. The other was the *X-Men*. I really was having a hard time deciding which title to give up. But the choice was quickly made easy for me.

Sitting at a desk just outside my office in those days was one Christopher Claremont, one of my editorial assistants and a rising young writing star in the Marvel firmament. As I wondered out loud to all and sundry which title I should sacrifice, Chris' hand went up and started flailing around like a windmill.

"Oooh, oooh, give up the X-Men," Chris shouted, sounding not at all unlike Gunther Toody from the late, lamented TV series, *Car 54, Where Are You?* "I'll take the X-Men book," Chris pleaded, "I'll do it."

Now, remembering how enthusiastically Chris had *kibbutzed* about the *Giant-Size* #1 plot—it was Chris' suggestion that we squirt the living island Krakoa into space—giving him the book made total sense. I kept the Hulk, left the editor-in-chief's job some months later and went back to writing and editing my own books as Roy had. Chris took over the *X-Men*, first dialoguing issues #94 and 95 over my plot, then working hand-in-hand with Dave Cockrum to plot and write the book from that point on.

Working first with Dave, then with artist John Byrne, Chris continued to write his butt off month after month. The sales were good; nothing to set the world on fire, mind you, but certainly much better than the original version of the X-Men's, and certainly enough to warrant continued publication. And thus it may well have remained.

But then Chris killed the asparagus people.

A whole blamed planet full of asparagus people. Frankly, I didn't care. If he'd killed a planet of Brussels sprouts people, I might have been a little upset. I mean, I *like* Brussels sprouts. But asparagus people? Hey, them's the breaks.

Fortunately for the X-Men and the comics-buying world, Marvel's then-current editor-in-chief Jim Shooter didn't agree with me.

There had been a lot of changes in the X-Men book under Chris' aegis. A number of other new mutants had been introduced. A number of original mutants had returned to the X-Men fold. One such was Jean Grey, once known as Marvel Girl, who was possessed of not-inconsiderable telekinetic power.

In saving a space shuttle full of X-Men—don't ask, you'll just have to read the story for yourself—something had happened to Jean, and her powers were amped up considerably. Now she was no longer Marvel Girl, but an almost godlike entity which called itself the Phoenix. It was the Phoenix, flaunting her powers, who had incinerated the planet of asparagus people. Chris, as I recall, had intended to end this storyline by using this crime as a reason for greater forces to considerably reduce Jean's power. Jim Shooter disagreed.

Jim argued that Jean had committed genocide on a planetary scale and had to pay the ultimate price for her crime. No mere slap on the wrist would do. Jean Grey had to be executed.

Now, had this occurred on a busy news day, nothing much would have happened. But, much like the day DC decided to kill *Superman* for the 47th time, nothing much else was going on in the world (thank God), and the story made the newswires. It spread like wildfire. People who didn't even normally read comics were suddenly clamoring to get their hands on the issue where a superhero actually died.

As a result, the circulation of *X-Men* #137 tripled, maybe even quadrupled, and a tremendous number of people got to sample what they had been missing all this time. And, to no one's surprise, a large number of them decided to stick around. Suddenly, the X-Men went from a solid mid-level title to the best-selling title in the line, outstripping even such stalwarts as Spider-Man. Apparently, it has remained so to this day. And thus are lucrative franchises grown.

As of last month, there were—count 'em—nineteen different X-Men and X-Men-related titles being published by Marvel Comics. Over the years, practically every prominent member of the team, from Nightcrawler and Colossus to such lesser lights as Mystique and Emma Frost, has had his or her own ongoing or mini-series. The term X-Men has entered the daily lexicon and there's nobody I meet who doesn't know who Wolverine is.

Still, the question remains: Why? How did this unlikely group of societal misfits with extraordinary powers come to symbolize a generation and force their way into the common consciousness? Why do we find who they are and what they do so endlessly fascinating? As I said, it's just mutants, right?

Yeah. Right.

In the pages ahead, seventeen of today's foremost authorities dissect and discuss the magic of the X-Men mythos for your entertainment and enlightenment. I suggest you get settled in your most comfortable chair with a hot cup of tea or cocoa and read on. It promises to be a most unusual ride.

Oh, and if you happen to hear the sudden belch of imploding air and start to smell the stringent stench of brimstone, I'd duck for cover if I were you.

Remember, these days the X-Men are everywhere.

Len Wein
January, 2006

WRITING THE X-MEN

Playing God and Discovering
My Own Mutanity

JOE CASEY

I can't begin to tell you how many times over the years I've crossed paths with someone who, upon learning what I do to put bread on my table, has said to me, "God, writing comic books has got to be the coolest job I've ever heard of. What I wouldn't give to write comics for a living." In the following confession, fellow comics scribe Joe Casey reminds us to always be careful what we wish for.

LADIES AND GENTLEMEN, writing comic books is a strange way to make a living.

I know this from experience. For close to a decade now, it's been my primary source of income. From a simple childhood dream to the career that eventually allowed me to buy a home and travel the world (if, by "the world," you mean most of the United States, Mexico, the United Kingdom and parts of Europe), writing comic books has not only been my job, it's been my life. And I pretty much love my life.

But a career in *anything* is a journey. It contains ups and downs, highs and lows, triumphs and disappointments. Just like good comic book stories, I guess. And like any other career, there are stages of advancement, a proverbial ladder of success wherein a writer can climb from relative obscurity to the top of his or her field, sometimes

in an alarmingly short amount of time. And in the realm of mainstream comic books, that usually involves writing the X-Men.

By now, you've probably all seen the movies. Maybe some of you
have seen the animated cartoon series from the early '90s. And, obviously, there are those of you who read, or at least knew about, the
comic book series that spawned it all. You all know the concept of
the X-Men—"mutants" born with extraordinary abilities, hated and
feared by the world they are sworn to protect. Most of you are probably familiar with X-Men perennials like Wolverine, with his feral
nature, his unbreakable adamantium claws and his unrequited love
for fellow X-Man Jean Grey (y'know, the chick who died in the second film). You know about Professor X, founder of the Xavier Institute and an incredibly powerful telepath who is also bald—because,
y'know, if you have incredible mind powers, your hair will obviously fall out—and confined to a wheelchair. You probably know about
Cyclops and his optic beams, which can only be controlled by wearing a ruby quartz lens visor. But not everyone is aware that, for the
majority of the past twenty-five years, the X-Men have dominated
the comic book market. The various X-Men series and their spin-
offs have consistently been top sellers, so much so that some writers
have made (literally) millions of dollars in royalties writing the comic book adventures of these unique mutant characters.

Not *me*, of course. I've never made millions writing comic books.
But whatever.

For a while there, X-Men fans were undoubtedly the largest audience a writer could be exposed to in the monthly comic book medium. Because even when the series dipped in quality over the years,
people still bought it. Maybe they were buying out of habit; maybe
they simply loved the characters; maybe they only liked the artwork
and didn't pay attention to the oftentimes uneven quality of the writing; maybe they only liked the writing and didn't pay attention to
the varying quality of the artwork, or maybe they actually liked often
confused plotting and occasionally overwritten dialogue.

Or maybe this massive reading audience simply connected to the
X-Men metaphor on such a deep emotional level, they weren't even
conscious of it. They just needed to maintain the connection. But
more on that later.

In the early years of writing comic books professionally, I never thought much about my "career," per se. I was so happy to even be invited to the party, I never thought much about the long term. And then, at some point a few years in, it hit me: if I wanted to keep doing this, I needed to get my business head on a little straighter. I needed to swing for the fences a bit more, professionally speaking. The ladder was there... I just needed to step on and start climbing. I needed to finally treat this thing like a business. I needed to get serious. I needed some concrete career goals.

And that's where the X-Men come in. They were the brass ring. They were the ticket to stardom and security in an otherwise volatile industry.

I started modestly, pitching—and eventually writing—a six-issue miniseries called *Children of the Atom*. It was an in-depth exploration of the original X-Men's origins, updated from their original mid-'60s milieu and adapted to modern times—in this case, the late '90s and the turn of the millennium. An artist was lined up, industry legend Steve "the Dude" Rude, and I dove into my research. That entailed not only reading lots of old comic books, but peeling back the layers of the characters, the concept and the metaphor to discover exactly *why* the X-Men had always seemed to touch such a nerve in so many readers worldwide.

As I prepared to write this series—which I was certain was going to rocket me to the top of the comic book writer heap—a cold, hard fact became all too apparent to me: *I never really liked the X-Men.*

See, when I was a kid, I was more of a "classic" superhero fan. Captain America. Iron Man. Thor. The Avengers. Daredevil. The Fantastic Four. These were the comic books I tended to go for during my more impressionable years. As I researched for *COTA*, I had to ask myself, "Why didn't I connect as strongly to the X-Men as so many others of my generation obviously did?"

And so we come to the aforementioned metaphor. Mutants are outcasts. Disenfranchised. Shunned by society. They often look different. Freakish, even. "Normal" people are afraid of them, and the government wants to destroy them. A *superhero underclass*, for lack of a better description. When you write the X-Men, you're supposed to be writing about racism and intolerance—big social ills that are an embarrassing blight on our shared society. At least, that's what we were all led to believe. In writing the miniseries, I decided that the metaphor was slightly different from the socially forward-thinking party line that Marvel used to spout so often. I'm not a racist or a homophobe, and I'm not trying to work out any of *those* kinds of issues, so I settled on "Mutants Equals Teenagers." Admittedly a bit thin as metaphors go—certainly not as strong or righteous as the racist metaphor—and yet it felt right somehow. I had found my way into the material simply by connecting the idea of being a mutant with the idea of being a teenager. The way I see it, every teenager feels different. Every teenager feels special. Every teenager feels misunderstood. Every teenager feels like an outcast. From the prom queen to the punk rocker, we were *all* disenfranchised. At that age, we were *all* mutants.

Completing the *COTA* series, I felt a sense of relief. It was a rough road, laced with editorial interference and artistic instability (three artists in six issues). One distinct memory of writing the series still stays with me. I'm at my desk, slaving over the script for issue number two, while the television displays the live news coverage of the shootings at Columbine High School. Obviously, there was something happening in America that my work on *COTA* could tie into. The American teenager was suddenly placed under a harsh spotlight, and I finally knew what I was writing about. My editors at Marvel Comics, however, tended to get a little nervous when I put the words "X-Men" and "Columbine" in the same sentence, even in a casual conversation. Here I was looking to make an artistically important, culturally relevant statement, and all they really wanted was a cute little X-Men story that would satisfy the fanboys and not make any waves. Unfortunately for them, that wasn't the kind of writing I liked to do. So there were conflicts. There were tense moments. But I stuck to my vision. I fought for my art. It was a work experience I wouldn't want to repeat anytime soon.

Despite the headaches involved, I still consider *Children of the Atom* to be something of an achievement. It sold well enough, but, more importantly, I felt good about what I'd done, overall. I felt like I accurately served the X-Men metaphor. I felt as though I'd actually crafted some cogent commentary on the modern teenager, how teenagers view themselves and how others view them. And, most importantly, I felt like I'd said my piece on a pop culture concept about which I honestly didn't think I'd have much to say.

But the X-Men weren't finished with me. Not by a long shot.

Cut to a few years later and an editorial regime change at the mighty Marvel Comics that you could describe as much more "creator friendly" than what I'd experienced while writing *COTA*. And here's where the good ol' "ladder of success" comes back into play. Opportunities at what I labeled as "New Marvel" were sprouting up all over the company's line of books, giving creators a chance to enter the House of Ideas and make a significant impact on top-flight characters. Careers were skyrocketing to great heights as already respected comic book writers like Garth Ennis, Grant Morrison and Peter Milligan were allowed to take on venerable Marvel properties and make them sing again. Newer writers like Brian Michael Bendis were also finding a home there, with much success. In a fit of self-interested career-mindedness, I wondered if there might be a place for me at New Marvel. Turns out, there *was* an opening. . . .

Writing *Uncanny X-Men*. It was one of the two "flagship" X-Men titles and at that point, probably the highest-selling comic book in the direct market. One of my favorite comic book writers, Scottish maverick magician Grant Morrison, had signed on to write the other flagship title (simply called *X-Men*, but not for long), and Marvel was looking for the appropriate partner in crime to aid in shaking up the X-Franchise, which the new regime believed—and rightly so—had become fairly stale. They needed a creative kick in the ass, and they needed a few brave souls to do it. Just the kind of high-profile assignment my career was waiting for. And for anyone else, it would've been a no-brainer.

But as you might expect—because if you haven't noticed by now, I think about these things way too much—I was a little reluctant to dive in and take the gig. I had to admit to myself, I'd said all I thought I could say with the *Children of the Atom* miniseries. And I'd barely made it through *that* experience with my eternal optimism still intact. I'd been quite happy to leave what we in the biz like to call the "X-office" far behind. I still had some artistic integrity. I still felt cool. I didn't need the X-Men.

Of course, the *other* side of my brain—the ambitious, career-oriented ladder-climbing side of my brain—wanted to kick my integrity's ass up and down the mountain. I mean, this was my ticket to fame and fortune, wasn't it? This would ensure a permanent spot in the Top Ten sales chart. I would be an industry titan! Besides, a couple of my good friends in the business had done it a few years previous, and they hadn't completely turned into blubbering sellouts (although they did end up quitting after being mucked with one time too many by the old editorial higher-ups). And, hey, if Grant Morrison was willing to belly up to the bar and take his shot at this franchise, why not me? Ultimately, I swallowed my many reservations because I couldn't ignore the simple fact that it was a good career move for me. It was the very tip-top of that proverbial ladder. I signed on and we were off to the races. They sent me Grant's massive "Morrison Manifesto," which outlined his ideas for his book. They were impressive. They were right on the money. Hell, this was an X-Men book *I* would actually want to read. And here I was, blessed with the opportunity to come up with stories and ideas for the other X-Men title...

...and I had nothing.

Oh, I figured I could fake it real good. I thought I knew enough about how superhero comics work that I could toss out a few half-baked ideas, string them together over six or eight issues and hope that inspiration would hit somewhere down the road. So, that's what I did. And, God bless 'em, the new "creator friendly" Marvel Comics gave me just enough rope to hang myself with. Thus, the comic book world was treated to such diverse gems as the X-Ranch, where humans went to be...well, *serviced* by mutant prostitutes, one of whom ended up joining the X-Men. Next up was the Supreme Pontiff, an evil, superpowered papal figure who headed up his own mutant-hating religion, the Church of Humanity (original, eh?). Then, of course, there were the mutant transformative party drugs made from mutant DNA that I affectionately dubbed "Designer Genes" (say it out loud and join me in a sarcastic chuckle). There was the X-Corps, a militant branch of the X-Men ideal that was originally supposed to border on mutant fascism. Sigh....

Something else I can look back on now with a bit more clarity was the fact that I wasn't really *connecting* with the characters I was writing. And I was writing some cool ones: Wolverine, the most popular X-Man by far. Nightcrawler, the demonic-looking, acrobatic tele- porter made famous by actor Alan Cumming's portrayal in the *X2* flick. Another character seen in the movies, Iceman, able to turn his body into pure ice. Archangel, a winged man who—due to some sort of convoluted comic book logic that had nothing much to do with him being a mutant—had blue skin. These are good characters, but for some unknown reason, I wasn't really able to breathe much life into them. I wasn't connecting with them as a writer, much in the same way I hadn't connected with them as a reader during my child- hood. In many ways, I was somehow avoiding my chance as a writer to even *make* those connections. Curious, indeed.

In any case, I wasn't exactly firing on all pistons, creatively speak- ing. Especially when I was being compared to the minor miracles be- ing performed by Grant Morrison on *his* book, now smartly re-titled *New X-Men*. Where I was struggling and failing to bring new ideas to the X-Men concept, Grant was being subversively intelligent in his approach to writing the X-Men. Basically, he was reinterpreting and reintroducing classic elements of X-Men continuity in a new, original way. The Sentinels, Magneto, the Shi'ar Empire, the Hellfire Club, all that good stuff that X-Men readers have always loved. In other words, he was giving the fans exactly what they want. What they *al- ways* want.

X-Men fans are a curious bunch. And a sensitive bunch. Not to mention a *vocal* bunch. The word "devotion" is a gross understate- ment when it comes to these folks. The word "fan" is short for "fa- natic," and in *this* case, that absolutely applies. I give them a lot of credit for not only sticking with their beloved X-Men through thick and thin but also for being quite capable, thanks to the Internet, of making their collective voice heard. If the fans didn't like something, they let you know it right away. And they did. They came out swing- ing, and I was their primary target.

At the time, I remember I was just a wee bit incensed. No one likes to be attacked. No one likes to have his nose rubbed in his own mis- takes, like a dog that's just gone to the bathroom on the living room carpet. The dog may be confused, but it's still angry. And so was I.

But in hindsight, I don't blame them one bit. They were X-Men fans and I wasn't, and yet I was the one steering the bus. And you gotta love the bus if you're going to have the balls to step up and steer it.

After just under two years, I was done. Fried. Finished. One thing I recall thinking at the time was how confused and terrified I was that the fans—the ones who read and disliked my *Uncanny X-Men* run— were behaving just like...well, like typical comic book fans. And, by that, I mean they were acting exactly like the absolute cliché of the anal-retentive, shut-in fanboy, resistant to change, afraid of having their weird little world disturbed in any way, fearful of all things new and different. Despite what I knew damn well was a lack of quality in my own work, I can honestly say I was genuinely befuddled by the high level of displeasure being expressed in my direction.

But you live and learn, right? As it turns out, writing the X-Men was *not* my ticket to fame and fortune. Sure, there was some money, and if *infamy* counts as fame, then fine, there was a bit of that, too. It was an experience, and at the time, I wasn't quite sure what I'd gotten out of it. Not to mention the fact that I was actually questioning why I'd even taken on the gig in the first place.

And then, a few years later, I guess you could say I had a minor epiphany. A breakthrough that had somehow escaped me even back in the day when I was honestly and diligently struggling with the X-Men metaphor, while writing *Children of the Atom*. Apparently, I'd gotten it all wrong.

A brief aside: Every so often in the X-office, the editors would suggest, "How about we create a gay X-Man?" After all, they'd had African American X-Men, Native American X-Men, etc. They often enjoyed displaying cultural diversity in their X-Men characters. I guess it made them feel good about their own white, middle-class identities (the comic book industry is predominately white and middle class, but that's another topic for another day). Every time I would hear one of these ideas, I would always ask myself, "What's the point of being so specific? A gay mutant? An African American mutant? An HIV-positive mutant? Oxymorons, all of them." To my mind, mutants are *all* those things simultaneously. They're *every* oppressed minority and disenfranchised subculture, all rolled up into one metaphor. That's why the comic speaks to such a wide fan base, right? Because it's representative of all of these groups.

Turns out, I was wrong. About all of it. The metaphor was something much more specific than homosexuals, African Americans or even teenagers. Mutants may be able to touch on these social categories, but it's all by happy accident. There's something much, much *deeper* at work here.

What mutants are *truly* metaphors for...are comic book fans. And, in realizing that—and we're talking about years after I'd left the job writing X-Men comic books—I realized that the metaphor had hit a lot closer to home than I had ever wanted to admit...which is probably why I never really embraced the concept as a kid.

Because when I was a kid, if you read comic books religiously like I did, you were labeled a geek. A nerd. A spaz. A weirdo. You were both hated and feared by those around you. Basically, you were a mutant.

Growing up, I tended to be the self-protective type. I hid my passions—for comic books, for movies, for rock 'n' roll—for fear of exactly the kind of social exclusion that so-called "geeks" the world over have suffered (until very recently, but more on that shortly). I didn't grow up in a very "artistic" part of the country. I had enough problems in my childhood without actively and purposefully compounding them by flying a four-color geek flag on top of everything else. So, I guess you could say I was a self-loathing mutant. I tried to be "normal." I joined the school's football team for a few years. Played Little League baseball. Ran cross-country track. Granted, it kept me physically fit, but I was obviously wearing a mask. I was hiding in plain sight. Part of me might've thought (hoped?) I was fitting in, but the deepest, most honest part of me knew the truth. The *real* truth.

I didn't confront that "real truth" until long after I'd begun getting paid for the very same things I had kept so hidden as a kid. It was almost as though I needed that validation to allow myself not only to *admit* my passions, but to *revel* in them. In addition, I'd moved to Los Angeles, California, where geek culture rules more and more each day (a change in environment can do wonders for your self-perception). And, in a weird, convoluted way, it was actually *writing* the X-Men that finally helped drive that point home once and for all.

These days, I embrace my mutant status. I embrace the geek in me. I embrace my inherent uncoolness because it's such a fundamental component of who I am. As a kid, I was afraid of that basic truth, so much so that it kept me away from enjoying a comic book series where the appeal was all about connecting to a worldwide readership comprised of people that were *just like me*: comic book fans.

In these early years of the twenty-first century, the rest of the world has finally caught up to all us die-hard superhero aficionados, and the movies and television shows that define popular culture are merely re-gurgitating ideas and concepts that the rest of us were reading in comic books twenty years ago. The geek has inherited the Earth.

Of course, an inevitable side effect is that X-Men comic books are no longer the dominating cultural force they once were in the comic book direct market, outside of the series' nostalgia value—that makes it a great place for a big-name writer like Joss Whedon to celebrate *his* mutant status. But the fact that Joss is able to come in and write a year or two of X-Men stories proves my point even further: the very passions kids like us hid from the rest of the world have lifted us to some greater glory of self-acceptance and, dare I say, *pride*. Being mutants clearly paid off.

Finally, I know what the metaphor is. It took me twenty-five years, but I get it now.

But that doesn't mean I ever want to write the X-Men again. Then again, I no longer *need* to, do I … ?

REFERENCES

Casey, Joe (w), Essad Ribic, Steve Rude, Michael Ryan and Paul Smith (p), Andrew Pepoy and Paul Smith (i). *Children of the Atom.* Marvel Entertainment Group (Marvel Comics), 1999, 2000, 2001.

Joe Casey is the writer and co-creator of comic book series such as *Automatic Kafka, Gødland, The Intimates, Codeflesh, The Milkman Murders* and *Secret I.D.* He has also written for the major superhero franchises at both Marvel Comics and DC Comics, including *Uncanny X-Men, Avengers: Earth's Mightiest Heroes, Fantastic Four: First Family, Adventures of Superman, Wildcats, G. I. Joe: America's Elite, The Incredible Hulk, Batman: Tenses* and *Iron Man: The Inevitable.* He lives and works in Los Angeles, California.

X-ing the Rubicon

How Marvel's Mighty Mutants Conquered Animation...and the World!

ROBERT N. SKIR

The X-Men have been remarkably successful in virtually every medium into which they've been translated. The field of TV animation is by no means the least of them. Here, veteran animation writer and one of my dearest friends Robert N. Skir leads us on the perilous journey from the printed page to the pixilated screen.

THE X-MEN SERIES remains the single biggest publishing phenomenon in comics history. Its ongoing popularity, as well as its ability to succeed in every medium into which it is translated—from comics to animation to motion pictures to television to video games and beyond—stems largely from two sources: compelling characters lovingly written and illustrated, and the title's ability to serve as a rich, resonating metaphor for a variety of universal human experiences.

THE ORIGIN OF THE SPECIES

Despite its pedigree as a Lee/Kirby creation, *Uncanny X-Men* spent its first decade as a third-tier series, a lesser light for Marvel Comics that fell into reprints by the early '70s. In 1975, it enjoyed a "Second Genesis" beginning with the "All-New, All-Different" *Giant-Size X-*

Men #1 ... and over the next ten years grew from a solid title into a juggernaut that outpaced Spider-Man, the Fantastic Four and all of Marvel's other flagship characters, evolving from bestseller into an ongoing publishing phenomenon.

And in the early 1990s, the time came for the X-Men to conquer an all-new, all-different audience....

LET'S GET ANIMATED

In the 1990s, the popularity of the X-Men increased exponentially, thanks to the animated series produced by Saban Entertainment for the Fox Kids Network. Overnight, the comic book phenomenon gained a huge TV audience, and Wolverine, Rogue and Storm won lifelong fans among people who would never even own a comic book.

Viewers expecting a superhero show with hard-hitting battles and apocalyptic confrontations got exactly what they wanted, and long-time X-Men fans were surprised by the respect for the source material provided by the writers and artists working behind the scenes, who were themselves comics professionals and/or fans.

Comics legend Len Wein, who co-created many of the X-Men's most outstanding characters—including Wolverine, Storm, Colossus and Nightcrawler—contributed scripts to the series, as did many fans who became professional writers, such as David McDermott and Steven Melching. Likewise, producers Will Meugniot (creator of the DNAgents) and Larry Houston were longtime devotees of the X-Men and made sure that, by the end of the show's run, virtually every character from the Marvel Universe had made a cameo in one form or another. Many of the character designs were handled by Frank Brunner, whose artwork graced some of Marvel's most revolutionary comics, including *Doctor Strange* and *Howard the Duck*.

As a rabid X-Men fan since *Giant-Size X-Men* #1, I personally served as an unofficial X-Men X-Pert for the first two seasons. Helping provide the character breakdowns during the show's early development stages, I was determined to make sure that powers and costumes didn't define the characters but that their personalities did; I outlined their loves, hates, flaws and relationships and only then got around to their powers. For instance, I described field commander Scott Summers as a young man carrying the burden of Xavier's dream on his shoulders; if Scott fails, he'll not only be letting down his friends and mutantkind, but (yet more importantly) his surrogate father. Scott is the personification of Xavier's dream, and it takes a heavy toll on him. I then described Scott's relationship with his fellow X-Men such as Jean, for whom he has strong romantic feelings he is reluctant to act on because of his fear of losing focus on leading the team. I then talked about how he's continually being provoked and challenged by Wolverine, who just loves tweaking Scott because a) it's fun, and b) underneath it all, Wolverine respects Scott and knows that he will grow into a great leader. (I likened Wolverine to a seasoned sergeant who likes to needle young, inexperienced Lieutenant Scott.) Only then did I talk about Scott's force-beams (they are not, not, *not* heat beams!), how powerful they are and Scott's great fear of losing control of them.

I wrote detailed breakdowns for all of the major X-Men—including many who did not make the cut for the television series, such as Kitty Pryde and Psylocke. If this series was to succeed, it had to treat the X-Men as people first, and superbeings second.

And with seasoned story editor Eric Lewald speerheading the development of the series as well as overseeing every single script from initial idea through polished final draft, that's exactly what happened over the show's ninety-plus episodes.

"I HAVE A DREAM" VS. "BY ANY MEANS NECESSARY"

The 1990s' animated *X-Men* proved to be more than just an excellent superhero show. It was a show, at its very core, about civil rights. From the very first episode, in which incipient-mutant Jubilee was hunted by Sentinels, the series highlighted the plight of mutants as persecuted minority. As they had become in the comics over the course of the '80s, the X-Men were portrayed less as students than freedom fighters, defending humanity from threats by evil mutants and defending good mutants from oppression at the hands a frightened, often hatefully bigoted, humanity. Magneto and his cohorts (herein rechristened the "Brotherhood of Mutants"; Magneto was only trying to help mutantkind, and would never have labeled himself or his compatriots as "evil") were determined to ensure that *Homo superior* won this evolutionary struggle.

The show was produced for Fox Kids Network, with executive Sidney Iwanter overseeing development and production. Far from the stereotypical Network Executive Who Just Doesn't Get It (an image propagated by Gene Roddenberry in his tirades over NBC's (mis)handling of the original *Star Trek*), Fox's Iwanter truly *got* the X-Men.

Iwanter similarly understood DC's vaunted Caped Crusader; during the production of *Batman: The Animated Series*, Iwanter insisted that Warner Brothers recruit Alan Burnett to oversee the writing. Burnett then hired Paul Dini, Michael Reaves and Marty Pasko as story editors, and together their stories redefined an icon.

While Iwanter was making sure the Broadcast Standards and Practices Department (which monitors scripts and all phases of production to ensure that nothing objectionable or imitable, or which might otherwise expose the network to litigation or cause it embarrassment, gets on the air) didn't prohibit tommy guns or the action that Batman needed, he was also ensuring that, in the case of *X-Men*, Morph could die (like Thunderbird before him) to give the show resonance and really demonstrate what jeopardy the X-Men were facing.[1] So much for the stereotype of the network executive as purveyor of homogenization and the dumbing-down of shows!

During development, Iwanter had countless story meetings during which he demanded that X-Men be as hard-hitting and intense as possible. He wanted action, adventure and a truly unique "take" on the superhero genre, all of which X-Men provided. But more than that, he wanted to explore how society itself would be affected by the emergence of mutants. The show became, under his guidance, an allegory about race relations, with mutants persecuted in the same manner as African Americans in pre–civil rights America (albeit heightened to superheroic, science fiction levels). Professor X thus became a Martin Luther King figure: Each man had a dream of mankind looking past its differences to live together in harmony (consistent with the comics but revolutionary for a Sat-

---

[1] Though Morph did end up returning for an episode or two a season later, thanks to a Marvel-style resurrection prompted by his popularity among viewers.

urday morning cartoon). Magneto was Malcolm X, seeking to liberate his people from oppression by any means necessary (again,
consistent with the comics but revolutionary for a Saturday morning cartoon).

On another level, the series maintained tight focus on its characters, with the personal/B-story soap opera elements often taking pre-
cedence over the action/A-story ones. Ongoing relationships were
affected directly by the characters' mutant powers: Rogue remained
eternally isolated from everybody else because her mutant ability to
absorb people's memories and powers merely by touching them also
made it impossible for her to enjoy the slightest human contact. Her
first kiss put her boyfriend Cody into a coma, prompting her horri-
fied father to disown her. And clearly, as much as Rogue and Gambit had the hots for each other, consummating their relationship
remained forever impossible. (I'm guessing that if Rogue loses her
powers for just an hour, Gambit won't even survive.)

Whereas strict continuity, season-long story arcs and soap opera–
style relationships are not hallmarks of American animated shows
in the early 1990s[2], in order to retain the spirit of its Marvel Comics
source, the X-Men series embraced these elements. Each thirteen-ep-
isode season contained a strong ongoing story arc: the Beast's incar-
ceration in the first season; Xavier and Magneto's imprisonment in
the Savage Land—and the effects of their absence on their respective
teams—in season two.

One of the major recurring relationships throughout the series
was the love triangle between Cyclops, Jean Grey and Wolverine.
This is an element for which I personally lobbied and which was introduced in the fifth episode, "Captive Hearts." It was based on two
panels from the Byrne/Claremont era wherein Wolverine lamented
first the (apparent) death of Jean after a battle with Magneto and
later her actual demise after the Dark Phoenix saga. In both cases,
Wolverine made it clear that he had romantic feelings for Jean; yet
neither Claremont nor any other writer ever followed through on
this. The Fox animated series put this relationship very much on the

---

[2] Anime had been doing this for decades, but in the States it was as yet unheard of, and considered
anathema to the daytime-television demographic of two- to eleven-year-olds—not that we were
ever trying to pander to them.

front burner, and it remains a defining element for Wolverine in the comics and motion pictures. (I love it because it gives Wolverine a really visceral way to annoy Cyclops. Always a plus.)

Personal stories with resonance. A fundamental metaphor about racial tolerance. Reverence for the source material. And lots of things blowing up. No wonder Fox's *X-Men* had ratings that went right through the roof, expanding the title's popularity and helping pave the way for the hugely successful film franchise.

And that film series gave rise to yet another animated series in 2000 on Kids' WB: *X-Men: Evolution.*

BACK TO THE EGG, OR . . . OH, MY GOD: ZITS!

Called upon to develop a new X-Men series set to air fast on the heels of the first feature film, I felt that this series had to be fundamentally different from the Fox animated series, largely because that show had been done *right*, and covered the ground it chose so completely.

How were we supposed to make this new series unique?

The answer came immediately: take the X-Men back to their beginnings, when they were just scared kids trying to understand their strange new powers, and Xavier's mansion was not yet a mutant stronghold, but a school.

And thus was born the Xavier Institute. ("School For Gifted Youngsters" just sounded too lame by this point. It made the students sound *special*, in the very worst sense of the word.)

This idea fit neatly into Kids' WB's programming slate; they wanted a young cast of characters to help them hook their core demographic, shows starring teens or tweens with whom their seven- to eleven-year-old viewers could bond. Kids' WB also requested that the mayhem and violence be greatly de-emphasized.

Basically, they wanted a less angst-driven, less intense version of X-Men.

On the other hand, Marvel needed the X-Men to act like X-Men, protecting a world that hated and feared them. They wanted the show to be dynamic and packed with the kind of action that has long defined the title.

Done. And done.

The way to meet both parties' needs was simple: scale down the scope of the series while keeping the characters (it's all about the characters; it's *always* about the characters!) consistent.

We thus agreed to begin the series with the birth of the X-Men, with Professor X welcoming the first mutants into his mansion and slowly expanding the cast as Xavier filled the Institute over time. The mutants were there to refine their powers so they would not be a threat to themselves or others. It thus became a show about the *training* of mutants.

And, of course, stopping bad mutants from doing bad things.

From this came the show's single most eccentric decision: to have our teen X-Men going to not one but two different schools! The Xavier Institute was a facility for honing mutant powers. But during the weekdays, Xavier's students went to another school, Bayville High (named after the town next to my native Oyster Bay—since there was no such thing as Bayville High School in New York, I figured that we could use the name without fear of getting sued by a school district that didn't want to be portrayed as being blown up on a regular basis), so that they could interact with normal kids. After all, if the show was about trying to control crazy powers, where was the jeopardy if our X-Men were safely isolated in their mansion? I mean, so what if Scott loses his powers in front of Jean Grey; she already knows he's a mutant and accepts him just fine. On the other hand, in a normal school, there's always the fear that their classmates will discover that they are freaks. And that provides *endless* potential for drama. And comedy.

I likewise proposed that "evil" mutants such as Blob, Avalanche and Toad be aged down to teens going to the same school as our X-Men, and basically treated as a rival gang. Doing so gave the teen X-Men plenty of opportunities to engage in battles while at the same time struggling desperately to maintain their secret from their normal classmates.

And thus, the X-Men were still trying to save the world...albeit in a high school microcosm!

Same battles. Same stakes. Smaller arena.

The X-Men's chief concern was mastering their powers while trying to live as (and among) normal teens. They lived in fear that the world would find out about their powers and brand them as freaks, because the very thing that made them special also marked them as freakishly different.

The central theme behind *X-Men: Evolution* thus became that being a mutant was analogous to being a teen, just trying to figure out how to fit into a big, scary world. I mean, who couldn't relate to being afraid of being branded as a freak by your whole high school? And, as teenagers, weren't we all afraid that our friends would find out the truth about us, who we really are deep down inside, and then reject us because of it?

As a central metaphor, it worked like a charm.

Story editors Bob Forward and Greg Johnson spearheaded the writing of the series, and they did a spectacular job. The characters were consistent with their portrayals in the comics (even when they were radically changed, as with Forge, their personalities were essentially consistent), and the stories and the themes were rich with resonance.

Likewise, animated Batman veteran Boyd Kirkland produced the show, writing and directing many of the episodes. He was also responsible for the character designs, which were intentionally less faithful to the Marvel Comics designs than the Fox series (this series had to look different in order to distinguish itself from what had come before) but inherently more animation-friendly. The show looked great, and it moved great, too.

Working together, their handling of the show's themes was masterful.

Jean Grey began the series with a major crush on quarterback Duncan Matthews, who later discovered that she was a mutant and rejected her. Nightcrawler, the single most freakish X-Man (and thus a must for this series!), personified fear of rejection most directly: he used an image inducer (Tony Stark's, which I pilfered from the original Claremont/Cockrum run) to holographically mask his appearance. And in a later, poignant episode, afraid of losing his Bayville friends, Nightcrawler sided with the bigoted, normal kids in ostracizing outed mutants Jean and Scott. Betraying one's friends for fear of losing one's popularity is exactly the sort of conflict kids face every day in every high school.

Their handling of Rogue's decision to join the X-Men instead of the Brotherhood perfectly mirrored the choice so many kids have to make between hanging out with the good kids or the bad kids, and the lifelong consequences of such a decision. Likewise, they gave Kitty Pryde and Avalanche a *West Side Story/Romeo and Juliet*–style relationship, which evolved over the run of the series. After all, who hasn't had a relationship with somebody outside his or her clique? And him being a villain? *Awk-waaard!*

The metaphor of mutants as Those Awkward Teenage Years continued throughout the run of the series. However, as the series evolved, the X-Men became outed, and mutants went from being rumors into being a full-blown source of fear…leading to lots of prejudice. And the battles went from local to global, thus returning the metaphor closer to Fox's and Marvel's conception of X-Men as persecuted minority and global guardians.

The series was a huge hit for Kids' WB, lasting four seasons.

It also seeded an audience raring for a feature film franchise that has, in its first two films (as of this writing), found a yet more global audience: now people who've never held a comic book or watched a Saturday morning cartoon are huge fans of Wolverine, Storm and the rest of the X-Men.

The success of both animated series came because of their fidelity to the source material. The characterizations in the shows were entirely consistent with their portrayals in the comics, such that even if the strict continuity of the comics was not followed, it scarcely mattered. Cyclops was still Cyclops, with nary a compromise to his rich personality, inner conflicts and past demons. The same was true for Rogue, Storm, Magneto, Mystique…*everybody*. Whether in comic books or animated television, feature films or games or anywhere else, Marvel has always endeavored to ensure fidelity to the characters we've known and loved for well over forty-five years.

The other reason for X-Men's enduring success is that the metaphors behind each successive incarnation of the series have not only added richness to the stories, but made the stories and characters universally relatable.

As of this writing, a third animated series is going into production, and will undoubtedly introduce the X-Men to an entirely new generation of viewers. *X3* has finished shooting in Vancouver, and will hopefully continue to expand on the scope of the X-universe (as *X2* greatly expanded it over the original *X-Men*), thus furthering its global popularity. The X-Men have grown from cult-comic success into a mainstream myth embraced by the world. And accordingly, that myth will continue to grow as long as fidelity is paid to the core of the characters, and the stories continue to find new metaphors to explore.

Clearly, the X-Men are here to stay.

Robert N. Skir grew up in Oyster Bay, Long Island. His love of all things fantasy, science fiction and horror led him to make animated films at fourteen, latex masks at sixteen and short stories throughout high school. He majored in English at the University of Virginia and earned a master's degree in screenwriting at UCLA.

He has written many episodes of animated television, including *Beetlejuice*, *X-Men*, *Batman* and *Superman*, and has served as story editor and writer for *The Mask*, *Extreme Ghostbusters*, *Godzilla* and *Transformers: Beast Machines*. His short story "Singularity Ablyss" was published in the 2005 anthology *Transformers: Legends*. He has taught animation writing at UCLA.

Cable's Grandfather

An X-Men Paradox

ROBERT WEINBERG

Poet and philosopher Ralph Waldo Emerson once wrote, "A foolish consistency is the hobgoblin of little minds." If that sainted sage had ever spent an hour trapped in an elevator with your typical comics fan, he would have known how right he was. Herewith, novelist and erstwhile comics writer Robert Weinberg attempts to unravel the twisted history of one particular X-Man without losing his sanity in the process. I'm told visiting hours are Tuesdays and Thursdays.

ONE AFTERNOON IN THE LATE FALL OF 1999, I received a most unusual e-mail from Peter Franco, an assistant editor of Marvel Comics. He and his boss, editor Mark Powers, had read a trilogy of vampire novels I had written for White Wolf Books, and they wondered if I might be interested in scripting a four-part supernatural comic book miniseries for Marvel. Needless to say, as both a professional writer and a longtime comic book fan, I found the idea intriguing. The next morning I called Mark. We talked for an hour, and a deal was made. Thus began my three-year stint as a comic book writer.

Powers and Franco, I soon learned, were the lead editors for the X-Men titles, which were, at that time, the best-selling comic books in the world. They wanted me to write a story in which a half dozen of the mutant heroes and heroines battled some new, incredibly evil menace so powerful that it threatened to wipe out all life on Earth. The miniseries was scheduled for the following October.

Cannibalizing an old idea of mine for a novel never written, I came up with a four-part saga I titled "The Citadel of Night." The script featured a vast, living cube, a mile on each side, that traveled from dimension to dimension, gobbling up all life on each version of Earth it landed upon. In my story, the cube materializes in the middle of an Indiana wheat field a week before Halloween. Only a small team of X-Men recognize the horrible danger threatening the town, the state and the country. Cut off from the outside world by a powerful energy field surrounding the living Citadel, the X-Men find themselves engaged in a life-or-death battle with a monster so huge that not even their most savage attacks can harm it. It was a fun concept, and I had a great time writing the scripts. Alas, it was never to be.

I outlined the entire series and finished two of the four scripts for the miniseries. They were bought but never used due to a massive shake-up at Marvel Entertainment. Sales were in decline and the editor-in-chief of the comic book division decided that the entire X-Men lineup of titles needed a drastic change. The publicity department called this change the "X-Men Revolution." Chris Claremont, the writer most responsible for the incredible popularity of the mutant heroes but who had left Marvel several years before, was rehired and given control over the two lead titles, *X-Men* and *Uncanny X-Men*. Warren Ellis, known for his offbeat and outside-the-box approach to superhero comics, was put in charge of three other X-Men spin-off comics. And, in a bold and unexpected move, I was asked by Mark Powers if I'd like to write a monthly title, which was how I came to write the continuing adventures of the X-Man known as Cable.

Cable had seen his share of writers over the past few years, and with good reason. Like most Marvel superheroes, he had an involved, complex backstory that anchored him firmly in the X-Men universe. It wasn't uncommon for such characters to be involved in a half-dozen unresolved plotlines, all spinning at the same time, while forging ahead fighting new villains each month. But, where most Marvel heroes had headaches, Cable had migraines. His adventures had subplots that had subplots that had subplots. In simple terms, Cable's life was a mess.

It hadn't always been that way. Originally, Cable had been created by Marvel editor Bob Harris, writer Louise Simonson and artist/writer Rob Liefeld for *New Mutants* #87. A grizzled old mercenary with a bionic arm and eye and a love for huge guns, Cable crossed the path of the New Mutants while tracking down a group of evildoers. Impressed by the young team's talent but unimpressed by their organization and skill as a unit, Cable took it upon himself to transform the group into a top-notch fighting force known as X-Force.

All proceeded well and good over the course of a year's worth of comics as Liefeld and Simonson revealed tantalizing glimpses of Cable's past. The huge mercenary had once been part of an elite fighting force known as the Six Pack and actually came from some time in the future, only returning to the present to hunt for a mastermind known as Stryfe. And, most surprisingly of all, Cable and Stryfe looked exactly the same; one man was evidently the clone of the other.

About that time, Liefeld and Simonson departed from the series *X-Force*, and a parade of different writers, all filled with new and divergent ideas for Cable, took over. Within months, the big mercenary's life grew a lot more complicated, and he got his own comic book, appropriately titled *Cable*, in which old mysteries were explained and new ones introduced. Within a few short years, Cable's life turned from a one-act show into a three-ring circus. In a matter of months, the mysterious cyborg-hero was transformed from a man with no past into a man with a past, present and future, tangled together in a mix that spanned both space and time. Cable became the centerpiece of a time-travel epic that encompassed the entire X-Men universe. In the process, he also turned into the hero with the most complicated background in comic book history.

His real name was Nathan Christopher Dayspring Summers, and he had come back from 2,000 years in the future to change the course of history. The son of Scott Summers, the X-Man known as Cyclops, and Madelyne Pryor, a clone of Jean Grey, the Phoenix, Nathan had been born in the present but was transported as a baby into the far future to save him from a deadly techno-organic virus that threatened to turn his body into a machine. It was then, twenty centuries after his birth, that he had been raised in secret by rebels battling a monstrous, near-immortal dictator known as Apocalypse. A mutant born in ancient Egypt, Apocalypse had spent thousands of years in suspended animation, waking every few centuries to see if the Earth was ripe for conquest. He finally struck in the fortieth century, plunging the world into a new Dark Age and establishing himself as undying dictator of the planet until Nathan, while just a teenager, used his incredible mutant powers to destroy him.

Years and years after that fateful battle, Nathan returned to the present as an adult, calling himself Cable and hoping to defeat Apocalypse in modern times, thus altering the future. After many, many encounters and missed opportunities, Cable finally did get the chance to confront and annihilate Apocalypse in the twentieth century. That encounter completed Cable's mission to the present and fulfilled his lifelong dream. By defeating Apocalypse in the twentieth century, the dictatorship of the fortieth century would never take place. The future was no longer fixed...though there were some rumblings about Cable's existence now that he had destroyed his own future. The comic series was without direction and without purpose, and it was the perfect time to bring in a new writer with a new perspective on Cable: me. I was given the reins of the series by Mark Powers and told to go ahead, do something new.

The challenge didn't worry me, because I knew that in the Marvel Universe there were always villains to be fought and quests that needed to be fulfilled. What did concern me was that Cable was living on borrowed time. Sooner or later, he would vanish from sight, taking his part of the Marvel cosmos with him. Because, in crafting a time-travel adventure without considering the perils of twisted logic, Nathan's previous scribes had entwined him in what the science fiction community calls a "grandfather paradox," leaving me with the task of getting him out.

Some readers might ask, why bother? Since time travel is merely science fiction and Cable's just a comic book character, why go to the trouble? Why didn't I just continue writing the comic, ignoring the mistakes of the past or treating them as if they didn't exist? It's a reasonable question and it deserves an answer—two answers, actually.

The first and most important one is that a writer has an obligation to his audience. Whenever an author writes about a world, whether it is the real world or some imaginary place, that world needs to obey certain rules of logic and order. If a story takes place in the Middle Ages, the hero can't rescue the heroine by driving up to the castle and shooting the bad guys with a machine gun. By the same token, if the laws of science apply to the Marvel Universe, even though they are routinely stretched, bent and twisted out of shape, those rules of science must always apply, whether the stories feature the X-Men, the Fantastic Four, the Incredible Hulk or a mutant named Cable. The story, the setting and the characters need to be consistent. If a mistake is made earlier in a story, it has to be fixed or explained later. Anything less is cheating the reader, and no writer wants to do that.

The second answer is a lot simpler. Who says that time travel is impossible?

Not Albert Einstein, that's for sure. Studying Einstein's general theory of relativity, it's clear that there's nothing in advanced physics that proves time travel is impossible. And, in our universe, if something is not impossible, then it's possible... though that doesn't mean it's easy. There's no evidence that time travel has ever taken place, and no one is exactly sure how it could be done, but there are theories.

The most popular version of time machine travel depends on a creating a wormhole, a rip in the fabric of the universe that usually connects two black holes, or a black hole and a white one, to create a tunnel into the past. Unfortunately, creating a wormhole big enough for a spaceship to enter requires more energy than could be generated by the sun in several billion years. Whether such technology might exist two thousand years in the future during the reign of Apocalypse is questionable. Still, it's not absolutely impossible. Which returns us to the original problem: how to save Cable from the grandfather paradox.

The grandfather paradox is a time-travel paradox that has been used in science fiction stories since the early 1940s. In its simplest form, it asks the following question: assuming that you could travel backward in time. If you returned to the past and killed your grandfather before he met your grandmother, would you have ever been born? The answer at first glance seems to be no, but that leads to complications. If you were never born, then how could you have grown up, built a time machine and then traveled back in time to kill your grandfather? Since you were never born, none of that happened. But if none of that happened, then you didn't kill your grandfather. So your grandfather did meet your grandmother and you were born, thus starting the circular chain of events all over again.

The same scenario occurs in Cable's case. Nathan Summers is transported to the far future, where he grows up in a world ruled by Apocalypse. Years later, Nathan travels back in time to the twentieth century and kills Apocalypse. Thus, Apocalypse never conquered the earth, and the future where Nathan grew up no longer exists. If that future never existed, then Nathan could never have grown up there, and thus he would have never gone back in time to kill Apocalypse. And so on and so on, as existence and nonexistence flutter on and off for all eternity. It's a puzzle without a solution: a paradox. Fortunately, the universe is even more complicated than the grandfather paradox. All I needed to rescue Cable from the grandfather paradox was a basic understanding of the Novikov self-consistency principle and a smattering of knowledge about quantum mechanics. And I possessed both.

The Novikov self-consistency principle was proposed by Dr. Igor D. Novikov in the mid-1980s to solve the problem of paradoxes in time travel. In its simplest form, the Novikov principle asserts that if an event exists that would bring about a time paradox, then the probability of that event taking place is zero. In other words, the universe will not allow a time paradox.

Seeking to prove this rather astonishing statement, Novikov resorted to a model that could be examined using advanced mathematics. He hypothesized that a billiard ball being hit into a wormhole in a certain direction would travel back in time and hit itself, thus stopping it from entering the wormhole in the first place. Studying the problem, Novikov discovered that there were many trajectories that could result from the same initial conditions, and which did not end up in creating a paradox. From this result, Novikov reasoned that the probability of such consistent events was nonzero. Since that was true, he therefore concluded that the probability of inconsistent events was zero.

Applying the billiard ball solution to normal time travel, Novikov reasoned that whatever a time traveler might do in the past, he would never be able to create a paradox.

Unfortunately, while Novikov's principle asserts that the grandfather paradox can't happen, it doesn't actually explain exactly how it is stopped. There have been dozens and dozens of science fiction novels and short stories written about the strange ways the universe prevents paradoxes from occurring, but none of them provide a reliable, all-encompassing solution.

For that, we need to look to quantum mechanics and the Many Worlds interpretation of quantum theory as proposed by Hugh Everett III in 1957. According to Everett's theory, whenever a number of possibilities exist in a quantum event, the universe splits into multiple worlds (i.e., universes), one for each possibility. Each one of these worlds is real, and everything is identical except for the one different choice. From the moment that choice is made, the worlds develop independently of one another. Moreover, each world exists simultaneously, while remaining unobservable to the others.

Under the Everett interpretation of quantum mechanics, our world (or universe) branches endlessly. Our reality is part of an uncountable and vast number of parallel worlds, every one of them different. Everything that could or can happen does, in one of these multiple worlds.

The Everett interpretation is a popular idea in modern science fiction. Stories about parallel worlds usually focus on what has become known as "alternate histories." In such stories, history is changed when a particular event doesn't take place and a different possibility does. A typical scenario in alternate history is one where the South won the Civil War. Other popular alternate worlds include ones where the Nazis won the Second World War, Jesus was never born, or the American Revolution failed.

Alternate histories are fine examples of Everett's interpretation, but they aren't perfect. Most importantly, alternate world stories rely on some major event in history not happening and thus changing the nature of reality as a result. Everett's theory doesn't deal with important events, but with actions on a quantum level. The Many Worlds theory suggests that unique universes exist for every motion made by an electron circling a nucleus inside an atom for every atom in the universe. It's a conclusion that suggests the number of parallel universes in the cosmos is beyond human comprehension. Events notable on a human level of interaction are not necessary—merely the movement of electrons is enough to bring a new world into being.

Not everyone is so entranced by Everett's theory. Many physicists prefer the Copenhagen interpretation of quantum mechanics, developed by Niels Bohr and Werner Heisenberg in Copenhagen, Denmark, in the late 1920s. This theory says when no one watches a system, it evolves naturally, but when someone watches a system, the act of observing it changes that system. Albert Einstein was a particularly vocal critic of the Copenhagen interpretation, expressing his doubts in the famous line, "God does not play dice."

Another group that finds Everett's interpretation of quantum mechanics troubling is the Catholic Church. The Many Worlds interpretation implies that everything that can happen in the universe does happen somewhere, implying that there is no one correct path to salvation—that people can act in many different ways, none of them any more probable or important than any other. The idea that every choice that exists is made in some alternate universe is a very different concept than that of free will, and one that's not in keeping with the teachings of any religion based on a specific path to salvation.

Fortunately, Cable was not very religious. Applying the Everett interpretation to his adventures in the past made perfect sense, and that's exactly what I did when I started writing his adventures in March 2000.

When Cable traveled back in time to kill Apocalypse, he achieved his goal in one possible universe but not another: at the moment he fought Apocalypse in their final battle, two versions of Cable were created. In one quantum world, Cable failed to defeat the villain and reality remained unchanged. Young Nathan grew up in a future where Apocalypse ruled and the grandfather paradox never occurred.

In the other possible quantum world, Cable destroyed Apocalypse and the world of the future from where he had come was immediately wiped out. The Apocalypse in that universe never succeeded in conquering the world. Still, Cable didn't disappear when the future did, as predicted by the grandfather paradox, because the future in that second quantum world was not the one he had come from. He instead came from the first reality, which still existed even if he could no longer access it.

Splitting Cable into two identical people in two separate realities managed to satisfy all the conditions of the grandfather paradox without violating the basic laws of the universe. Cable still existed in a future ruled by Apocalypse while, at the same time, his alternate form managed to destroy that future.

Continuing with that same line of reasoning, I decided that it would be fun to further explore the unlimited possibilities offered by the Everett Many Worlds theory. Thus, I involved Cable in a war between two alternate realities, each struggling in the past to enact a certain event that would guarantee the survival of their parallel world in the future. Of course, since Everett guarantees all realities, the battle wasn't what either side hoped for, but I felt it best not to raise the point in the comic and cause more confusion than necessary. From there, my stories hopped, skipped and jumped forward, based on the long-range concept that not only could anything happen in Cable's future, but that everything would. I plotted and played with quantum mechanics and had a grand old time. And, hopefully, entertained my readers.

Not everyone, however, is so fascinated by the Many Worlds theory and quantum mechanics. Many people consider the grandfather paradox a strong argument against the possibility of time travel. While comic books are far from believable, they do need (as mentioned earlier in this piece) to maintain an internal consistency. Featuring a lead character who violates one of the basic laws of the universe is a sure way of destroying the slightest illusion of reality.

I always knew that if someone suddenly decided that time travel did not work in the Marvel Universe, Cable, as a visitor from the future, could no longer exist. Or if he did, it would only be after a complete and total makeover of his character and his biography. That's exactly what happened about a year after I started writing Cable's adventures. The editor-in-chief of the comic book division decided that time-travel stories were too unbelievable and complicated for the readership and banished them to limbo. I was given several months to finish up my ongoing Cable adventure in parallel worlds. A new writer and a new artist took over the series and turned Cable back into a globe-trotting mercenary who never once mentioned time travel.

Or at least, that's what happened in this reality. I like to think that somewhere else, in a parallel world that's very close to this one, a quantum step away, I'm still writing about Cable's adventures traveling in space and in time. But exactly what stories I'm telling, even I don't know.

Robert Weinberg lives in Oak Forest, Illinois, a suburb of Chicago, and is the author of sixteen novels, fifteen nonfiction books and dozens of short stories. As an editor, he's compiled over 150 anthologies. Bob's a two-time winner of the World Fantasy Award and has won two Bram Stoker Awards, given by the Horror Writers Association, of which he is also a member. He's perhaps the only horror writer ever to serve as the Grand Marshal of a rodeo parade.

A Plea for More Mystery

KAREN HABER

Years ago, at a convention in Birmingham, England, I was surrounded by a group of fans who demanded I tell them how Nightcrawler's powers worked. Such powers, I was told, defied the laws of physics that applied to mass and the conservation of energy. So how does Nightcrawler teleport, they chided. How, huh? How? "It's simple," I replied, "Nightcrawler can teleport because...I say he can." The fans started to back away from me as if I had something contagious. "No, really," I continued, "it's comic books. We make this stuff up. It's not rocket science, it's fantasy." The fans ran screaming. Here, the lovely and talented Karen Haber attempts to make more sense of comic book physics and the consequences thereof than I ever bothered to.

Q: *What do these things have in common?*
   The Pyramids
   Greta Garbo
   The Big Bang

A: Mystery. They remain fascinating enigmas, untouched by years of analysis and speculation.

Q: *What do these things have in common?*
   Paris Hilton
   New Orleans Sewage System
   The X-Men

A: Media overexposure. The more you look at them, the less interesting they become.

Icons are, by their very nature, mysterious. And they should stay that
way. Spend too much time analyzing and demystifying them, and
poof, the magic goes away.

So it is with the X-Men. They should be cherished as romantic exponents of wish fulfillment rather than placed under scientific scru-
tiny. They can't hold up to the bright light of science.

I should know. I'm the coauthor of *The Science of the X-Men*. And
if there's anything I learned from that book, it's that certain characters deserve to be given space and have their secrets preserved. Like
Garbo, they want to be left alone.

The fad for "scientific" books linked to popular television shows and
movies began with *Star Trek* and the admirable wish to combine a little education with readers' mega-helpings of pop culture. Unfortunately,
these books are the printed equivalents of candy bars enriched with anti-
oxidants in the fond hope that what we enjoy can also be good for us.[1]

For example, take this excerpt: "Many of the X-Men have powers
that seem to defy the laws of physics. They have access to incredible amounts of energy and that energy is of a completely unknown
type. It is like nothing in this universe...and that is the key to understanding what science could lie behind it."[2]

It seems to me, upon mature reflection, that what this statement reveals is how pointless it is to attempt to analyze the powers of the X-Men.
They have access to incredible amounts of energy? No question. And that
energy is of a completely unknown type? Yes, because it has no ground-
ing in science as we understand it—because it's fiction, not science.

---

[1] I'd be curious to learn just how many readers of these "Science Of" books were spurred to pursue
careers in science as a result of their reading. I'm willing to put money on it that there were fewer
than five. Perhaps none.

[2] Haber and Yaco, *The Science of the X-Men*, 66.

Of course the X-Men have amazing, inexplicable powers. That's the entire point of them, isn't it? They're mutants. They're not like us.

The superpowered "mutant" is a time-honored trope of science fiction and comic books. The iconic, romantic antihero outsider is a character with whom alienated readers identify and, as such, the character takes on mythic, compelling importance.

Such characters transcend mundane explanation, and rightly so. They were never intended to stand up under the analytic spotlight. They are romantic icons, the projection points for wish fulfillment and escape. They aren't meant to be subjected to scientific analysis any more than Greta Garbo was meant to be seen in color without her screen makeup.

MYSTERY IS SEXY

Mystery is, yes, let's face it, *sexy*. The unknown is often a large component of attraction between people and the things (including comic books) they love.

The effects of mystery are many, not least of which is the sustained interest and curiosity of others. Think of, well, Greta Garbo. Mata Hari. And, until recently, Deep Throat.

Consider the benefits of mystery: peace, calm, quiet, coolth. Less information. Fewer bright lights.

I'm sure we can all think of a few people who could benefit from a bit more mystery: Pat Buchanan, Monica Lewinsky, Tom Cruise. Picasso.

In fact, I can only think of two individuals who should be given less mystery: Jack the Ripper and Osama bin Laden, and, unfortunately, only one of them is dead.

So yes, right here, right now, I'm making a straightforward unabashed plea for more discretion. Bring back bashfulness. I want it all: Ladies' hats with veils. Half-lit faces. Sentences that trail off into silence. More mystery, please. A double helping. In this age of facelifts performed on TV and public presidential polyps, mystery is the one thing that hasn't lost its appeal.

The information explosion has led a few of us to run for earplugs and blindfolds. Too much information is available, 24/7. I can't go to the dentist without being subjected to commercials for his services in the waiting room. I can't go to the supermarket without listening in on several personal telephone conversations per aisle and, instead of Muzak, ads for the food I'm actually buying and the store in which I'm actually already shopping. (Who would ever dream that I'd miss Muzak so much?) I can't go on vacation without being offered Internet capabilities in my hotel rooms. Too much information. Too much visual noise. As Wolverine might say, snarling, "Put a cork in it."

So it is with looking too closely at that voodoo that those X-Men do. A word to the would-be wise: *never* analyze the golden goose. It might stop laying those lovely eggs. Leave the X-Men alone. The X-Men have captured popular imagination with a potent cocktail combining sex appeal, mediagenics, tight costumes and terrific lighting. They're good-looking oddballs capable of evening the score with any bully in any metaphorical schoolyard.

On film, the X-Men are all about action, style and, as we've already said, s-e-x. The tremendous visceral power of film as a visual medium lends itself most easily to concentrating on the externals.

In the comic books, the reverse is true. Despite their visual nature, the X-Men comics are basically story-driven, emphasizing—to varying degrees—both text and subtext. The internal lives of the characters, their interior worlds, are easily as important as the mega-clobbering dominating each splash panel. This psychological visibility is an undeniable component of the characters' peculiar allure. It makes them compelling objects of wish fulfillment and projection.

Let's posit that your average reader of X-Men comics is/was an alienated adolescent. Further, let's assume that after a bruising day at school and monosyllabic exchanges with the 'rents, said adolescent's favorite moment of the day is spent alone in his or her room with the door closed, reading about and/or being someone else.

The identification of reader with comic book subject is a well-known, powerful and potent experience. Half a century ago, psychiatrist Fredric Wertham, of *Seduction of the Innocent* fame, was well aware of the power of the printed word and image. He became convinced that comic books were a dangerous influence on developing minds and psyches and in 1948 ran a symposium, "The Psychopathology of Comic Books," that received a great deal of attention.[3] Although his initial target was the admittedly lurid crime comics of the immediate postwar era, Wertham soon discovered he could make a good living by attacking superhero comics. Before he was pacified by the institution of the Comics Code, there were public burnings of comics in places like Binghamton, New York.

Dr. Wertham went off the tracks in claiming that comic book readers would grow up to become sociopathic dangers to society. However, in at least one area he was correct—as much as that admission may pain some of us. Comics *do* have lasting effects on their readers—you, dear reader, are holding the evidence in your hands right now. Several decades after first reading comics, many kids-in-adult-bodies are still discussing them, writing about them and making movies about them.

Do comics' powers reside solely in their appeal as escapist literature? I think not. Comics are many things to many readers: art, nostalgia, an escape hatch. The need for escapism persists into adulthood, and perhaps those things associated with earlier, more innocent times have an even more potent allure than when first encountered. Who wouldn't prefer to leap over a tall building in a single bound rather than spend eight hours inside it, crunching numbers? However, the power of comic books is more than just a good trapdoor into an alternate universe. Within the safety of a familiar realm, iconic figures clash over important—nay, fundamental—issues: good versus evil, love versus hate. Powerful stuff. No wonder, forty years down the road, we're still talking about 'em.

The hypnotic, transcendental power of a good long story has been known since Homer first sang of Achilles. The human animal seems to require tale-telling, perhaps as a means of processing and accepting the hierarchical challenges and demands of real life.

Comic books may be a very simple, contemporary variation on meeting this need. With a few words and pictures, the reader is absorbed, transported and comforted. No wonder we keep coming back for more.

---

[3] Jones, *Men of Tomorrow*, 239.

DON'T COME ANY CLOSER

Just what makes the X-Men so appealing? They are outsiders—special outsiders, who are better than the majority of "normal" folk who fear and shun them.

In other words, the X-Men symbolize alienation with a capital "X." They are the ultimate misfits.

What pimpled, anguished teenage kid can't relate to that?

Misunderstood and feared, the X-Men have suffered because of their otherness, have lost friends and family. They have learned to be cautious and private. They have miraculous powers that are difficult to fathom. Theirs are the powers of gods.

Of course, if we shine too bright a light on these mutants, we might not like what we see. Why disperse the illusion? Scientific explanation undercuts the very elements that make these characters so alluring. Do we really want to pull back the curtain and see who's behind it? If we break the illusion, the suspension of disbelief—that oh-so-necessary component to every good science fiction and fantasy tale—dissipates. The illusion is key to accepting the fantasy, to buying into the dream.

For example, think of the movie *Casablanca*. It's a classic romantic tale filled with marvelous performances by iconic actors. To learn that the entire thing was considered a failure by those involved (until the public saw the movie and set them straight), that the actors thought it wouldn't be any good and that the screenplay was cobbled together with a wink and a nod, diminishes the experience of the entire movie.

Or consider another Bogart performance, in the original movie version of *Sabrina*. He does a very nice job as the dour older brother of the dashing William Holden. But did you know that he got the role after Cary Grant turned it down? Now try to watch that movie and not compare the actors in your mind's eye. Not quite the same experience, is it?

As for the X-Men, there *is* a bit of a paradox in the mix here regarding the known and unknown. The X-Men are mutants, yes, and superpowered. But they live together as humans, with human-sized desires and disagreements. In fact, in certain respects, they are an extended, quarrelling, dysfunctional family. (Perhaps the X-Men at home aren't really so different from their readers.)

What, then, do readers want? Should their comic book heroes be mysterious and yet not *too* mysterious? Must heroes tread the high wire between familiarity and predictability? Do readers *want* them to have psychological visibility? Do they feel an emotional intimacy with them? And is there a significant difference between being known and being *too* well-known? Perhaps it's the difference between intimacy and contempt.

Perhaps readers *do* want to know the X-Men, at least to a point. They want to know them while still continuing to admire them. They may not want to know how Iceman freezes up the nearest villain, but they do want to know about his social life (or lack thereof). The reader wonders how Cyclops feels about losing Jean Grey. And what about Wolverine and his former Japanese fiancée, Mariko Yashida? As for Professor Xavier, he can't walk. That's got to be frustrating, even for the mastermind of the X-Men.

Marvel comics characters have frequently been characterized by a certain emotional angst and psychological skewedness. This is certainly true of the X-Men. Despite the fact that their psychological visibility might be a component of popular comic book cult status, I can't help wondering if these superheroes might be at risk of overexposure. Are the X-Men in danger of becoming just one long ongoing soap opera?

THE MYSTERIOUS X-MEN

Let us consider a few of the X-Men who are more shrouded in mystery than most, and how this works—or doesn't. (And, perhaps, consider a few who might benefit, in my opinion, from a bit more mystery.)

Wolverine

Here's a guy who's part mineral—mind those adamantium claws—part animal and part who knows what. Wolverine/Logan is one of the *most* mysterious X-Men, and one of the most dangerous. He's literally capable of ripping off someone's face.

Now, be honest: do you *really* want to know how those adamantium claws got into the back of his hands? Of course not. How much do we need to know about his sense of smell, his endocrine system and the effects of hormones/testosterone on aggression and hair growth? I, for one, don't want to see his medical chart; I want to see him take his shirt off.

Wolverine is a mysterious guy, compelling and powerful. Shine a bright light on the mystery and it might just dissolve into endless looping story-line spirals. Was he a government agent once? Is he also a mutant? Does it really matter?

Part of Wolverine's appeal is that he's unknowable and unpredictable. Although his friends call him Logan, no one really knows his real name, age or where he was born. And, frankly, who cares? More interesting to me is the disparity between his in-print and on-screen appearance. The Wolverine of comic book fame is a short, ugly spark-plug of a guy with seriously weird hair and enough in-your-face attitude to fill several taller mutants to the brim. He talks—and fights—like a soldier of fortune.

Fade to black, and bring up the lights on Hugh Jackman as Wolverine on-screen in the X-Men movies. The thin, elegant, six-foot-four actor is not exactly a perfect physical match for the character. (He must find it a real challenge to play shorter, wider and coarser.) Happily, the result of Jackman's casting—and viewers' willing suspension of disbelief—is that he's made the character extremely physically appealing. For me, at least, it was a revelation: Wolverine as boy toy. It complements the comic book character's early aura of mystery perfectly—now Wolverine's physical image matches his character's psychological allure.

When Marvel editors made the decision to create and describe Wolverine's backstory, it backfired on them. The result was a character whose power and appeal was diminished by too much information. This is the area where psychological visibility shades into True Confessions. (Actually, there is one mystery I *would* like resolved regarding Wolverine: who's his barber? Now *there's* a brave guy.)

Storm

Is she a goddess? Is she a mutant? Can the two coincide? Is it just a matter of semantic and cultural interpretation?

Storm controls the forces of nature on a vast scale but can narrow her focus down to the molecular level. Such elemental elements are at work within her and are within her control that she is one of the most frightening and inhuman of the X-Men, utterly unknowable, more goddess than mutant.

Who is she? What does she enjoy, besides a good lightning storm and playing adoptive mom to Kitty Pryde? And where did she get that white hair and those big blue eyes?

Mythological gods have long been credited with the ability to control weather and the elements. Think of Zeus and his lightning bolts, Loki and fire. No one questions where Zeus got his powers. So should it be with Storm.

In *The Science of the X-Men* we posited that Storm uses telekinesis to manipulate dust particles in the air, which seed cloud and trigger rainfall. It follows, then, that she has to be aware of air quality at all times in order to bring off some of her more awesome climatic effects. Now ask yourself: does the beautiful Storm look like someone who stays up-to-date on the dust quotient in the air at all times? Okay, maybe she does indeed manipulate dust to seed storm clouds, or has an instinctive "dust" sense. What does it matter? Let's call her a rainmaker and leave it at that.

Did she spend her childhood as a thief in the streets of Cairo? Was she a secret agent for Interpol? Is her costume waterproof? Never mind.

Let's keep things mysterious and glamorous. She's descended from an ancient line of magic-wielding African priestesses and she can fly on the wind. She's been worshipped as a goddess and when she gets angry, tornadoes appear. And she looks absolutely fabulous in an evening gown. Don't ask questions about Storm; just worship her.

Jean Grey and Mystique

Alas, poor Jean, we knew you way too well. This original X-Man (X-Woman?) suffered so many plotline indignities that killing her off was a mercy for both the fans and the character herself.

Mystery is the last thing I think of when I think of Jean Grey; she was killed, reborn, cloned, hypnotized into becoming an evil version of her own ancestor (don't ask) and transmuted into an unstable, universe-endangering force. The only mysterious thing left about her, now that she's dead, is which name she preferred: Marvel Girl, Redd Dayspring, Phoenix, Dark Phoenix or Lady Jean Grey/the Black Queen?

A super-telepath, Jean Grey nevertheless suffered more manipulation by bad guys than most of the other original characters combined. While her powers really do defy explanation in that time-honored "don't ask me, she's a mutant" tradition, she's been hypnotized, analyzed and pulverized. Her love life is the talk of the comic book world. We know her parents. Her children. She's a one-character soap opera. R.I.P., Jeannie.

On-screen, Jean Grey doesn't really have much impact as a character, although both Cyclops and Wolverine lust after her. Famke Janssen is lovely and, for all I know, a brilliant actress. But she isn't exactly given a great deal to do. Compare poor Jean to her shape-shifting antagonist, the fabulous Mystique, as portrayed by the equally fabulous Rebecca Romijn. Now *there's* mystery made sexy and dangerous. We don't know anything about Mystique except that she's naked under her shape-shifting disguise. And that's all we need to know.

Magneto and Professor Xavier

Magneto controls the powers of magnetism and, perhaps, much more. We don't know him very well, and that's probably why he seems far more compelling than his Boy Scout rival (at least in the films), Professor Xavier.

Magneto's roots go back to WWII, but luckily he's been rejuvenated. He's ageless, implacable, has half-Gypsy children, might have been Jewish and, played by Ian McKellen, is a foxy grandpa who hasn't yet run out of tricks with which to bedevil his fellow mutants.

We can't even fault his motivation, at least in the comic books. After surviving concentration camp internment during the war, Magneto lost his beloved child to a fire when he was prevented from saving her by an anti-mutant mob. His devastated wife left him soon after. The inhumanity of humanity has convinced him that mutants should inherit the Earth, and he's not interested in waiting for that to happen. His motivation is understandable, even if the result of his actions is often lamentable. But we can't hate this fascinating, complex character.

Professor Xavier certainly suffers by comparison: the headmaster who knows too much. How sexy is that? The movies haven't yet allowed him a love interest, although in the comic books he's already absconded with a fabulous alien queen.

Professor X is a telepath, and it's really difficult to make telepaths sexy on-screen. When they utilize their superpowers, they tend to frown, or close their eyes, or touch their foreheads. The next thing you know, they're scheduling appointments for Botox shots. And then there's that silly Cerebro helmet the Professor favors. Frankly, it's not a good look for him. Perhaps what Professor X needs is a makeover. But Patrick Stewart can't be faulted for his immaculate interpretation of the good Professor. Perhaps good, and the visibility that comes with it, just isn't sexy.

A PLEA FOR MYSTERY

The X-Men have endured many different interpretations and incarnations, as in Neil Gaiman's recent, fascinating *Marvel 1602*, a limited series fantasia in which the X-Men and other heroes invented during the Silver Age of Marvel comics are transposed to the time of Elizabeth I to play out a doom-laden drama. The X-Men really transcend time and science. They are the essence of heroism and alienation. Their origins are mysterious, their lives are fraught with fear and rejection, and their powers are staggering and strange.

Much of their appeal is because of their larger-than-life nature. Accordingly, they should be cherished as romantic exponents of wish fulfillment for both reader and viewer, and admired for their remarkable abilities and physical appeal. It doesn't matter how they do what they do. What's important is that they do it.

They may be at risk of overexposure from their angst-generating writers, at least in the medium of comic books. The threat is diminished in the movies, where psychological visibility is more difficult to convey. On film, some of the mystery is retained. And in a world where we hear all too often about suicide bombers, cadaver dogs and intestinal contents, what remains mysterious should be protected and praised. The fragile bond between character and reader deserves to be respected and unsullied by metascientific attempts to explain what are, after all, tales of the unexplainable.

REFERENCES

Haber, Karen, and Linc Yaco. *The Science of the X-Men*. BP Books, Inc., 2000.

Jones, Gerard. *Men of Tomorrow: Geeks, Gangsters and the Birth of the Comic Book*. Basic Books, 2004.

Karen Haber is the author of eight novels, including *Star Trek Voyager: Bless the Beasts*, coauthor of *The Science of the X-Men* and editor of the Hugo-nominated essay collection celebrating J. R. R. Tolkien, *Meditations on Middle Earth*. Most recently she has helmed *Kong Unbound*, a book of essays and an official tie-in to the new movie, published by Pocket Books in October 2005.

Her short fiction has appeared in *Asimov's Science Fiction* magazine, the *Magazine of Fantasy and Science Fiction* and many anthologies. She reviews art books for *Locus* magazine and profiles artists for Locus publications including *Realms of Fantasy*. She also coedits the *Best of Science Fiction and Fantasy* anthologies series with Jonathan Strahan.

Her newest science fiction novel, *Crossing Infinity*, a tale of gender confusions between worlds, was published in November 2005.

Infinite Mutation, Eternal Stasis

JAMES LOWDER

Both my computer and my PDA have reset buttons. I'm extremely happy about this since, at least once a week, one or the other of them freezes up, and it's only the reset button that allows me to return to the technological wonderment of the twenty-first century. In this next piece, James Lowder discusses the consequences of living in the Marvel Universe and the dangers of pressing its hypothetical reset button once too often.

IT WAS *GIANT-SIZE X-MEN* #1 that hooked me. A friend had recommended that particular comic book because it featured a menacing giant monster—Krakoa, the Island That Walks Like a Man—and such oddly named behemoths were always guaranteed to grab my interest. Monsters like Krakoa had been an important part of Marvel's history back in the fifties and early sixties. Wonderfully rendered by Jack Kirby and Dick Ayers, lumbering, hyperbole-spouting beasties with bizarre names like Fin Fang Foom and Zzutak, the Thing That Shouldn't Exist, had tromped through *Strange Tales* and *Journey Into Mystery* in the years before the Human Torch and Thor took up residence in those pages. Marvel's monsters were nostalgia items by the mid-seventies, the stuff of reprints and the occasional guest appearance in second-tier titles like *The Incredible Hulk*.

The X-Men shared their rather sad fate for a time. Before *Giant-Size* #1, five years had passed since the last original story appeared under the X-Men logo. Apart from reprints, the mutant heroes had kicked around the Marvel Universe rather aimlessly during that time, popping up now and then in places like *Marvel Team-Up*, where they played supporting roles to more popular characters. Len Wein and Dave Cockrum changed all that. In their relaunch of *X-Men*, they struck a workable balance between the expectations of readers new to the series and those familiar with Marvel's increasingly complicated continuity. The new stories gave fans of the sixties comics a way to keep tabs on their old favorites, like Cyclops and Marvel Girl, but also a venue in which to encounter such interesting new creations as Nightcrawler, Storm and Colossus. Little wonder that the "All-New, All-Different" *X-Men* quickly gathered a devoted audience and, after Wein and Cockrum handed over the creative reins to Chris Claremont and John Byrne, established itself as the flagship of an incredibly successful mutant franchise.

I was a devoted reader of the X-titles myself from the late seventies to the mid-eighties. For nearly a decade after reading *Giant-Size* #1, I snapped up each new issue of *X-Men*—soon to be re-titled *Uncanny X-Men*—as soon as it hit the stands. When Marvel debuted *New Mutants* and *Alpha Flight* as spin-offs in 1983, I added them to my subscription list at the local comics shop. I was invested in the characters by then, had followed along as their backstories were revealed and expanded, so the decision was an easy one. Then the miniseries craze swept through the Marvel offices, and even more spin-offs flooded the marketplace. I kept up with them for a while, too, but with each passing month, each new batch of X-comics, I found myself less and less enthusiastic.

By 1985, I'd had enough. It wasn't just the growing number of titles being pumped out or the steady creep of cover prices. As Marvel strove to establish their mutants as a bona fide franchise, they hyped each title and major story arc with a breathlessness that simply grew wearying. The mutant heroes raced from issue to issue, series to series, in a perpetual state of crisis more pervasively dire than that faced by any other costumed do-gooders. To be certain, superhero comics thrived on puffed-up potential catastrophes, and death and disaster had always loomed large for the X-Men. But the calamities depicted in the single X-title that ran throughout the sixties, or even the first few issues of the seventies relaunch, had seemed very different from the constant chaos buffeting the franchise in the eighties.

Professor Charles Xavier first "died" in 1968. His passing gave writers Roy Thomas, Gary Friedrich and Arnold Drake a reason to move the slow-selling title in new directions, splitting up the team after the elimination of their near-omnipotent protector. According to Thomas' introduction to the *Marvel Masterworks* volume reprinting the death story, the intention at the time had been to make Xavier's demise permanent, and the company's actions seem to support that idea. Marvel even went so far as to downplay the X-Men logo on the title's covers for seven months, highlighting instead individual heroes or even villains. Xavier remained dead for two years, returning just before the original series' hiatus started in 1970. The plot twist used to resurrect the professor—that it was not Charles Xavier, but someone else disguised as him who had been killed in *X-Men* #42—was the sort of awkward retroactive plot revision that would become commonplace in the eighties. For the two years preceding that clumsy reveal, though, Xavier's death essentially remade the one and only X-title.

Death continued to make its presence felt in significant ways after the series' relaunch in 1975. The Native American hero Thunderbird died in *X-Men* #95, a mere two issues after his introduction in *Giant-Size* #1. A few months after Thunderbird's death, Jean Grey sacrificed herself to save her friends, only to be transformed into the cosmically powered Phoenix. Like Xavier's first death, these events infused the series with a sense of danger and surprise. They also had long-lasting impact. Thunderbird stayed dead for over twenty-five years—and remains dead, if you discount the alternate-world version of the character that popped up in 2001's *Exiles* #1. Either way, John Proudstar has served as a fairly fixed symbol for the potential peril the mutant heroes face each time they rush into battle. And Marvel Girl's transformation into Phoenix in *X-Men* #100 and #101 still ranks as one of the most important story lines in the series' forty-year history. Even if subsequent writers have tinkered extensively with the precise nature of her metamorphosis, the transformation itself, like Thunderbird's death, remains as close to a constant as can be found in Marvel's mutant continuity.

The way in which the X-titles dealt with death and other supposedly weighty dramatic conflicts changed by the mid-eighties. Calamity battered the mutants several times each month. The cycle of death and resurrection, "final" defeat and startling return, accelerated so much that the niceties of pacing and structure were all but abandoned. In remarkably short succession, a central character like Storm was shown giving in to her evil impulses and becoming "Dark Storm," dallying with Dracula a couple of times, suffering the implantation of a killer alien embryo, dying and merging with a space whale before being reborn, only to lose and finally regain her weather control powers. As the series has progressed, radical, life-changing events have impacted the story line for shorter and shorter spans. The crises are experienced, then forgotten the moment the next hyperactive plotline overtakes the heroes. The emotional and physical scars these traumatic experiences inflicted on Storm proved no more lasting than the new hairstyles and costumes she adopted and summarily abandoned.

This isn't dramatic conflict leading to change, but rather conflict creating the illusion of change. And before too long, the observant reader catches on to the fact that the publisher or an individual writer can—and will—hit the narrative reset button and return everything to the expected, familiar form just as soon as someone undermines the status quo too substantially.

Such narrative resets serve a purpose in the marketing of a franchise like the X-Men. The repeated shifts back to the status quo allow the various books to appeal to fans who might have missed a few issues or even those who stopped reading the Marvel mutant saga for a long stretch. If the latest issue or miniseries depicts a favorite hero as a villain, or villain as a hero, gives him flashy new powers or strips his powers away completely, don't worry. All will soon return to normal. If an X-fan dislikes a story arc, the direction in which a writer has taken some fragment of the franchise, he can rest assured that the book will eventually circle back to recognizable depictions and familiar narrative turf, sometimes with remarkable speed.

Consider the chaos wrought by Kulan Gath in *Uncanny X-Men* #190 and #191. The evil wizard magically recast Manhattan and its inhabitants into medieval analogues. Guns became swords; cars, horse-drawn carriages. The X-Men and the other spandex-clad supers caught loitering around the island when the spell took effect remained warriors, but like almost everyone else, could not remember their lives before Gath's sword-and-sorcery makeover. Only Spider-Man recalled what the city had been like only a day before; an earlier encounter with the self-proclaimed Master of the Dark Runes had shielded him from the sorcery somehow.

During the course of the two-issue tale, Kulan Gath fused Professor X with the mutant Caliban, warped the body of the mystic Dr. Strange so that he could not wield magic and transformed the Wasp into a soul-drinking demon. Casualties in the climactic battle included such long-established characters as Rogue, Colossus and the Vision. But it was the use—or, rather, abuse—of Spider-Man that stuck with most readers. Gath tortured the hero, gathering his life essence to power his spells, then crucified him. Several panels focused on Peter Parker's suffering, including a close-up of his screaming, bloodied face before he met an agonizing end.

All the suffering, all the noble sacrifice, turned out to be empty show. At the story's conclusion, Dr. Strange and Illyana Rasputin used Kulan Gath's own spell to create a "temporalspacial claudication," turning time back upon itself and restoring the world to the moment before Gath was loosed upon Manhattan. The end result was the introduction of the mutant-hunting Nimrod into the continuity, but the deaths were undone—never occurred, in fact—and the world at large was left blissfully ignorant of what had transpired. A few characters remained conscious of the "time slip," but were unaffected by it. Their dialogue even one panel removed from the carnage was flat and coldly philosophical, as if the ordeal they and their dearest comrades had just endured held no more meaning than an idle chat about lunch menus.

As spectacle, the Kulan Gath story worked well enough—apart from the cheat ending, anyway. The action was nonstop and the bloodletting sadistic enough to sate fans of Grand Guignol–style entertainment. Within a series involving popular, even beloved, characters and structured around a detailed continuity, though, such a tale can be profoundly unrewarding. Spider-Man shouldn't be handled in the same way as the interchangeable victims lined up for Technicolor slaughter in a low-budget slasher flick. Readers are too invested in his character after all these years to see him suffer without that sacrifice having a point. But the pat dismissal of the chaos caused by Kulan Gath's villainy, the easy way in which the awful events were negated, punished readers whose sympathies were aroused and undermined their confidence in the surrounding story line. If seemingly ambitious plots are revealed to be nothing more than straw men to be toppled and plowed under—with brutal crucifixions inflicted and then erased, cities twisted and reformed, memories wiped and reprogrammed—the narrative integrity of the entire series is cast into doubt.

For much of the last twenty years, the X-titles have spun endlessly through similar, if less compact, epic story lines cross-marketed among the dozens of mutant-themed titles released each month. They promise long-lasting impact on the Marvel Universe, but deliver temporary sparkle and buzz that fade just in time for the next big marketing push. "The X-Tinction Agenda" and "The X-Cutioner's Song," "The Age of Apocalypse" and "Onslaught" and "Operation Zero Tolerance": through all these multi-issue, multi-title epics, the familiar characters plodded along like high-functioning amnesiacs, capable of remembering whatever bits of their long and complicated histories were necessary for the narrative-in-progress, but forgetting everything else that might have muddied the story or complicated their return to the comforting familiarity of the status quo.

And the pattern shows no sign of slowing. 2005's *House of M* story line reads like the Kulan Gath yarn on steroids: driven mad by the realization her children never existed, the once-heroic Scarlet Witch used her powers to remake the world into a mutant utopia; only a few select heroes recalled how things had been, and had to fight to return reality to its proper configuration. Marvel has promised the series will have long-term repercussions, with hundreds of mutants stripped of their powers and the status quo reset forever. In the context of the franchise's history, of course, "forever" has a definition you won't find in the *Oxford English Dictionary*. Here the word means something like "until the next shift in editorial or marketing philosophy dictates otherwise."

How soon that shift might occur depends upon sales of the various X-titles in the wake of *House of M* and, more importantly, the success of the franchise in the larger media marketplace. Income from subsidiary uses of the X-Men intellectual property, for films and animated shows and novels, action figures and T-shirts, is vital to Marvel's bottom line, so the comics won't be allowed to undermine the general consumer's concept of the characters. Corporate consciousness of this wider marketplace can create a secondary strain upon the narratives spun in the comics, too. Since gaining even a fraction of the movie audience would increase the comics' sale significantly, the company may periodically nudge the four-color X-Men closer to their big-screen incarnations.

For a time, author Grant Morrison's run on *X-Men*—re-titled *New X-Men*—did just that. Black leather outfits like those in the films replaced the heroes' brightly hued spandex uniforms. Professor Xavier's School for Gifted Youngsters finally seemed to operate like a school, with a full roster of students. The stories were stripped of some of the more wildly fantastic trappings and given a more sober science fiction approach. The point of all this seemed to be to attract more mainstream readers. As such, they would be unfamiliar with the tangled comics' continuity. The cinematic incarnation of the mutant heroes provided their status quo.

Such overt overtures to the mass market stirred resentment among the comics' longtime fans—the aging, hardcore types who make up so much of the comic book audience these days—and by 2004, familiar X-scribe Chris Claremont had returned to *Uncanny X-Men*. The changes Morrison had wrought were largely undone within a year, and the story line had returned yet again to more familiar territory. Where *New X-Men* had aimed to bring in fresh readers, Claremont's *Uncanny X-Men* appealed almost exclusively to an audience comfortable with the pattern of empty crisis and quick reset, characters who waver between dramatic shows of angst and a flippancy about the disconnect that gapes between their actions and their experiences. "I was dead," noted Betsy Braddock (a.k.a. Psylocke) in *Uncanny X-Men* #462, "got better. Changes your perspective." Then she went on to catalogue how such resurrections were commonplace among her friends and family. Indeed, in such circumstances, death and suffering mean little, to either the mutant heroes or the readers tempted to sympathize with them.

Of recent creative teams assigned to X-franchise titles, writer Joss Whedon and artist John Cassaday have come closest to achieving the sort of balanced appeal to new readers and old that Len Wein and Dave Cockrum managed all those years ago in *Giant-Size #1*. Their twelve-issue run on *Astonishing X-Men* was spiced with moments designed to appeal to longtime fans, as when the newly resurrected Colossus hurled Wolverine at a fleeing spacecraft, playing out the "Fastball Special" maneuver used in dozens of stories throughout the eighties. At the same time, the issues featured a storytelling style less frantic than that of the typical X-title, with an emphasis on character reaction and cinematic pacing, making the narrative far more accessible to the casual reader. While Whedon and Cassaday didn't have the luxury of introducing an entirely new team of heroes, as Wein and Cockrum did in 1975, they did the next best thing: reintroduced a long-absent character, Kitty Pryde. She was the ideal guide, a figure capable of inspiring feelings of nostalgia from veteran X-fans and presenting new readers with a surrogate explorer, thanks to her years away from the mansion and its inhabitants.

Straddling the worlds of nostalgia and novelty as she did, Kitty seemed quite aware of the cyclical nature of her existence and that of all of Marvel's mutants. "Nothing has changed," she noted as she stood before Professor Xavier's mansion in *Astonishing X-Men #1*. She had quit the team more than three years earlier, after the death of her one-time love interest, Colossus. In the interim, the mansion had survived assaults by alien soldiers and rioting students, before suffering total destruction in *New X-Men #147* at the hands of Magneto—later revealed, in a bit of very awkward continuity revision, as an imposter. And yet, as Kitty entered the mansion, she saw that "it looks like nothing has happened. No time has passed."

Kitty understood the reason Professor Xavier would rebuild the mansion as a duplicate of the original: the setting offered his students a sense of stability. Entering the reconstituted mansion conjured memories for Kitty, glimpses of her past that obliterated time and made her feel like a child again. The same could be said for readers of the X-titles; they're afforded the welcoming embrace of continuity by the mansion's seemingly familiar confines.

Whedon's characters also expressed the darker aspects of this continuous reassertion of the status quo. Unlike Claremont's Psylocke, they seemed to recognize the cycle's oppressive emptiness. Though Colossus had supposedly sacrificed himself years ago to save the world's mutants from the fatal Legacy Virus, he was discovered alive by Kitty Pryde in *Astonishing X-Men* #5. Tears streaming from his eyes, he fell at Kitty's feet and begged, "God, please...am I finally dead?" Surely many a Marvel mutant, slaughtered and resurrected and slaughtered yet again, has secretly uttered the same plea since *X-Men* #1, way back in 1963.

Kitty and Colossus shared a moment of quiet reflection as the first story arc wrapped up in *Astonishing X-Men*. Standing beside his old flame, Colossus somberly observed, "I leave the world in terrible turmoil. I come back, same turmoil. Nothing different at all." And yet, everything was different—or, at least, it should have been, if all the suffering and joy the characters experienced in the years since Colossus "died" in *Uncanny X-Men* #390 really meant anything. The stability upon which both he and Kitty commented is, in fact, illusory. Read any issue of any X-title and the evidence is there before you: a panorama of furious heroic struggle, frenetic incident after frenetic incident that makes any absolute stasis impossible. To be certain, the status quo will reassert itself—as the quiet scene between the supposedly retired Kitty Pryde and the supposedly dead Colossus itself demonstrated—but any stability imparted by this reassertion will be as false as the latest Xavier Mansion, and wrought for the same purpose. Its artifice can trick visitors into the comforting embrace of nostalgia, but that reassurance is based upon a lie. No matter how much the place might seem like the original, that building is long gone.

As the writers and artists creating new X-Men comics struggle to simultaneously fulfill the tripartite expectations of dramatic novelty, fan nostalgia and mass-market accessibility, endless mirror images of once-familiar characters and locations are created. These are not dramatic progressions, but rather doppelgangers, like the Xavier Mansion Kitty Pryde found at the start of *Astonishing X-Men* #1 or Krakoa on the cover of *Exiles* #67. The momentary frisson of excitement I felt upon seeing the Island That Walks Like a Man, thirty years on from his appearance in *Giant-Size X-Men* #1, could not be sustained by the story itself. This was not the monster I so fondly remembered, grown more interesting because of adventures lived since being hurled into space all those years ago. Rather, this Krakoa was the inhabitant of some parallel Earth, a stranger with a co-opted shape, removed from his own history. So, too, all the other heroes and villains in the myriad X-titles. Their stories circle back time and time again to places I think I recognize, populated by characters that seem familiar, but they're really only phantasms, pale reflections of creations caught in a story cycle forever turning at furious speeds, but getting nowhere.

REFERENCES

Bedard, Tony (w), James Calafiore (p), and Mark McKenna (i). "Destroy All Monsters, Part 2." *Exiles* No. 67. Marvel Comics, September 2005.

Bendis, Brian Michael (w), Olivier Coipel (p), John Dell, Scott Hanna, Rick Magyar, and Tim Townsend (i). *House of M* Nos. 1–8. Marvel Comics, June–November 2005.

Claremont, Chris (w), Dave Cockrum (p, i), and Sam Grainger (i). "Greater Love Hath No X-Man…" *X-Men* Vol. 1, No. 100. Marvel Comics, August 1976.

———. "Like a Phoenix from the Ashes." *X-Men* Vol. 1, No. 101. Marvel Comics, October 1976.

Claremont, Chris (w), Alan Davis (p), and Mark Farmer (i). "Season of the Witch, Part 1." *Uncanny X-Men* Vol. 1, No. 462. Marvel Comics, September 2005.

Claremont, Chris (w), John Romita, Jr. (p), and Dan Green (i). "An Age Undreamed Of." *Uncanny X-Men* Vol. 1, No. 190. Marvel Comics, February 1985.

———. "Raiders of the Lost Temple!" *Uncanny X-Men* Vol. 1, No. 191. Marvel Comics, March 1985.

Claremont, Chris, Len Wein (w), Dave Cockrum (p), and Sam Grainger (i). "Warhunt!" *X-Men* Vol. 1, No. 95. Marvel Comics, October 1975.

Lee, Stan (w), Jack Kirby (p), and Stan Reinman (i). "X-Men." *X-Men* Vol. 1, No. 1. Marvel Comics, September 1963.

Lobdell, Scott (w), Salvador Larroca (p), Scott Hanna, Danny Miki, Lary Stucker, Tim Townsend, and Dexter Vines (i). "The Cure." *Uncanny X-Men* Vol. 1, No. 390. Marvel Comics, February 2001.

Lobdell, Scott (w), Leinil Francis Yu (p), and Mark Morales (i). "One Tin Soldier Rides Away." *New X-Men* Vol. 2, No. 110. Marvel Comics, March 2001.

Morrison, Grant (w), Phil Jimenez (p), and Andy Lanning (i). "Planet X, Part 2: Magneto Superior." *New X-Men* Vol. 2, No. 147. Marvel Comics, November 2003.

O'Neil, Dennis (w), Neal Adams (p), and Tom Palmer (i). "Before I'd Be Slave." *X-Men* Vol. 1, No. 65. Marvel Comics, February 1970.

Thomas, Roy (w), Don Heck (p), and George Tuska (i). "If I Should Die." *X-Men* Vol. 1, No. 42. Marvel Comics, March 1968.

_____. Introduction. *Marvel Masterworks: The X-Men Vol. 4*. Ed. Cory Sedlmeier. New York: Marvel Comics, 2004. vi–vii.

Wein, Len (w), Dave Cockrum (p, i), and Pete Iro (i). "Second Genesis." *Giant-Size X-Men* No. 1. Marvel Comics, May 1975.

Whedon, Joss (w), and John Cassaday (p, i). "Gifted." *Astonishing X-Men* Vol. 3, Nos. 1–6. Marvel Comics, July–December 2004.

Winick, Judd (w), Mike McKone (p), and Mark McKenna (i). "Down the Rabbit Hole." *Exiles* No. 1. Marvel Comics, August 2001.

James Lowder has worked extensively on both sides of the editorial blotter. His novels include *Knight of the Black Rose* and *Prince of Lies*, and his short fiction has appeared in such anthologies as *Shadows Over Baker Street* and *The Repentant*. As an editor he's helmed ten anthologies, including two collections of superhero tales. His nonfiction writing on film and comics has seen print in *Amazing Stories*, *Sci-Fi Universe* and the BenBella collection *King Kong Is Back!*

HEROES AND

VILLAINS

"The Best There Is...Isn't Very Nice"

Complex Dualities in Wolverine

CHARLIE W. STARR

What is it that makes a hero? Scholars and philosophers have been de-bating that particular question since Gilgamesh was still in swaddling clothes. Here, Charlie W. Starr picks apart everybody's favorite Canadi-an brawler to find out what makes him tick. This, of course, is much like poking a rattlesnake with a sharp stick to see if it's asleep. However rea-sonable the question, you're not gonna like the answer.

THE GREAT QUESTION in pop-culture studies is "Why?" Why *Star Wars* and why baseball? Why *The Matrix* and why Madonna? Why Sponge Bob and why Big Macs? Why do these things capture our cultural imagination? The "Why?" of comic books was addressed in M. Night Shyamalan's 2000 film *Unbreakable*. There he sees language as originating in pictures. Says the Samuel Jackson character:

> I believe comics are a last link to an ancient way of passing on history. The Egyptians drew on walls. Countries all over the world still pass on knowledge through pictorial forms. I believe comics are a form of history that someone, somewhere, felt or experienced.

In *Unbreakable*, Shyamalan offers a theory of myth as a concrete picture language that precedes modern language forms. These images, surviving in a kind of collective human unconscious, intrude into contemporary culture through comic art. What it reveals is an archetypal or universal pattern of the hero, what the great myth theorist Joseph Campbell called the *monomyth*: a single story being told over and over again in all the stories of heroes from all throughout time.

Think of atoms—those tiny high school chemistry building blocks from which all the physical objects in the universe are made. Certain stories are like that. They're made up of a series of unchanging elements (like atoms), producing patterns (like molecules) that repeat over and over again. There are atoms of human experience which, when put together, create patterns which C. G. Jung called *archetypal*. These archetypal patterns are blueprints to the hidden nature of reality itself, blueprints that are revealed in the stories we tell. Call them archetypal or mythic, certain kinds of stories appear all over the world, all throughout history—these are the stories that take hold of the foundations of the world.

It's a theory that also appeared in the 1920s in the work of Owen Barfield, whose book *Poetic Diction* had a profound influence on the thought and writing of his friends J. R. R. Tolkien and C. S. Lewis. What Owen Barfield found in studying the history of language was that a strong distinction between a sign (like the word "cow") and its signified (the actual cow) is new to human thinking. For people before the modern era (even up through the medieval period), to name a thing was to invoke it. Speech had physical consequences in the world; words were what they signified. According to Barfield, language was much more like concrete reality for the majority of human history than it is today, which is to say that language had the same kind of power over us that pictures (and music) often have now.

In other words, for most of human history, language has been, like any picture, as much an object as the things it refers to. It should be no wonder to us, then, that we constantly push language to adopt more concrete forms—combining words with music or with pictures in comic books, movies and computer programs (computers, for instance, only became a widespread cultural phenomenon when they became less about abstract symbols and more about pictures, their program structures altered from the confusion of DOS to the clarity of Windows). Comics about superheroes may be less than a hundred years old, but stories of superior heroes are not, and neither are pictures of their exploits. We've simply translated them using modern technology, converting our oldest myths into comics and movies. Comics are a product of our mythic mind, a way of thinking older than science or philosophy, and thus more primal in what they reveal.

But if one "Why?" has been answered, we are nevertheless left with many more. My question is, "Why Wolverine?" Superman, Batman and Spider-Man have entered the American psyche—moving past the subculture of comic readers into mainstream awareness. At the fringe of that awareness lies the hero who has replaced Spider-Man as the popular "top dog" of the Marvel universe among that comic-reading subculture. But like a creature roaming the edge— that place where civilization and wilderness meet—Wolverine waits to claw his way into our mass cultural vision. Or perhaps, as his presence and popularity in the X-Men films suggests, he is already there, but the creature that he is forces us to exile him to that edge, to the place in our collective, civilizing consciousness where we can safely coexist with what the Wolverine is. This then is the quest: to know why Wolverine matters to us, by discovering what he is.

BEGINNINGS

Created by Len Wein and John Romita, Wolverine leaped into comic history on the last page of *The Incredible Hulk* #180, sent by the Canadian government as their "Weapon X" to do battle (in *Hulk* #181) against the great green behemoth. Marvel's strongest hero, unstoppable even by such superstrong characters as the mighty Thor or *Fantastic Four*'s Thing, is taken on by a five-and-a-half-foot scrapper with no superstrength at all. And Wolverine holds his own!

Wolverine was then brought to the *Uncanny X-Men*, his primary home for decades, by Wein and Dave Cockrum. The X-Men comic had struggled for ninety-three issues, relegated in the end to the place of mere reprints. Then, in 1975, *Giant-Size X-Men* #1 launched the series' rebirth with half a dozen new X-Men, including Storm,

Nightcrawler, Colossus and Wolverine. The new series was a huge success, and all origins were quickly explained: these were mutants, born with special powers. But that was hardly enough to explain Wolverine.

I titled this section "Beginnings" because it isn't exactly proper to speak of Wolverine's origins. For twenty-five years he had none, which is to say Wolverine's origins have been slowly revealed over decades—the mystery of his past has always been part of his character's power. First he was only Wolverine, without a name. Even that took several issues to reveal, and then only one name: *Logan*. It was then some time before we learned his claws come out of his hands, not some apparatus in his gloves. Then we learned he may have had a decades-old past of which even he was unaware. Then came the *Weapon X* miniseries, showing how he got his adamantium skeleton and claws, then flashbacks to previous adventures (including adventures in the Canadian Secret Service and even a World War II team-up with Captain America) and then his mysterious past relationship with Sabretooth. Finally, some twenty-six years after his entrance into *X-Men* popularity, the six-issue *Origins* comic revealed his absolute beginnings to mixed reviews, ranging from those purists who said Wolverine's origins should never be told, to those who agreed it should be known some day but thought the approach, in the style of a nineteenth-century romance novel, to have failed miserably, to those who thought three decades was bloody long enough to wait and so were just plain happy to have any definitive Wolverine origin at all!

Personally I'm a semi-purist. I acknowledge the right, yea verily the need, for Wolverine's story to continue in comics, but, for me, the great years are those of the late seventies and on through the eighties when Chris Claremont (with some formative help from Frank Miller) defined the Wolverine character at its mythic best. So much of what has followed has been retread or an attempt to find something else to do with him, and so it is on the Claremont years that I concentrate.

THIS AIN'T NO DISCO

Wolverine's roots may be archetypal, but his cultural beginnings are in the antihero sentiments of the 1970s. We were fresh out of Vietnam, where the presence of news cameras demanded a permanent change in the way wars are waged. In our collective guilt we either condemned war heroes or ignored them, wanting the whole thing to go away. Add to this two factors: First, the more obvious one: the feminist revolution of the sixties and seventies which, while creating opportunities for equality, demonized all things masculine, rejecting such qualities as courage and heroism in favor of sensitivity and emotional expression. The problem with men was that they weren't enough like women.

The second factor was more subtle, has been part of our culture much longer, but came to a head at the same time. In a 1961 short story called "Harrison Bergeron," Kurt Vonnegut imagined a future America in which absolute equality was required absolutely. Strong people were chained with heavy weights, beautiful people were forced to wear ugly masks, dancers had their legs fettered, newscasters spoke with a lisp and people who were overly intelligent wore an ear piece which blasted various noises into their heads, confusing their ability to think. Everyone was forced to be equal.

Because of the American love of equality, ours is a culture that tears down the heroes we raise up, that rewards success but then accuses the successful of arrogance and greed. It's a culture that spends millions on making underachievers feel special while eliminating educational programs for highly talented students. This equality mentality, a kind of hierarchiphobia, was one of the main themes of the recent superhero story *The Incredibles*. If we take away our superheroes so that we can all feel equally important, the results are obvious: "If everyone is special then no one is special." Deep thoughts from the minds of Disney....

So out of a mix of postwar angst, forced mediocrity and gender-bending castration with its resulting backlash of macho stupidity, the seventies raised the antihero hero: Eastwood's Dirty Harry, Burt Reynolds' Bandit, Stallone's Rambo. Batman became a truly dark knight, Superman and Captain America became unbelievable caricatures, and a psycho man-animal with claws and fits of "berserker rage" began his rise to the top of the comic hero popularity pyramid. Even in a decade when we rejected heroes, we still had to have them. So we made them very good at being bad and made them a little bit psychotic, like Wolverine: "I'm the best there is at what I do. But what I do best isn't very nice" (*Uncanny X-Men* #163).

WOLVERINE-NESS

Chris Claremont has said that he was handed a Wolverine around whom everyone had to walk on pins and needles: "Say hi to him the wrong way, he'll take your head off." That was fine for a few years, but Claremont quickly realized he was faced with a serious question: how do you make a psycho interesting? (*X-Men: The Legend of Wolverine*). His answer, whether conscious or not, was to find those qualities of archetypal humanness in Logan that would have made him as relevant to the storytellers of the ancient past as he was to those of us who loved his dark goodness in the seventies, and as he is to everyone who remains fascinated by his claws today.

For Claremont, making Wolverine for himself meant making the *Wolverine* miniseries in 1982 with the legendary comic writer/artist Frank Miller. The concept, according to Claremont, was to envision Logan as a "failed Samurai." His struggle is between an ideal image of himself and some chemical imbalance inside him that pulls him back at the moment the ideal is almost met. He must forever pursue that ideal (whether he achieves it or not) or else "yield to the dark side of his nature."

The archetypal quality in Wolverine is this dual nature. He is utterly noble and completely savage. He is us at our absolute best and worst and the best there is at being the absolute worst. But this duality is always complicated in Logan, never simple. He is an isolated loner standing off against society, but he is also a partner. Alone in his first miniseries, in his second Wolverine was paired with Kitty Pryde. Teamed in the *X-men*, Wolverine eventually earned his own series (and possibly, as rumor has it, his own movie). As Batman became Superman's dark other in the eighties, so Wolverine has been the *other* to many: Kitty, Colossus, Nightcrawler, Rogue and more.

Understood correctly, myth is a kind of storytelling that instru
without allegorizing. Into an allegory, an author places one-for-one
correspondences—each character and object representing a single
idea. In myth, meanings are fluid and multiple. Wolverine does not
represent simple opposites but rather a *complex duality*, pairs of relationships that sometimes oppose but are sometimes in harmony—
the kinds of relationships to be found in all of human experience.

Those of us who believe in universal right and wrong find times
in life where black and white turn to shades of gray. Those who believe that morals are relative, believe so with absolute conviction—
fundamentalist surety. We love nature but want our houses warm in
winter. We hate routine but plan out our lives on elaborately detailed
calendars. We fall in love forever but hate old flames with heartfelt
bitterness. We have great aspirations but hide secret sins. Human experience is often the experience of paradoxical truths. Some of the
most foundational of these truths are embodied in stories of complex
duality like Wolverine's. & BATMAN's

Among Wolverine's complicated dualities is a "Beauty and the
Beast" pattern in which he can love women and be loved by them
in a variety of ways, yet cannot have them. His first great love was
Jean Grey, but she belonged to Scott Summers, Cyclops. They both
lost Jean when her Phoenix form died (*X-Men* #137). Logan neared
marriage and happiness with the Lady Mariko Yashida, winning her
through a war against her own father that culminated in a death duel
where Wolverine rose to the height of his nobility, only to lose her
just before marriage, first to the illusion-making powers of Mastermind and then to Mariko's own nobility when, in her shame, she
decided she must first restore clan Yashida, breaking the clan's under-
world ties and correcting evils committed while under Mastermind's
power (*Uncanny X-Men* #176). Another woman, Lady Deathstrike, is
one of Wolverine's greatest enemies. Young women, Kitty Pryde and
(in the X-Men movie) Rogue, are among his closest friends. His loves
for women range from noble to needy, from romantic to fatherly. He
loves, he rescues, he loses.

Another of Logan's complex dualities revolves around the idea of
self-knowledge. His mystique for decades has been his fragment-
ed memory. Wolverine, like the whole of humanity, has never quite

[margin note: TRUTH ← EMBRACE ALL PARTS OF YOUR-SELF TO EXPERIENCE LIFE. IT IS ALL THINGS GOOD, BAD HAPPY, SAD RIGHT, WRONG. I have lived.]

known who he is. Not only are his memories incomplete, sometimes they are false. His identities are multiple and sometimes contradictory. But he frequently knows others better than they know themselves. He can, first of all, peg true identities: he can tell by sight, smell and sound that an ally is in fact an enemy in disguise—a robot or a shape-shifter. But it goes deeper. He recognizes even personality traits, as when Kitty Pryde was possessed by her future self (*X-Men* #141) and Logan was convinced she was telling the truth, or when Rachel Summers, the alternate timeline daughter of Cyclops and Jean Grey, came from the future into a different past and Wolverine sensed Jean's personality in her daughter (*Uncanny X-Men* #193). In the first powerful Brood story, Logan was the only one of the X-Men who could not be hypnotized by the Brood, but rather saw them for who they were (*Uncanny X-Men* #162). He alone was able to save his friends—which leads to another duality, this one a real paradox.

Wolverine is often the first into battle and the first to get pasted. He may be the "best" but he often loses. And yet sometimes he won't join a battle at all and so must turn the tables by himself when the other X-Men lie in unconscious defeat. Utterly impulsive or utterly self-controlled, there is no middle ground for Wolverine.

One of his most entertaining moments of inaction occurred when he took Peter Rasputin, Colossus, to a bar to get him drunk and beat him up over his recent treatment of Kitty Pryde. When the X-Men's strongest enemy, the Juggernaut, showed up at the same bar and began a slugfest with Colossus, Logan sat back, drank his beer and watched the show. It was one of the best lessons Colossus ever learned (*Uncanny X-Men* #183). In another great moment of restraint, Wolverine ended an alien invasion of Earth with a bluff while playing poker: he bet his life against the alien leader's and the guy folded (*Uncanny X-Men* #245).

Wolverine smokes and drinks constantly, enjoys getting into fights, butchers the Queen's English with words like "bub," "babe," "fracas," "yup," "an'" for "and," "o'" for "of" and the suffix "-in'" for any word ending in "-ing." He is also a dictionary of punctuated Hollywood one-liners:

To Ororo: "I'm made for killing—you're not." (*Uncanny X-Men* #152)

Of the Brood: "No deadlier beings exist in the universe. 'Cept maybe me." (*Uncanny X-Men* #162)

On fighting the Brood: "They do their best. I do better." (*Uncanny X-Men* #162)

On fighting the Silver Samurai: "I survive his first cut. He survives mine." (*Uncanny X-Men* #173)

To Sabretooth: "You were right, Sabretooth. You're the killer. I'm a *man* who sometimes kills." (*Uncanny X-Men* #212)

Having lost his healing power and sure he's about to die on the island of Genosha, as he enters battle: "I might as well go with style. An' lots o' company!" (*Uncanny X-Men* #238)

Even so, his wisdom is far-reaching. A recurring theme in his stories is one of educating others. Logan frequently teaches his partners the nobility and nature of the true warrior. Bar bum he may be, but he is also sensei, master. He taught Kitty Pryde to overcome her fear (*Kitty Pryde and Wolverine*), Storm to restrain her own rage (*Uncanny X-Men* #152), Professor X to allow Storm to lead the X-Men and stop getting in her way (*Uncanny X-Men* #181), Dazzler to be a hero (*Uncanny X-Men* #228), and Colossus to control his power (*Uncanny X-Men* #231). Logan is to his friends a classic archetype: the wise fool.

And he is also the archetype of one half of an ages-old conflict, the one between nature and the city. It's there in the oldest story ever written, *The Epic of Gilgamesh*, where Enkidu (who shows striking resemblances to Wolverine) stands in for nature, and Gilgamesh for the city, in a struggle to find balance. The theme frames the Bible as well: it begins in a garden and moves to a post-Eden wilderness, but then Cain kills his brother and, for protection, builds the first city. The tension between nature and city continues throughout the biblical story to the Apocalypse of John where a new heaven and earth come together in a single place, a city, the New Jerusalem, at the center of which Eden's Tree of Life grows—the unity of the two worlds complete. It's a theme in the *Iliad*, where Greek and Trojan warriors battle to forge themselves into nations built by law instead of only tribes joined by blood. It is a mythic pattern forever at the heart of human endeavor: to live in harmony with nature while refusing to accept her limitations.

Logan is on the nature side of this duality. In the opening of the first miniseries, Wolverine tracked down a bear that had killed some people and mercifully ended its life with hand and claw. Then he tracked down the hunter who shot the bear with a poison arrow, driving it to madness and slaughter. Logan quipped, "The bear lasted longer." In *Uncanny X-Men* #245, the team had moved to Australia, where they discovered an underground base used by enemies they had defeated. Wolverine sensed danger in the vast complex, even in the very technology, the computers around them. Another team member suggested that it was "maybe the 'natural man' reacting to all this technology?" To which Logan replied, "There's a reason I trust my senses over these toys." And yet, true to the idea of complex duality, Wolverine is, himself, augmented by technology, the byproduct of civilization—his body is laced with artificial adamantium, the product of Frankensteinian science. In Wolverine, technology and nature are forever wedded.

HIS THREE SELVES

One archetypal duality stands out to me as the central Wolverine story line—again, another duality more complex than mere light and dark, yin and yang. So many of the archetypal human stories, the great recurring myths, are stories of the human aspiration toward divinity. Mankind longs to achieve godhood or at least find his way to God. Hercules, son of god and mortal, eventually achieves *apotheosis*, godhood. Achilles, whose mother is a goddess and father mortal, was destined, had he been born of gods only, to dethrone Zeus, king of the gods. His struggle in the *Iliad* is a struggle between his humanity and the divinity he will never achieve. But there is a second struggle coexisting with the first: the ascent from animal to man. It is Enkidu's story in *Gilgamesh*; it is the story of Tarzan; it is an integral archetype of Greek myth: fauns and satyrs, centaurs and minotaurs, and the story of Euripides' *Bacchae* in which Dionysus draws the women of Thebes into animal existence in the wilderness. It's even in the Bible: in Daniel 4:31–37, Nebuchadnezzar, emperor of the mighty Babylonian empire, falls to an insanity in which he becomes like an animal, running wild and naked, eating grass like cattle.

The central theme to Chris Claremont's Wolverine was this pair of coexistent archetypes, this complex duality: the progression *from* beast *to* man and the struggle *in* humanity *for* divinity. In a battle against Dr. Doom, the Fantastic Four's chief nemesis made use of Logan's heightened senses to try to drive him mad with rage (*Uncanny X-Men* #147). Logan remembered nearly attacking his first mentor, James Hudson (the leader of Canada's Alpha Flight), and how Hudson helped him reduce his berserker rages. He remembered Hudson's words—"You're a man, not an animal"—and his memory helped him control himself long enough to escape. In his first miniseries, Wolverine sank to his lowest animal self in his confrontations with Mariko's father, Yashida Shingen, but he rose to the same grand conclusion: "I'm not an animal. I'm a man" (*Wolverine* #4).

Logan always suffers from an animal self, a *Wolverine self* if you will. The berserker rages remain a part of his psyche; when killing is required he never hesitates, and his heightened senses tax his sanity, even in the latter Claremont years. But his character is not limited to a Wolverine self, claws extended, versus a *Logan* self, whose retracted claw hands are human. He is more. We might go so far as to identify an animal self, a human self, a *mutant self* (the healing power and heightened senses that make him *Homo superior*, evolution's answer to godhood) and even a *Promethean self*,[1] (an amalgam of metal and flesh, made a god in the image of a materialistic universe). But I suggest that three selves are sufficient: Wolverine the animal, Logan the man and his highest ideal, the *Samurai self*. Logan's greatness is that he somehow *is* the best there is at what he does. Though he may think himself a failed Samurai, his greater nobility appears throughout the X-Men series. His own Mariko said, "You are an honorable man, Logan, with the soul and inner grace of a true Samurai" (*Uncanny X-Men* #162), and a dying woman whom he comforted called him a Samurai as well (*Uncanny X-Men* #181). And in his first recorded confrontation with Sabretooth, even Logan recognized this

---

[1] Prometheus gave man technology in the Greek myth; Mary Shelley's *Frankenstein* was subtitled The Modern Prometheus.

third self: "I've changed. I've learned about honor. A hard road more often than not. But worth the effort" (*Uncanny X-Men* #212).

Wolverine is an archetype of complex human dualities: of lust and romance, of desire and restraint, of insight and self-deceit, of goodness and wickedness, of success and failure, of acting and being, of wisdom and *earthiness*, of teaching and learning, of nature and civilization (each, again, in both harmony and discord), of animal and machine (each both in harmony and discord) and most of all of the human creature: an animal created with a divine spark, who sometimes forgets his spiritual self to sink into his animal flesh, or sometimes forgets his mortality to elevate an arrogant soul. He struggles between heaven and dirt, between angels and slugs, looking for the place of balance where he can say, as Wolverine does, "I am a man."

(margin handwritten note: The battleground of Heaven within each of us.)

When Chris Claremont quit *X-Men* after #279 in 1991, those who followed undid much of the character development he had accomplished with Wolverine. The subtle maroon and burnt orange costume he'd picked up in *X-Men* #140 was traded again for the old gaudy yellow outfit he used to wear, and his animal nature reasserted itself. Essentially, they started over. Perhaps a makeover ruined him, but that's what happens with a character we don't want to let go. But then, we can't really let go; the story is an archetype as old as the stories we've told since creation. Like it or not, we will constantly write Wolverine, whether for good or ill. We've been doing it for four decades and for four thousand years.

REFERENCES

Barfield, Owen. *Poetic Diction: A Study in Meaning.* Middletown, CT: Wesleyan UP, 1973.

Byrne, John, Chris Claremont (w), John Byrne (p), and Terry Austin (i). "Days of Future Past." *X-Men* No. 141. Marvel Comics, January 1981.

———. "Rage!" *X-Men* No. 140. Marvel Comics, December 1980.

———. "The Dark Phoenix Saga: The Fate of the Phoenix." No. 137. Marvel Comics, September 1980.

Claremont, Chris (w), Dave Cockrum (p), and Josef Rubinstein (i). "Rogue Storm!" *Uncanny X-Men* No. 147. Marvel Comics, July 1981.

Claremont, Chris (w), Dave Cockrum (p), and Bob Wiacek (i). "Beyond the Farthest Star." *Uncanny X-Men* No. 162. Marvel Comics, October 1982.

————."Rescue Mission." *Uncanny X-Men* No. 163. Marvel Comics, November 1982.

Claremont, Chris (w), Jim Lee (p), and Fabian Nicieza (i). "Bad to the Bone." *Uncanny X-Men* No. 279. Marvel Comics, August 1991.

Claremont, Chris (w), Rick Leonardi (p), and Terry Austin (i). "Deadly Games!" *Uncanny X-Men* No. 228. Marvel Comics, April 1988.

Claremont, Chris (w), Rick Leonardi (p), and Dan Green (i). "Dressed for Dinner." *Uncanny X-Men* No. 231. Marvel Comics, July 1988.

————. "The Last Run." *Uncanny X-Men* No. 212. Marvel Comics, December 1986.

Claremont, Chris (w), Rob Liefeld (p), and Dan Green (i). "Men!" *Uncanny X-Men* No. 245. Marvel Comics, June 1989.

Claremont, Chris (w), Bob McLeod (p), and Josef Rubinstein (i). "The Hellfire Gambit." *Uncanny X-Men* No. 152. Marvel Comics, December 1981.

Claremont, Chris (w), and Allen Milgrom (p). *Kitty Pryde and Wolverine* Nos. 1–6. Marvel Comics, November 1984–April 1985.

Claremont, Chris (w), Frank Miller (p), and Josef Rubinstein (i). *Wolverine* Nos. 1–4. Marvel Comics, September–December 1982.

Claremont, Chris (w), John Romita, Jr. (p), and Dan Green (i). "He'll Never Make Me Cry." *Uncanny X-Men* No. 183. Marvel Comics, July 1984.

————. "Tokyo Story." *Uncanny X-Men* No. 181. Marvel Comics, May 1984.

————."Warhunt Two." *Uncanny X-Men* No. 193. Marvel Comics, May 1985.

Claremont, Chris (w), John Romita, Jr. (p), and Bob Wiacek (i). "Decisions." *Uncanny X-Men* No. 176. Marvel Comics, December 1983.

Claremont, Chris (w), Mark Silvestri (p), and Dan Green (i). "Gonna Be a Revolution." *Uncanny X-Men* No. 238. Marvel Comics, November 1988.

Claremont, Chris (w), Paul M. Smith (p), and Bob Wiacek (i). "To Have and Have Not." *Uncanny X-Men* No. 173. Marvel Comics, September 1983.

Jemas, Bill, Paul Jenkins, Joe Quesada (w), Andy Kubert (p), John Roshell, and Saida Temofonte (i). *Origins* Nos. 1–6. Marvel Comics, November 2001–July 2002.

Smith, Barry Windsor. *Weapon-X* Vol. 1, Nos. 72–84. Marvel Comics, 1991.

Unbreakable. 2000. Dir. M. Night Shyamalan. Touchstone Pictures.

Wein, Len (w), and Dave Cockrum (w, i). "Second Genesis." *Giant-Size X-Men* No. 1. Marvel Comics, May 1975.

, Len (w), Herb Trimpe (p), and Jack Abel (i). "And the Wind Howled...Wendigo!" *The Incredible Hulk* No. 180. Marvel Comics, October 1974.

———. "And Now the Wolverine." *The Incredible Hulk* No. 181. Marvel Comics, November 1974.

X-Men: The Legend of Wolverine. Marvel and Buena Vista Home Entertainment, 2003.

Charlie W. Starr teaches English, humanities and film at Kentucky Christian University in eastern Kentucky, where he also makes movies with his students and family. He writes articles and teaches Sunday school and has published three books, including a book on Romans, a science fiction novel and *Honest to God*, which was released by Navpress in the summer of 2005. His essay "The Silver Chair and the Silver Screen" is the lead chapter in the book *Revisiting Narnia*, released by BenBella books in October 2005, and his essay "Of Gorillas and Gods" appears as a chapter in another BenBella book, *King Kong Is Back!*, released in November 2005.

He enjoys writing, reading classic literature and watching bad television and movies of every kind. His areas of expertise as a teacher include literature, film and all things C. S. Lewis. Charlie describes his wife Becky as "a full-of-life, full-blooded Cajun, who can cook like one, too." They have two children: Bryan, a high school senior who wants to be the next Steven Spielberg, and Alli, a seventh grader who plays a pretty mean piano. You can find more on Charlie's books and look at some of the movies he's made at his Web site: http://campus.kcu.edu/faculty/cstarr.

Pryde and Joy

KEITH R. A. DECANDIDO

Kitty Pryde burst onto the scene long after my own involvement with the X-Men book was over. Call her Ariel, call her Sprite, call her Shadowcat, there's always been something I've found endlessly appealing about her. I've just never been able to figure out for sure exactly what that certain something is. In the following character study, Keith R. A. DeCandido explains Kitty's continuing appeal to the both of us.

WHEN PEOPLE TALK ABOUT the X-Men, they usually are talking about Wolverine, the group's most popular character since he joined the team in 1975. Or perhaps they're talking about Rogue or Gambit or the Beast or Phoenix or Storm or Jean Grey/Phoenix/Marvel Girl/whatever-the-heck her-name-is or Cyclops, the founding member and, in many ways, the heart and soul of the X-Men, even during those periods when he wasn't with the team.

But to me, the embodiment of the X-Men has always been and always will be a young genius named Katherine Pryde, nicknamed "Kitty," who went through several code names (Sprite, Ariel) before settling on Shadowcat.

Kitty has never been the most prominent member of the team. There was also a lengthy period of time where she was associated with the British branch of the X-Men, Excalibur—indeed, she was a founding member of that team, and remained with them for as long as they existed. But still, she has endured and, to my mind, is really what the X-Men are all about.

From the very first page of the very first issue of *Uncanny X-Men* in 1963, the center of the X-Men mythos has been a school: once Professor Xavier's School for Gifted Youngsters, now the Xavier Institute for Higher Learning. The X-Men's home and headquarters has almost always been this school, and even on those occasions when they abandoned it, whether for the outback of Australia or an island in the Bermuda Triangle, they always returned there eventually.

> XAVIER: The human race is not yet ready to *accept* those with extra powers! So I decided to build a haven...a school for *X-Men*! Here we stay, unsuspected by normal humans, as we learn to use our powers for the benefit of mankind—to help those who would distrust us if they knew of our existence![1]

The school theme is one of the main things that separates the X-Men from other superhero teams. Ultimately, when it comes to mission statement, there really isn't a lot that separates the X-Men from the Avengers or the Fantastic Four or the Defenders or the New Warriors or, for that matter, X-Force, X-Factor, Excalibur or any of the other X-spin-off teams, or, if it comes to that, the Titans, the Justice League or the Outsiders: they're superpowered beings who protect humanity from the bad guys. The one thing that makes the X-Men stand out is that they function against the backdrop of an institute of learning. They are not just in it to be superheroes; they are in it to learn—and to educate.

The X-Men are a team of mutants, people who are *born* with superpowers, and the theme of prejudice has always been at the forefront of the comic books, as mutants are discriminated against by normal humans who fear what is different. Not only do the X-Men beat up the bad guys, they also train young mutants in the use of their powers—and try to educate the world at large to the fact that humans and mutants *can* live together in peaceful coexistence.

---

[1] Lee et al., "X-Men."

Cyclops: We have unique gifts—but no more so, and no more special, than those granted a physician or physicist, or philosopher or athlete. It could be due to an accident of nature or divine providence, who's to say? Are arbitrary labels more important than the way we live our lives, what we're supposed to be more important than what we actually *are?*[2]

The problem the X-Men comics have always faced is that mainstream comic books really thrive on fights between good and evil. Issue after issue of kids in a classroom isn't something that's going to fly off the newsstands. Tellingly, the earliest incarnation of the X-Men, which had the team as teenaged students attending Xavier's School and all wearing matching blue-and-yellow "school uniforms" for costumes, was never particularly popular. The book never caught on to the same extent as Marvel's other books, and in the late 1960s, after sixty-six issues, the book was canceled.

In 1975, when the comic book was relaunched with an almost entirely new team—a more broadly based team, culturally speaking (the original X-Men were four white guys and a white woman), and a more grown-up one—the school subtext was largely abandoned and the book rocketed to the top of Marvel's sales charts, a position it has occupied fairly permanently, and rarely with any challenge, for over twenty-five years.

However, the focus of Xavier's as a school was too unique to ignore for long. In 1980, two new mutants were introduced as part of a larger story line involving the X-Men's battle against a new foe called the Hellfire Club (which would remain one of the team's most tenacious villains from then on). One new mutant, called Dazzler, was a disco singer, introduced for the purpose of spinning her off into her own comic book (one that went from being immensely popular to crashing and burning; the character later joined the X-Men before disappearing from the comics for many years).

The other was Kitty Pryde.

A thirteen-and-a-half-year-old girl from the suburbs of Chicago,

---

[2] Claremont et al., "God Loves, Man Kills."

Kitty reintroduced the idea of the X-Men as a group for teaching mutants, and Kitty eventually joined the team as an X-Man-in-training. She even got a blue-and-yellow outfit just like the original team, though she was not always permitted to go on missions. Eventually, she became a full member, albeit with many fits and starts.

I first started regularly reading X-Men comics at the age of thirteen, so the character of Kitty was fascinating to me because she was my age. What's more, I identified with her as the smart kid trying to fit in. In many ways, I grew up with Kitty as she faced various and sundry trials and tribulations.

Most interesting was watching Kitty develop her powers, and this was one way in which she perfectly exemplified what the X-Men were about. Kitty was constantly learning new facets of her powers, adding them to her arsenal and improving them as she went along. In an interesting twist, a story called "Days of Future Past" (*X-Men* #141) was done very shortly after Kitty joined the team. In it, a much older Kate Pryde in a horribly dystopian New York City was able to send her consciousness back to her teenaged self in order to prevent an assassination. During this story line, Kate showed a much greater facility with her ability to phase through solid matter than Kitty had at that point—or than she would have for some time. Over the course of the next several years, writer Chris Claremont showed Kitty developing her powers slowly, allowing them to grow organically and sensibly with each new experience rather than giving her perfectly realized powers all at once. Letting characters learn new ways to use their powers has always been a facet of Claremont's writing but it was especially prevalent with Kitty, who really was learning. That last word is the key: she was a student, after all.

I think, though, what I always liked best about Kitty was that she had spunk. This goes back to her first appearance. Both Xavier's School and a boarding school run by a member of the Hellfire Club were competing to have Kitty attend. While Xavier gave Kitty's parents the sales pitch, Storm, Wolverine and Colossus took Kitty to a local malt shop, where they were attacked and captured by Hellfire Club operatives.

Kitty had only discovered her powers earlier that afternoon, when a migraine went away after she phased through her bed and bedroom floor and wound up in the downstairs living room of her house. Her second use was during the attack, when she jumped back in shock and went through the malt shop's wall. But the really gutsy thing she did was to then sneak into the Hellfire Club's hovercar and stow away on it, returning with the villains to their headquarters. Kitty herself was astonished at her own gumption, but her hero's instincts were already in place—reemphasizing an idea as prevalent in the X-Men as in other superhero comics: it is not just power that makes you a hero, but what you do with that power. Kitty chose to go after her new friends at great risk to herself.

Kitty managed to stay one step ahead of the Hellfire Club, and when they finally did catch up to her, the remaining X-Men not only rescued her, but had her aid in rescuing their captured teammates.

That ability to think on her feet has served her well. On more than one occasion, she wound up in the position of being the field leader of both the X-Men and Excalibur, and did quite well every time it happened. (This wasn't a given—Claremont in particular has never been afraid to put people out of their depth and have them fail. Nightcrawler's first foray as the X-Men's leader was a disaster, and Magneto failed in his attempt to replace Xavier as headmaster of the school.)

One of Kitty's finest moments, to me, came in an adventure involving both the X-Men and the New Mutants in Asgard. At the climax, Kitty stood up to Loki, the god of mischief and not exactly somebody to be trifled with.

> LOKI: My patience is at an end, and with it, your pathetic lives.
>
> KITTY: Sez you, weasel-face! There are maybe a *score* of X-Men and New Mutants loose in Asgard. We know the truth—and so do the Valkyries! Either you call it quits—right now—you send us home, with all curses lifted and no more vendetta, or we scatter! You can't catch us all! Sooner or later, somebody'll reach Thor or Balder or Heimdall or Freya or the Warriors Three—and *poof* go your precious ambitions to be big boss here, and maybe a whole lot more!
>
> LOKI: Art *threatening* me, youngling?
>
> KITTY: You *bet*cha![3]

---

[3] Claremont et al., "There's No Place Like Home."

That's just one example of many where Kitty shows a maturity and ability beyond her teenaged years. And you gotta love a character who tells off one of Marvel's oldest villains by calling him "weasel-face."

After joining the team, Kitty's first baptism by fire came during an attack on the mansion by a demonic creature known as the N'Garai. Alone in the mansion, Kitty was forced to fend off this monster all by herself, using her phasing ability—a fairly defensive power, particularly in those early days—and the mansion's own devices to stop it. She continued as a trainee member of the team, honing her abilities—right up until the X-Men were taken by the Brood, a race of alien predators from another galaxy.

The X-Men were believed to have been killed; Xavier was despondent for a time. He eventually decided to reopen the school, but only as a school—the "New Mutants," as he called them, would not be a team of heroes going on missions, but instead trainees.

When the X-Men returned to Earth, Xavier put Kitty on the New Mutants. His logic was sound—Kitty was a trainee, the New Mutants were trainees, and indeed, some of them were older than she was. It seemed like a perfect fit. Kitty herself was furious at the demotion.

> KITTY: We're a *family*, don'tcha see? The X-Men are as close to me as my own parents—in some ways, closer—but by shifting me to the New Mutants, the Professor's saying that isn't so! It's tearing me up inside, Stevie, I don't know anymore what to do![4]

However, Kitty handled herself against some alien intruders to the mansion, and Xavier relented—he'd never seen her in action before (he was not present for most of her best moments on the team, whether helping rescue the team in Chicago, her fight against the N'Garai or the battle against the Brood).

At that point, she finally got her own costume—a nice green number designed by Paul Smith—and a new code name. She had gone by Sprite at first, a nickname the arrival of which was marked by bad cola jokes and which never really clicked. The issue in which Xavier put her back in the X-Men, amusingly entitled "Professor Xavier is a

---

4 Claremont et al., "Professor Xavier is a Jerk!"

Jerk!" was the swan song of that code name, and she went by Ariel for a time after that. According to an interview with Claremont, Ariel was his original code name choice—after the ethereal character in Shakespeare's *The Tempest*—but he went with Sprite after realizing that Ariel was a male character. Apparently, he later changed his mind.

However, the name Ariel didn't work much better than Sprite. Tellingly, every time the character was referred to in promotional copy, or when she appeared in *Marvel Team-Up* alongside Spider-Man or as the title character of a miniseries, she was always referred to as "Kitty Pryde." In fact, the miniseries that gave her the code name that she has retained for the two decades since—Shadowcat—was called *Kitty Pryde and Wolverine*. Even now, two decades after she got the code name, she's still associated with her real name first. A recent miniseries starring the character, *Shadow and Flame*, was billed as a Kitty Pryde series rather than a Shadowcat one.

In some ways, this represents more of the character's appeal to me. Yes, she's a superhero; yes, she's a genius; but she's also a real person. I know people just like Kitty, people with her sense of humor, people with her sparkling personality, people with her spunk. Yes, she's an idealized version, but that's to be expected in a comic book that deals in clichés and ideals.

But this also reflects a major facet of the X-Men. While they technically have both code names and given names, the whole notion of a "secret identity" is one they've more or less abandoned—partly because they all live and function in the school, and so don't really have lives outside the X-Men. Bruce Wayne and Batman are practically two different people, and Peter Parker and Spider-Man are different aspects of the same person, but Scott Summers and Cyclops are the same person. Kitty represents the embodiment of this. Her code name is all but irrelevant, little more than a nickname, Kitty Pryde is who she is. Given that Xavier's dream is for mutants to be accepted alongside humans, is it any wonder that one of the most appealing characters is one who's better known by her real name—who's recognized as a person first, and as the mutant Shadowcat second?

We've also seen her grow older. While the fickle time of comic books has meant that she hasn't gotten much older over the course of the twenty-five years she's been around, she has definitely grown up.

In addition to bearing greater responsibilities as a member of both the X-Men and later Excalibur, she also matured in her relationships. She had a crush on teammate Peter Rasputin, a.k.a. Colossus, which developed into true love—and then turned to heartbreak when Peter fell in love with another woman. Any chance of reconciliation was shattered when the X-Men were believed killed, the event that led to the formation of Excalibur.

While with Excalibur, Kitty formed a relationship with Pete Wisdom, a fellow teammate. Amusingly enough, Wisdom never had a code name, either. A former secret agent, he also went by his own name. (The pair made an odd couple. Where Colossus and Kitty were fairly close in age, Wisdom was a cynical, much older man, whose outlook on life seemed an odd pairing with Kitty's youthful enthusiasm. Though, in many ways, it works: Kitty's experiences had tempered her enthusiasm, and her youthful optimism was probably good for Wisdom.)

On top of all that, Kitty has her own dragon. This isn't exactly representative of what the X-Men are all about, but you have to admit, it's pretty cool. One of the most entertaining Kitty stories was called "Kitty's Fairy Tale" (*Uncanny X-Men* #153), during which she told Colossus' sister Illyana a bedtime story in which all the X-Men were turned into fantasy versions of themselves—starting with Pirate Kitty, who rode a big dragon named Lockheed. Later on, when they were on the Brood home world, a small fire-breathing dragon saved Kitty's life and then stowed away on the trip home after the X-Men destroyed the Brood planet, becoming Kitty's friend and protector. She named him Lockheed, as well.

KITTY: We can't send Lockheed home, Professor. He doesn't have one anymore. And since the X-Men were partially responsible for that, we owe it to him to look after him.
XAVIER: Eminently logical, Kitty. If I say no, will he eat me?
KITTY: Lockheed, don't you *dare*![5]

Most of Lockheed's dialogue consists of the words "Meh" and "Pfui," but he's a great character, and has stayed staunchly by Kitty's side ever since.

---
[5] Ibid.

One of Kitty's best moments was, ironically, in the *New Mutants* comic book series. Despite the fact that Kitty never liked the New Mutants and didn't want to be a part of it—she referred to the team often as the "X-babies"—it was in that comic, in a landmark issue entitled "We Were Only Foolin'" (*New Mutants* #45), that Kitty had one of her most impressive moments, in one of the most tragic and brilliant stories in the X-books' pantheon. Kitty reluctantly joined the New Mutants in attending a mixer at a local high school and met a young boy named Larry Bodine. Kitty and Larry got along very well—right up until he started telling "mutie" jokes, at which point Kitty and the New Mutants lost interest in being his friend. Only one of the New Mutants didn't believe his prejudice, thinking him a good soul.

Some of the local kids thought that Larry was a mutant, and jokingly threatened to call mutant hunters down on him. However, Larry really was a mutant—his making "mutie" jokes was a cover—and was scared to death by this threat, not realizing it was just a prank. Larry wound up killing himself. Kitty was the one to deliver the eulogy at his funeral, and it is an emotional, heartfelt speech, decrying the senseless prejudice that led a good kid to take his own life.

Claremont could have had any character give that speech—indeed, as an issue of *New Mutants*, it probably would've been more appropriate to have a member of that team give it. But it worked best coming from Kitty, the person who is, in many ways, the embodiment of what the X-Men are all about—not just finding mutants among humans and making their lives better, but finding heroes among mutants and giving them a chance to shine. Years later, this issue is still regarded by some fans as one of the best comics ever done regarding the mutant question, and Kitty Pryde was the heart of it.

So what we've got is a character who we've watched grow up from a spunky teenager into a valued asset to the X-Men, whose powers have developed over the years, who can stand up to any of the heavy hitters in the Marvel Universe and who (smaller point, I know) has her own dragon. She has endured the several thousand changes that have gone on in the X-books over the last twenty-five years, and she is at the center of one of the strongest stories in the pantheon.

Why isn't she more popular? Beats the heck out of me. But she'll always be my favorite. So here's to ya, kid.

REFERENCES

Byrne, John, Chris Claremont (w), John Byrne (p), and Terry Austin (i). "Days of Future Past." *X-Men* No. 141. Marvel Comics, January 1981.

Claremont, Chris (w), Arthur Adams (p, i), Alan Gordon, and Mike Mignola (i). "There's No Place Like Home." *Uncanny X-Men Annual* No. 9. Marvel Comics, 1985.

Claremont, Chris (w), and Brent Anderson (a). "God Loves, Man Kills." *Marvel Graphic Novel* No. 5. Marvel Comics, 1982.

Claremont, Chris (w), Dave Cockrum (p), and Josef Rubinstein (i). "Kitty's Fairy Tale." *Uncanny X-Men* No. 153. Marvel Comics, January 1982.

Claremont, Chris (w), Jackson Guice (p), and Kyle Baker (i). "We Were Only Foolin'." *New Mutants* No. 45. Marvel Comics, November 1986.

Claremont, Chris (w), Paul Smith (p), and Bob Wiacek (i). "Professor Xavier is a Jerk!" *Uncanny X-Men* No. 168. Marvel Comics, April 1983.

Lee, Stan (w), Jack Kirby (p), and Paul Reinman (i). "X-Men." *X-Men* No. 1. Marvel Comics, September 1963.

Keith R. A. DeCandido is on his fourth journey into Smart Pop Land, having deconstructed the first episode of *Firefly* for *Finding Serenity*, debunked the last line of *King Kong* in *King Kong Is Back!* and delineated the merits of the nine actors who've dramatically performed the role of Superman in *The Boy from Krypton*. Keith is also a best-selling novelist, veteran anthologist, ardent baseball fan and practitioner of *kenshikai* karate. Find out too little about Keith at his official Web site, DeCandido.net.

Magneto Attracts

CHRISTOPHER ALLEN

If a man can be measured by the quality of his enemies, then Charles Xavier is a most impressive man indeed. On the one hand, we have Magneto, perhaps the greatest of the X-Men's foes, capable of controlling all metal and reshaping it to his will, capable of making the Statue of Liberty walk and the Golden Gate Bridge dance the tango. On the other hand, there is Lucifer, who can…can….Well, suppose we let Christopher Allen tell us all about it.

LUCIFER. MAGNETO.

One conjures images of Faustian bargains, fire and brimstone. Horns on the head, a pointy tail and a villainous Van Dyke beard. The Number of the Beast discovered on the scalp, a hundred times worse than lice. The subject of countless heavy metal songs performed by cynical hedonists for confused teenagers who would rather hear anything but their parents' James Taylor albums.

The other recalls bad '50s inventions and ad copy. "Now in thrilling Magnetovision!" "Not just neato…MAG-neto!"

And yet, in the world of Marvel Comics, Lucifer is a villain given just two chances to shine before getting a one-way ticket to oblivion—literally—while Magneto has been the X-Men's greatest foe since day one, and was even given his own book. What gives?

Lucifer, the villain who took the spring (and more) out of Professor Charles Xavier's step, has come close to killing Xavier more times than most X-Men villains. So why the hell have you never heard of this guy? I mean, I know Satan tends to keep a low profile, but he's usually not embarrassing.

It's quite a puzzler, especially given Marvel Comics' propensity for bringing back every lame-o who has ever worn a tight costume to steal a purse, travel back in time to steal a pharaoh's purse or pander too late to fads like kung fu, disco and skateboarding. No love for the Luce Cannon?

The reasons for Magneto's attraction (yes, yes, pun intended) and Lucifer's, well, repulsiveness, break down to both conception—inspired versus not—and execution—dynamic versus indifferent and inconsistent.

To understand why Magneto became the nemesis to Professor X, while Lucifer became a no-name, a yahoo, rather than the yang to X's yin, let's look at the two main creators of the X-Men, Stan "the Man" Lee and Jack "the King" Kirby, who, along with artist Steve Ditko, were the prime architects of what would become known as the "Marvel Universe," beginning with the seminal *Fantastic Four* #1 in 1961. Utilizing what would become known as "the Marvel Method," Lee scripted nearly all of Marvel's output through the early '60s, providing a basic plot to an artist who would then expand it and draw it as a comic story. Because of his endless ideas and unmatched artistic dynamism, Kirby was Lee's greatest collaborator, and the lion's share of the work fell to them during this time. They were producing half a dozen comics a month, or more, and some of these were "split books," with two different serials each issue. The men were often so overworked that they were only plotting one issue ahead, and trying to make each issue as exciting on its own as possible. The idea of consistent continuity was given little consideration at first, with Marvel's modern mythology accreting in detail almost by accident and expedience. It made sense to use one hero's enemy in another hero's book rather than create a new bad guy each time, just as a large chunk of a story could be spent in having two heroes or teams meet, distrust each other, fight and then unite against a villain. Kirby designed the characters, often adding ideas and details that would inspire Lee, but on the rare occasions something didn't work very well, well, those deadlines still had to be met, and Lee and Kirby just had to hope for better next time. Simply put, Magneto was a character who worked, and Lucifer wasn't.

Kirby penciled just eleven issues of *X-Men* before going to just layouts for Werner Roth to finish, for six issues, and then, aside from the occasional cover, his input into the book was nil. Magneto debuted in 1964 in *X-Men* #1, and Lucifer in 1965 in issue #9, and though only eight issues (bimonthly for reasons not worth mentioning here, but probably a factor in the book's relative lack of popularity at the time) and a change in inkers separate them, there is a great deal of difference between the two. While it is true that most of the stories favored by X-Men fans, such as "The Dark Phoenix Saga" and "Days of Future Past," occurred much later and were done by different creators, it is also true that the long-running Marvel series all have their most important, enduring villains appear within the first year or two of their inception. Dr. Doom would fight the Fantastic Four by the fourth issue; Spider-Man wouldn't meet the Green Goblin until *Amazing Spider-Man* #14, but tangled with arguably his second most popular villain, Dr. Octopus, in #3.

In *X-Men* #1, Lee and Kirby have had time to work out their concept for a team of teenaged mutants operating in a world peopled by those who hate and fear them. It is eleven pages before we see Magneto, but in that time the reader is introduced to four of the X-Men in exciting training (in what would later become known as the Danger Room), as well as their leader, the mysterious, bald, wheelchair-bound Professor Xavier, the startling idea of a superhero team operating within a private school for the gifted, and the comely Jean Grey, who would become the fifth X-Man, Marvel Girl. In other words, Magneto got a good lead-in, and Lee and Kirby did right by him, presenting an oddly garbed man bent on world domination, with an impressive display of power that included turning tanks and guns against Army soldiers, binding the soldiers in a fence of invisible magnetic waves and taking over Cape Citadel by himself, all within moments. Magneto's commanding presence was formidable, and Kirby's design of his helmet, shaped to draw attention to the eyes, and costume, featuring a bolted chest piece to remind the reader at all times that the wearer was associated with metal and its properties, was unforgettable. And with the Cape and all its ordnance for use in the battle, Lee and Kirby not only provided a thrilling sequence, they also showed that, while he did not succeed, Magneto was a fearsome opponent, and his escape proved they thought highly enough of him that his return was a certainty. It was also a solid script throughout, with the aforementioned dramatic introduction of both hero and villain, the great battle and something else as well: a hint of depth. Magneto was shown to be the philosophical counterpoint to Xavier—a mutant who wanted to use his powers to dominate humanity, not help it. Great concept, great execution.

Lee and Kirby built upon Magneto's appeal with repetition. Nowadays, it's commonplace for superhero teams to have a new menace every month, but in *X-Men* the creators saw fit to make Magneto the central villain; he appeared in most of the first eight issues with his Brotherhood of Evil Mutants in various combinations. In #6, Magneto teamed up with the Atlantean Prince Namor, the Sub-Mariner, to defeat humanity—or as Namor phrased it, "the surface dwellers." Magneto showed his cunning by appealing to Namor as a fellow mutant, since the prince was half-human, half-Atlantean: he had pink skin rather than blue, and was able to breathe air. While Magneto did flee when Namor discovered his perfidy, he escaped with his dignity intact.

Giving a villain a team to lead could serve to diminish his power in lesser creative hands, but Lee and Kirby knew what they were doing. Among the many members of the Brotherhood were the brother-and-sister mutants Quicksilver and Scarlet Witch, who had reservations about the evildoing part of their work and were impressive enough to be chosen by Captain America in the first Avengers membership change, in *Avengers* #16. So not only had Magneto already returned to trouble the X-Men further, he was also established as such a leader that other powerful mutants were placed in his charge, to do his will. Retroactive continuity (a.k.a. *retconning*), would reveal that Quicksilver and Scarlet Witch are also Magneto's children, showing that this was a guy who was really committed to his cause. Even without this knowledge, it was evident that until Lucifer arrived, there was no other character even in the running to replace Magneto in importance. And by sheer volume of appearances in the early days of the series, Magneto was inextricably linked with the X-Men, and so, in later years, few writers who got to play in the X-Men sandbox could resist taking a crack at him.

And so, when Lucifer made his debut in #9, he had his work cut out for him—and unfortunately, Lee and Kirby hobbled him from the start with uncharacteristically subpar conception and execution. From the title, "Enter, The Avengers!" and its following legend, "Featuring: The Earth-Shattering Threat of Lucifer!" it was clear that the man wasn't being given enough room to shine. The splash page did display Lucifer in the center, circled by X-Men and Avengers, but significantly, none were looking at him. Instead, the teams were posed as if ready to battle each other, and Lucifer was drawn so small, and so overwhelmed by the large bomb-shaped apparatus he was hoisting, that only the diminutive Avenger the Wasp made less of an impression. It was a lot like two rival fraternities were about to throw down at a party, and oblivious nerd Lucifer showed up with a fresh keg to try to fit in. At any rate, he presented no threat in his first artistic depiction, whereas on the cover of #1, Magneto stood his ground against a full team attack under the banner, "The World's Most Powerful Super Villain!" Big boots to fill, Lucifer.

Rather than taking on the X-Men with a masterful scheme, Lucifer began his career in reactive mode, unleashing gimmicky weapons and traps for Professor Xavier, who had tracked him to his Balkan lair. And no, he couldn't seem to slow down an invalid on a treaded vehicle chugging along in a cave. What was worse was that for all of Kirby's skills at character design (the X-Men revert to their original yellow and dark blue every few years; Magneto retains his scarlet cape and costume, often with the purple accents, some forty years after his debut), Lucifer was just a lackluster design. He had a beard, barely seen between a fur-collared cape and a helmet that was reminiscent of both the old Jack Kirby/Joe Simon character Gangbuster/Guardian and of the phallic-foreheaded Buddha seen in the lighting treatments of many a sit-down Chinese restaurant. (If you've never noticed, consider yourself fortunate.)

Lucifer did have a plan of sorts, something to do with a thermal bomb, attuned to his heartbeat, with the ability to wipe out a continent, but for what gain was never made clear. It was revealed that the story was taking place now in Bavaria, not the Balkans after all, which seems a pretty clear indication of scripter Lee's lack of interest. Then, with no help from his X-Men, Xavier defeated Lucifer easily with his mental powers, then let him go as if he had no fear of him and could find him at any time to exact vengeance for the loss of his legs. Lucifer shuffled off panel like a scolded child, penile helmet hanging low. It should be pointed out that it's hard to become one of the top enemies of a super-team when one doesn't actually fight the team itself, instead tangling with their mostly stay-at-home leader.

Magneto went away for a while, allowing Lee and Kirby to finally add some other important characters to the X-Men universe, such as Xavier's unstoppable half-brother Juggernaut and the giant, mutant-hunting robot Sentinels. But then Magneto returned in fine style in #18, sending the defeated, bound X-Men up in a floating gondola while taking over their school and kidnapping the Angel's parents, who had arrived to visit their son. However, it looked like Lee had already lost hope for Lucifer by the end of issue #19, which advertised, "Next Ish: The Return of Unus! The Blob!—And The Mysterious Lucifer! 'Nuff Said!"

It's not enough that Lucifer got third billing to Jerk and the Fatman; by the time the long-promised story of how Professor X lost the use of his legs arrived in #20, Lee and Kirby had moved on to launch and create other books, leaving the low-selling X-Men in the hands of Lee-acolyte Roy Thomas, with penciling handled by "Jay Gavin," a.k.a. Werner Roth. Since Roth was a second- or third-tier Marvel artist never given the assignment of designing or redesigning characters, the task of rehabilitating Lucifer fell to the young Thomas, in only his first issue. With perhaps a similar lack of confidence in his villain, Thomas gave Lucifer some new mental powers (that perhaps could have prevented his defeat in his first appearance, if he'd had them), and had him manipulate Brotherhood members Unus the Untouchable and the Blob in a scheme to discredit the X-Men by having Unus and Blob dress up as them and commit crimes. It worked, giving our heroes the reputation of public menaces, and they tracked Lucifer down to his new Southwest mesa digs.

Lucifer used his new powers to control Professor Xavier, though Xavier was still able to mentally tell Marvel Girl the story of how Lucifer robbed him of the use of his legs when Xavier confronted Lucifer during his rule of a hidden Tibetan city. Thomas revealed that Lucifer is, in fact...an alien! But before you get excited by the promise of this exotic early episode, it should be noted that Lucifer paralyzed Xavier merely by getting him to stand under a dangling stone block (what was that doing up there, anyway?).

In contrast to the first conflict between Xavier's X-Men and Magneto, Thomas' story of the first Xavier/Lucifer meeting was fraught with problems. There was no apparent purpose for Lucifer's presence in Tibet other than to enslave a small group of primitive people, and mentally forcing one to try to drop a chandelier on Xavier wasn't terribly dramatic, nor was the simplistic manner in which Lucifer eventually defeated Xavier. A telepath defeating another telepath by dropping a heavy object on his legs is akin to a fencing match won by throwing dirt in the opponent's face: it's cheap and it's thuggish.

Thomas drove a big nail in Lucifer's coffin of a career by revealing him contacting his leader on a big screen. His leader! For all his "might," Lucifer was just following orders, minding the huge mind-control computer called Dominus as his Quistalian homies prepared for an Earth invasion. The guy giving the orders, "the Supreme One," looked much like Lucifer, but with a larger helmet (smarter) that had cool lightning bolt things on it (more powerful) where Lucifer's helmet was smooth and decal-free. Lucifer was diminished and redundant. No one ever ripped off Magneto's helmet and lived to tell about it, nor does Magneto take orders from anybody.

Our Quistalian Stallion suffered another ignominious defeat, this time at Marvel Girl's hands—she used telekinesis to wrap him up in his own cape. This was the last straw for 'Preme, who banished Lucifer to "a dimension where neither time nor space exists," and unlike many of even the lamest Marvel characters, he has never been brought back.

Given the fact that Lucifer cost Xavier the use of his legs, wouldn't this historical connection have been able to overcome the shortcomings of the character? Was it just Magneto's strong first appearances that secured his later standing? That has something to do with it, sure. Out of necessity, Marvel writers have had to adopt the notion that there are no irredeemably bad characters, since not every writer got to write the good ones, but it's also true that for every Green Goblin, there's a Red Ghost and a Purple Man and other characters "colorful" in name only. Magneto had a good foundation laid for him, and not only did Lucifer not, he was abandoned somewhere where it would require more work to bring him back than it was worth.

Magneto was a mysterious supervillain first and foremost, and continued to gain in complexity as the series went on. The added dimension to his character stemmed from his philosophical differences to Xavier, his belief that mutantkind must rule mankind and that they can never live side by side in peace. That there is evidence to support Magneto's belief makes him a villain of great depth, more so in later years as he tried Xavier's way for a time, as a teacher in Xavier's school for mutants. In *Uncanny X-Men* #161, Chris Claremont wrote the story of the real first meeting for Xavier and Magneto (then Magnus), when they both worked in a clinic for concentration camp victims in Israel. They ended up fighting former Nazi Baron Strucker and his terrorist HYDRA troops, who had come for camp survivor Gaby Haller, the only one who knew the location of the gold they were looking for. Magnus and Xavier worked together to track down HYDRA and the abducted Gaby, and Magnus showed his difference from Xavier by killing the terrorists. It isn't a classic story, but it was a decent attempt to add some shared history and friendship to the two to make their later conflicts a bit more poignant. Claremont and later writers would add more and more nuance to Magneto's character; he even took Xavier's place as headmaster at the school for a while, the supervillainous mass-murdering megalomaniac actually coming down from his high horse (in Magneto's case, his own space station, Asteroid M), to try *someone else's way* for a time. This lightening up worked with the chicks, too—he played "bend the fork" with X-Man Polaris, sort of the less powerful female version of himself. More importantly, Magneto has *his own country*, Genosha, a sanctuary for mutants, which fed that megalomania fire again while still doing some good. Lee and Kirby couldn't have predicted the turns Magneto's career would take, but they definitely laid the foundation for some of them from the start.

Lucifer, the poor devil, never had a chance. Dramatic but inappropriate name. Uninspired costume with a helmet that has set my therapy back months. Nonvisual powers. First battle with X-Men not actually with X-Men but with their bald, non-ambulatory leader. Creepy helmet. Switch in writers leads to awkward switch from would-be world-beater to point man in alien invasion, with similar-looking but more powerful boss and big machine that was more important to plan than he was. Foiled in second battle by Marvel Girl throwing his cape over his head. No asteroid. No evidence he could mate with human women, even Balkavarian ones. And did I mention the helmet?

Magneto has a great helmet. I have no issues with that helmet at all.

REFERENCES

Friedman, Michael Jan. *X-Men: Shadows of the Past.* I Books, 2000.

Lee, Stan (w), Dick Ayers, Jack Kirby (p), and Dick Ayers (i). "The Old Order Changeth!" *Avengers* No. 16. Marvel Comics, May 1965.

Lee, Stan (w), and Steve Ditko (a). "Spider-Man versus Dr. Octopus, the Strangest Foe of all Time...." *Amazing Spider-Man* No. 3. Marvel Comics, July 1963.

———. "The Grotesque Adventure of the Green Goblin." *Amazing Spider-Man* No. 14. Marvel Comics, July 1964.

Lee, Stan (w), Jay Gavin (p), and Dick Ayers (i). *X-Men* Nos. 18–19. Marvel Comics, March–April 1966.

Lee, Stan (w), Jack Kirby (l), Jay Gavin (p), and Chic Stone (i). ". . . And None Shall Survive!" *X-Men* No. 17. Marvel Comics, February 1966.

Lee, Stan (w), Jack Kirby (p), and Chic Stone (i). *X-Men* Nos. 1–11. Marvel Comics, January 1965–May 1966.

Thomas, Roy (w), Jay Gavin (p), and Dick Ayers (i). *X-Men* Nos. 20–21. Marvel Comics, May–June 1966.

Christopher Allen is the managing editor and founder for ComicBookGalaxy.com. He has also written for *The Comics Journal*, Kevin Smith's MoviePoopShoot.com, *Ain't It Cool News* and NinthArt.com, and is one of the 2006 judges for the comics industry's prestigious Will Eisner Comics Industry Awards. He has two children and lives in San Diego, California.

Magneto the Jew

MARIE-CATHERINE CAILLAVA

There are those who say that there really is no such thing as free choice, that a person's future is ultimately determined by the events of their past. If this is true, then can we really blame young Erik Lehnsherr for the crimes committed by the older Magneto in the name of Mutantkind? Here, Marie-Catherine Caillava offers us her views on the matter, and reminds us that, to this day, certain words still possess a terrible power of their own.

MAGNETO'S BEING A JEW is of paramount importance. It defines the very relationship between reality and fiction.

At least, it does to me.

Let me share with you a very personal story, that of my love affair with Erik Magnus Lehnsherr and of how he made me become a writer.

I grew up your standard European little girl, except for the fact that I was told stories about Jews (translate: very nice people) hiding in Grandpa's cellar, and of "nazees" (meaning: horrible monsters) finding them one night after the baby cried at the wrong moment and taking them away, never to be seen again. I would hide my teddy bears before falling asleep, out of fear that the same "nazees" would find them and do awful things to them. Being six years old, I was not too sure what those "awful things" would be. I remember that, after much painful pondering, I had decided that the most atrocious thing one could do to a teddy would be to tear its stuffing out while laughing sadistically, like the villains did in comics. Every morning my bears and I were so joyful—just like the heroes who prevailed on the last page of every single book I owned—because the "nazees" had not found us while we slept. Then, when I was eleven years old, I saw an elementary-school-level documentary about Auschwitz. I was sick and had nightmares for a whole week. Surprisingly, it was not the sight of the piles of corpses or the expression in the eyes of the captives that scarred me the most, but two facts that a bookworm kid like me had never managed to conceive. First, that the Nazis were human beings—I had so far taken the expression "inhuman bastards" literally—and they did not laugh sadistically while pushing families into the gas chambers. In fact, war criminals all said it was boring, smelly and difficult work that gave them no pleasure. Second, survivors were not "joyful" to have survived, but all had very complex emotions about it. Some actually felt guilty, while others spent every single minute of the day with their memories or lived frantically, feeling bound by a duty to the dead to be happy and make the most of life.

Villains and good guys in the real world had nothing in common with their fictional counterparts. I can't begin to tell you how deep the shock was to me. All the things I had learned from books were useless! Fiction and reality had no relation at all. Human villains looked like our next-door neighbor, while the good guys' reactions to their own victory held a complexity far beyond my young grasp.

I began looking into psychology and asking myself how to classify fictional characters. Captain Nemo, for example, sank ships, thus killing sailors, but I liked him. Did that make me a monster? Was my interest for the dark master of the Nautilus any different from being a real-world fan of the Nazis?

When you are eleven years old, these questions are overwhelming.

But some years later a mutant in tights stepped into my life and made me grow along with him.

Enter Magneto.

The first time I met him was in a friend's cellar, in battered copies of the first few issues of *X-Men*. The Master of Magnetism was a familiar figure, as villains go: arrogant, eyes shining, posing like a Kabuki character, talking about himself in the third person. His ghost army, while walking into San Marco, wore helmets and sported a flag, very unsubtle allusions to Nazis in WWII Germany. He talked about the superiority of the mutant kind and the rightful place they had as leaders of Earth—with him at the helm, of course.

It was far from love at first sight, but he felt reassuring; I could put a "villain bent on world domination" sticker on him and go on with my reading. How restful.

A while later, I discovered that Xavier and his team were still being published in a franchise now called *Uncanny X-Men*. Of all the characters that had carried over into the new series, Magneto had evolved the most. He now took his helmet off to show a very sad and human face, and in "And the Dead Shall Bury the Living!" (*Uncanny X-Men* #149) he spelt out his credo: "The money and energy devoted now to war will be turned instead to the eradication of hunger, disease, poverty. I offer a golden age the like of which humanity has never imagined." His ambition to become the ruler of Earth was just a means to reaching that noble end. I was intrigued.

But then, I flipped a page of the action-packed "I, Magneto" (*Uncanny X-Men* #150) and read as he said with tears in his eyes: "I remember my own childhood—the gas chambers, Auschwitz, the guards joking as they herded my family to their death. As our lives meant nothing to them, human lives became nothing to me."

I nearly had a fit, and began writing a rabid letter to the publisher: was the author mad? Making a tights-wearing comic book villain a survivor of Auschwitz was an insult to the dead! Putting my thoughts together for my letter, I quickly realized that I had to define the nature of the fiction/reality border before barking about fictional Magneto and his real-world past. I was about to discover why fiction was so capital to our reality, thanks to the immigration officer on the border, a tall lonely man called Erik Lehnsherr.

Human beings like you and me live in the world called reality, and we find it so excruciatingly painful and complex that we invent worlds of fiction to try and better analyze our universe, or at least make it seem more bearable for an hour or so.

No reality is more unbearable than the Nazi death camps and other organized mass murders: the most horrendous crimes—physical, emotional and cultural—bolstered by twisted rationalization. Hitler did it, Pol Pot did it. Both men were plain, real human beings—a terrifying notion.

On the other side of the border, we can find no fiction more remote from our reality than the superhero comics genre: muscular people in spandex tights, flying around while commenting on their fistfights: "Gosh, you've totally taken me by surprise with that blast ray, and now I'm plummeting to my doom!"

There is indeed something obscene in alluding to the death camps in such a potentially silly universe, one powered by soap opera–like plots in the "I am your father!" or "But you're dead, I saw you!" styles.

There are, of course, comic books dealing directly with the Holocaust, but they all serve an educational purpose. The most famous one, *Maus*, is a memorial to the victims of the Shoah, using the medium of comics and a deceptively childlike penciling to emotionally involve the reader. The same is true for comic books that address anti-Semitism. Will Eisner's *Fagin the Jew* was narrated and drawn with such tenderness in the ink lines and "real" details in the text that the readers could not resist identifying with that so-lovable scoundrel Fagin. The medium of comics was, in both cases, used in service of a duty to memory and education.

But when a word like Auschwitz appears in the speech bubble of the main villain in *X-Men*, does the Marvel franchise use the name to move us and make this week's fantastic plot more interesting, or is there another purpose, something more to it than promoting a comic book through allusion to one of the most horrifying events in our history?

We can only find that out if we first try to answer this question: is Magnus a Jew or not?

I've never met an X-Men enthusiast who did not have a personal theory about Magneto's identity.

"He is not a Jew but a Gypsy, see page *xyz* of issue *blahblah*."

"Lehnsherr is not his real name!"

"Read page *this* of issue *that*, he was in the Sonderkommandos in Auschwitz which, contrary to what the number of his tattoo implies—and this is where my analysis is so magnificently clever—might mean he arrived early and he's a Jew indeed!"

"Oh, c'mon, you're all nuts, it's clear the writers just messed up the continuity in issue *niki-nakt-nu* with that Gypsy allusion!"

And so on.

We X-maniacs could all write volumes about it, because we love the mutant universe and think of it as real. But it's all pointless: Erik is a fictional character in a fantasy world, born in the imagination of a succession of individuals who loved creating comics and aimed to fascinate their readers.

So let's have a look at Magneto's real progenitors, and by that I mean folks on our side of the border: Kirby, Lee and Claremont. Kirby and Lee, like the vast majority of comic book pioneers, were Jews of Central European origin. It's unlikely they would let a word like Auschwitz get into one of their publications without a lot of thought. As for Claremont, who developed the psychology and history of Magnus so brilliantly, he's known for the seriousness and wholehearted care he puts in his work. If he wrote Auschwitz, he meant Auschwitz. Why else use it instead of a generic "terrible place where my people were enslaved and slaughtered"? It would have done the trick if Claremont's aim had been solely to make Magneto both a victim and a bad guy. When artists like Lee, Kirby and Claremont use a precise real-world word, they know it's going to create an association in the reader's mind. That's their goal. We have seen enough movies about it and read enough history books; we don't need the whole picture.

When you say Auschwitz to people, they immediately think Holocaust, even though there were deaf people, Gypsies, communists and many other groups of people slaughtered there, too. But one million Jews were butchered coldly in that camp alone—one-sixth of the total number of victims of the Holocaust—and it has naturally become the symbol of the suffering of the Jewish people under Nazi rule.

In the same light, if you say, "He emigrated to Israel after escaping from Auschwitz," ninety-nine percent of people will think at once:

"He's a Jew who survived and joined the Zionist movement." Their first thought is not going to be "Hmm, I wonder if he's a Gypsy."

Whether Lee, Kirby and Claremont wanted the audience to deduce that Magneto is a Jew or not, the reader *does*. But let's assume, for the moment, that making Magneto a Jew was in fact their intention. Why would they even want Magnus to be a Jew?

Well, many Marvel characters have a strong personal culture; that's part of their charm. It was only natural that, between an Irish flying mutant and an African Goddess of the Clouds, we should have some Jewish superheroes. Kitty is Jewish, Sabra is an Israeli mutant and 007 from the Mossad, just like baby blue-eyed Thing in the Fantastic Four, was created to be the alter ego of Kirby: a nice Jewish guy from Brooklyn.

More importantly, making Erik Lehnsherr Jewish highlights the message of *X-Men*. One of the unique aspects of the X-Men universe is that it is a three-layer cake: layer one, the action and hype; layer two, the soap opera (my child!); and layer three, the underlying message about the world we live in. Like all high-quality fictions, *X-Men* is a comment on reality, more specifically on prejudice and being different. And that third layer is what has made the franchise such a long-lasting success while other comics have come and gone.

The coup de maître here is that it was not Xavier, Mr. Compassion-and-Rationality, who was given a childhood in Auschwitz, but Magneto, the—at first—grandiloquent bad guy. Of course, Xavier could be Jewish too; he worked in Israel, he's an intellectual, he fits several clichés. But had he been brought up in a death camp, he would not have been very different from what he is: he would have seen prejudice kill his family and would work for peace so that those horrors didn't happen to his fellow mutants. It could have worked as far as characterization goes, but it would not have added anything to the depth of the stories or his character. But to make *Magneto* be the survivor—what a world of contradictions in his head, what a wealth of human emotions to explore! Good and bad, remorse and anger—he could have wiped out Hitler's army with a thought, had he only been aware of his powers.

He is a bad guy, a victim, a dreamer, a loyal and honest friend, a powerful mutant, a man who has nightmares every night, a loving father and a nutcase plagued by uncontrollable fits of rage. If good fiction is indeed a reflection on our reality, no matter how entertaining that fiction may be, then Magnus is a fantastic tool for the exploration of human nature.

This bridge across the border between our world and the X-Men's is made irresistible by the creators. One of the reasons so many people love to enter the X-Men universe is that the franchise is about being different—or, for that matter, just feeling different. Any teen bookworm living among kick-boxing fans, any young gay man isolated in an aggressively heterosexual environment, any smart girl surrounded by male bullies and female airheads, almost anybody who feels different, can identify with Xavier's team. Unlike superheroes like Superman, the X-Men are not invincible or aliens; they are fully human, born of "normal" parents, and turn out to be mutants almost always unexpectedly. They are from all parts of the world, appearing apparently at random among the "normal" population.

This is another way making Magneto a Jew enriches the X-Men story. If one was to make a map of where mutants are on Earth in the X-universe (pre- or post-Genosha), there would be red dots everywhere, scattered over all the continents. The very same kind of map one would have ended up with in mapping the Jewish communities in Europe in the early nineteenth century: scattered everywhere, part of the countries they lived in but rejected and different, alone.

The lonely bookworm who identifies with the X-Men is happy to cross the bridge to their universe. And in that crossing is the opportunity for education and reflection. Today's Israel is a country where families try to avoid talking about politics, where fear and anger are part of the daily life. In many ways, it's like any other country in the world would be during a crisis. But there is another Israel, one that is incredibly related to Magneto. That other Israel is a dreamland, the utopia that was dreamt of by the Zionists in 1920s and '30s Germany.

Fiction is always far more simple than reality. The parallel between Magneto's Genosha, the African island granted as a haven for all persecuted mutants, and Israel is an obvious one, but the conclusions we draw from the X-Men universe are quite different than the ones we hear from most modern-day Zionists.

Mutants in the X-universe and Jews in the early twentieth century were in the same situation: isolated and persecuted. On the mutant side, as in all fictional worlds, we have two clear-cut, black-or-white positions: one man is saying, "We must live among them," and the other is saying, "We must go live elsewhere, or they'll destroy us."

In 1920s Germany, Jews—real people with far more complexity than comic book characters, no matter how well imagined—had thousands of lines of thought about their problem. They all agreed that there was a rise in anti-Semitism and that it was unlikely the Gentiles in Europe would change their attitude out of the blue. Some Jewish movements, like the Jewish Labour Union (a.k.a. the Bund), and intellectuals like Einstein advocated educating the goyim, showing people that the Jews and the non-Jews could live in harmony and learn from each other, rather than encouraging self-segregation by running away and creating a separate state that would be an easy target for anti-Semites. Xavier would have approved, of course. The other main movement was called Zionism and worked along the idea that Jews were too different from the goys (it's not a derogatory term; "goy" originally meant "nation" in Hebrew) and the goys too prejudiced for things to get better. The only solution was to create a state of Israel, where Jews could fully live along the lines of their own tradition and rebalance the pyramid of their society that was, during that period, almost entirely composed of intellectuals and artisans, including almost no proletariat.

This is where reality reaches a complexity that no invented situation could achieve. Even the very simple and basic question of where to create Israel was a matter of immense controversy. Some, for religious reasons, wanted it to be in historic Jerusalem; others, for even more religious reasons, wanted it to be anywhere *but* in Jerusalem (only God, and not men, can give life to Israel, according to their views). And other groups, some not religious and some frankly anti-religious, wanted a neutral place to be chosen. The United States had just closed its door to immigration and so was not a possible choice. Jerusalem belonged to the British and was of great strategic importance in their position against the Ottoman (Turkish) forces. There were talks of Africa, even of some islands. Of course we easily think of Genosha. Indeed, in analyzing Magneto the Jew and wondering if he would have been a Zionist, we are forced to ask the question, "Which kind of Zionist?" And this is where we can learn.

When we talk about Zionism in '20s Germany, we imagine that Hitler's rise to power and the rumors of a "final solution" to exterminate Jews triggered the growth of the movement: they are coming for us, let's go away and save ourselves and our culture. Many Jews reacted this way but, amazingly, not all. Anti-Semitism was such an everyday thing, and had been for so long, that some Jews did not fully realize the speed at which things were getting worse. Some Zionist intellectuals even thought that anti-Semitism was a natural thing. Jakob Klatzkin, of *Encyclopaedia Judaica* fame, said in 1925:

> If we do not admit the rightfulness of anti-Semitism, we deny the rightfulness of our own nationalism. If our people is deserving and willing to live its own national life, then it is an alien body thrust into the nations among whom it lives, an alien body that insists on its own distinctive identity, reducing the domain of their life. It is right, therefore, that they should fight against us for their national integrity.

Would Magneto still agree with this logic? We can't be sure; no concept in his universe is as complex as these different positions—and yet the problem is the same: a people scattered among packs of hungry wolves. We can even go so far as to wonder what the Master of Magnetism would have thought of the few Zionists who were so optimistic as to believe that Hitler could help them! Their reasoning was (my words, my oversimplifying): *Dear Mr. Hitler, You don't like us and want to be rid of us. As it happens, we want to go away from you and live freely according to our tradition. So, please help us create an Israeli state somewhere. We'll go away, you'll be rid of us and happy, and we'll be rid of you and happy too, far from any persecution or misunderstanding.*

It's heart-wrenching to think that a few intellectuals actually believed the devil could be reasoned with. Would Magneto ask the Sentinels to help build Genosha? Hardly. It's much more like a move that Xavier could have made.

Problems in fiction are complicated by the many twists and shades in the real world, but the important thing is that the fiction, which can be much more attractive than our own reality, leads us to wonder about our world. The lonely bookworm (yes, that's me) who feels like a mutant in a dull human world of bullies can, through the X-Men, identify, and accept or reject, the various options open to her in her real-life situation. This is not simply of historic interest, but of daily basic importance. By linking the world of the X-Men to our own world, and our own past, we illuminate our own mistakes and explore other ways of dealing with recurring social problems. If we don't study our past, then we are bound to reproduce it, becoming prejudiced ourselves or not uniting against prejudice when the opportunity arises. A particularly bright boy rejected by the brutes around him might learn a little from the X-Men, but he'll learn far more from the experiences of the blind community, or the Gypsies, or the Jews. All prejudice arises from the same source: people refusing to accept the fact that other human beings are not exactly like them.

Magnus can do good and evil things. He's a victim and a criminal. This makes him human, unlike many comic book characters who are fully evil or fully (and boringly) good.

It's only too easy to call the character Erik has become over the years a bad guy. Is he a man bent on becoming a dictator, or is he a take-charge guy who works only to protect his fellow mutants? Xavier fights him but calls him his brother, and he of all people should know. Magnus works alongside the peace-loving X-Men several times, even acting as Xavier's locum at one point. But each time events prove to him that being nice is not the solution, that humans won't accept mutants and that mutants will have to fight for their rights. Magneto is a complex and haunted soul who can hope and believe, who can despair when his dreams vanish, who wants the best for his people, who knows what pain is, who loves his children, who aches over his past actions and reputation.

He is human, full of human contradictions, just like the Israel we read about each day in the papers—any Jew who's been there will tell you there is an atmosphere of love, as if you were among cousins, everywhere. But at the same time, the internal disagreements are violent, sometimes physically so.

The more Magneto is linked to our world and our history, the more we can learn from him. If he were a generic victim, we could only learn so much. But by making him a Jew, we gain access to a wealth of history, experiences, hopes, mistakes, prejudice, rage and wisdom.

By learning from an essentially magical character living in a totally improbable world such as that of the X-Men, we can also see that the role of fiction is not only to entertain us, but also to make us think. The more one gets involved in a fictional creation, the deeper the desire to think will become.

This is why I consider Magneto to be a Jew.

This is why I love him: He is human, and he gives the universe of fiction its full meaning.

REFERENCES

Claremont, Chris (w), Dave Cockrum (p), and Joe Rubinstein (i). "And the Dead Shall Bury the Living!" *Uncanny X-Men* #149. Marvel Comics, September 1981.

Claremont, Chris (w), Dave Cockrum (p), Joe Rubinstein, and Bob Wiacek (i)."I, Magneto." *Uncanny X-Men* #150. Marvel Comics, October 1981.

Marie-Catherine Caillava is a mutant living in London. She's a ghost-writer, translator and radio critic specialized in SF. Her special powers are getting the printer stuck five minutes before the publisher rings at the door, and reading her dog's mind, especially at eleven P.M. when it's raining outside. Her hobbies are Zen calligraphy, kyudo and day-dreaming about peace on Earth.

THE X-MEN AND
OUR WORLD

Parallel Evolution

DON DEBRANDT

Ever heard of the Burning Man? No, he's not one of the X-Men's enemies, though with a name like that he'd make a good one. Rather, the Burning Man is a concept, an experience, a new or perhaps ancient way of looking at the world. The X-Men are the children of evolution. In some ways, Burning Man is the parent. Come along now with Don DeBrandt on a visit to Black Rock City, where mutation isn't just a concept; it's a way of life.

ON A SUNNY SATURDAY MORNING in the late spring of 2005, I found myself in a dark, cavernous warehouse in a semi-industrial area of Vancouver, British Columbia. I was there looking for mutants.

And I found them. These particular mutants were responding to an ad in the local paper asking for anyone of unusual appearance—tattoos, brandings, piercings, stature—to please come down and fill out some paperwork at a given address. No, this wasn't some Orwellian Mutant Registration Act; it was a chance to make some cash. It was, in fact, a casting call for the movie *X-Men 3*.

I must confess, I got there late. By the time I arrived, the line that had apparently stretched halfway around the building had shrunk to twenty or thirty hopefuls. There was at least one Little Person, a few people covered in tattoos and a guy who'd had his naturally long canines sharpened into actual fangs.

But why was I there? Well, I didn't figure they'd be impressed with my ability to bend my thumbs back to touch my wrists (though there was this Asian fellow who demonstrated something similar, bending his elbows backward; he claimed his father could do the same thing, raising the possibility his ability was, in fact, genetically derived), but I wasn't planning on handing in an application.

I just wanted to spend a little time with my tribe.

The best superheroes, the ones who speak to something deep in our collective consciousness, always have a metaphor at their heart. Superman is a savior; Batman embodies revenge. The Incredible Hulk personifies rage, while Spider-Man represents teenage angst and insecurity.

Superman was born a hero. Batman chose to become one. The Hulk and Spider-Man both had their unique abilities thrust upon them through the medium of radioactivity and circumstance—and Marvel Comics took this theme one step further when they introduced the X-Men, featuring characters as monstrous-looking as the Hulk and the same age as Spider-Man. The all-important difference was that these teens hadn't *done* anything to gain their powers; they hadn't thrown themselves in front of a gamma bomb or hung around any radioactive spiderwebs. All they'd done was reach adolescence.

And that was the genius of the concept. Every teenager feels like an outsider, a freak, someone who doesn't fit in. Your own body betrays you, sprouting hair and changing shape; your very bones stretch and ache. Every minor event in your life becomes high drama, punctuated by lust and despair.

Stan Lee took that framework and gave outward expression to inner turmoil. The clumsy boy growing too fast for his clothes and suddenly sporting a five o'clock shadow became the superagile Beast; the standoffish kid with the glasses became the optic blast-firing Cyclops. Lee gave his characters wings and the ability to read minds, to levitate objects and create walls of ice. The very things that set them apart, that made them outcasts, also made them heroes. He tried to demonstrate that the difference between a disability and a superpower is just a matter of perception.

This is how it was, in the beginning.

But things change.

Things *mutate*.

——— ———

The art festival now known as Burning Man was born on a San Francisco beach in 1986, midwived by artist Larry Harvey. It grew every year, and by 1990 it was attracting 800 people to the ceremonial burning of the Man. That year, though, the police shut them down— the crowd was just too big. The organizers responded by hauling the Man out to the alkali flats of Nevada, where he was torched in front of a much smaller group—ninety or so. Evolution is a natural thinning-out process, and only the dedicated crazies followed Larry Harvey out to the Black Rock Desert.

The first time, anyway.

Mutations occur constantly. You don't know whether the creature is a successful step up the evolutionary ladder or not until it survives... and propagates.

In 1992, 600 people attended Burning Man. In 1993 the number of participants reached 1,000, and then 2,000 in 1994.

In 1999, the citizens of Black Rock City numbered over 23,000 strong. The festival was thirteen years old, and a more manic-depressive, hormonal or impulsive teenager has never existed. Crazy, beautiful, bursting with creative potential and stupid self-indulgence, starry-eyed and cynical, stoned and drunk and dancing under the stars, bleeding imagination from every orifice and laughing in the middle of hundred-mile-an-hour dust storms in hundred-degree heat. Everything was bigger and badder and brighter, every interaction and consequence made more important by its intensity but meaningless by its transience. Black Rock City, like adolescence, is a temporary place that feels like the *only* place while you're there. It is a city of strangeness, of constant change and sudden shock, of unusual appearances and bizarre behavior.

It is a city of mutants.

——— ———

If there is a constant in the life of a teenager, it's an awareness of sex. Hormones flood through your body like radiation, changing everything from your skin to your brain. You are literally in the process of becoming a different person, one you don't know, one you're not even sure you like. And this new person seems to spend an awful lot of time thinking about what other people would look like without any clothes on.

Of course, this sort of subject matter wasn't exactly appropriate for a comic book in the 1960s, when the medium was still aimed primarily at children. Talking about teen angst was one thing; getting into sexual specifics was another.

But as I said before, things change. Things mutate. Even mutation itself shifts and alters, and the cultural matrix that birthed the X-Men underwent its own evolution. The X-Men of the silver screen are very different from the X-Men of the four-color page, and so are the concerns of their audience. In *X-Men 2*, the mother of a young mutant—on learning of her son's abilities for the first time—asks him plaintively, "Have you tried *not* being a mutant?"

Substitute the word "gay" for "mutant" and the parallel becomes obvious. The mother doesn't understand what it's like to be a mutant, just that it means her son will be persecuted and ostracized; she clings vainly to the hope that this is a choice he's made, because a choice can be reversed. The idea that this is who he is, that he doesn't *have* a choice, is not something she wants to consider.

Despite massive evidence that sexual preference is encoded in our genes, many people refuse to believe it. Equating a mutant—who, by definition, is a product of his genetic makeup—with homosexuality is a controversial statement. You are who you are, it says; your destiny is written in your DNA, not your decisions.

But that's oversimplifying a complex issue. Sexuality isn't as black and white as gay or straight; it's a rainbow of options that range from celibacy to promiscuity, from monosexuality to the transgendered. People may not choose what turns them on, but they do choose how they respond to those urges... and some places offer a lot more choices than others.

"We're in love," the young woman proclaimed proudly. I was having a drink at my favorite watering hole, the Starlust, and the couple next to me had both in their eyes.

"Where'd you meet?" I asked them.

"The Anus of the Goat," she said happily. "We had sex there, and we've been together ever since."

The Goat, I came to understand, was an art installation in the middle of the Black Rock Desert. The Anus consisted of a large artificial sphincter with a bed on the other side. The bed had been placed there specifically for the use the young couple had put it to, and the enjoyment of those who wanted to watch. Falling in love was optional.

There's a lot of sex at Burning Man. Sex in RVs, sex on dusty couches, sex in tents. Most of it is private, but some is quite public. For instance, it's not uncommon to see a Chinese basket swing set up in full view or to watch a public flogging. There are theme camps organized specifically around sex: mundane sex, polyamorous sex, gay sex, kinky sex...even spiritual sex. Whatever flavor you prefer—assuming it's consensual and at least semi-legal—someone in Black Rock City can satisfy your tastes.

For many people, this is a revelation. At Burning Man, sex doesn't carry the stigma it does in everyday society. It's part of the experience, like the casual nudity, and after a while it really doesn't seem like such a big deal.

Seven days in the desert. That's how long it takes for ingrained standards of public conduct to make a radical shift toward something different. And it's not just ideas about sex that Burning Man transforms; it challenges preconceptions of commerce, of community, of self-expression and self-reliance. Perceptions *mutate* under the relentless glare of the hot desert sun. . . .

But when attitudes evolve, they don't do so through chance. They evolve through *choice*.

———— ————

The more things change, the more important stability becomes. A solid core is vital when everything else seems to be random, swirling chaos. This essay, for example, may seem to ramble, but it *does* have a simple, central theme: the mutation of mutation. To keep that theme front and center, I'll use various methods to reinforce it: repetition, parallel structure, clear and obvious analogies. It's a form that's proved remarkably sturdy over the span of human civilization.

The X in X-Men stands—as it does in mathematics—for the unknown, for the unquantifiable factor in a mutant's DNA that gives him paranormal abilities or a radically different appearance. People fear the unknown and so fear mutants—and fearful people often turn to religion for comfort, guidance and a sense of constancy. This constancy of belief is often passed down via family, in a process as direct and linear as genetics.

But mutants are people, too, and they're even more afraid than the "normal" people around them. It makes perfect sense that they would turn to religion as well—and that, sooner or later, a mutant would become a spiritual leader of his own kind.

In *X-Men 2*, the mutant leader Magneto asks a young mutant what his name is. The boy replies, "John."

Magneto's response is, "What's your *real* name, John?"

And John says, "Pyro."

Taking a new name for yourself is a ritual used in many belief systems. It's an important step, because it symbolizes redefining who you are. Sometimes, a new name is assigned as a means of control, of telling the individual that his essence is now defined by the organization he belongs to, not himself—but some faiths allow you to choose your own name, thus defining yourself and your new relationship with the universe.

There are many Pyros out on the playa. "Playa" is the term for both the desert and the ever-present dust it's composed of, and "Pyro" is short for pyromaniac—also a component in abundant supply in Black Rock City. Not only are you likely to run across people setting things on fire—art, vehicles, themselves—you're also likely to meet people who introduce themselves with eerily appropriate names: Devilgirl, Dr. Pyro, Firepoet, Burnstormer, Sunburn, Firefly, Pyro Gyro, Firespider, Burnkitty. Playa names are an old and established tradition in BRC, though whether it's okay to name yourself or if someone else must give you your name is still a subject of much debate.

The same sort of dichotomy exists in the world of the X-Men. Professor X assigned the original students at his school code names:

Storm, Cyclops, Angel, Beast. The covert government agency that gave Wolverine his adamantium skeleton and claws also gave him his name.

Magneto seems to have chosen his own title—but then, Magneto is no ordinary supervillain. He is the self-appointed leader of a hated minority, one against which the government is waging an active campaign in an attempt to suppress or even exterminate it. More than grandiose schemes to extort money or conquer the world, Magneto offers a very brutal logic: he tells his people they are the future, they are *Homo superior*. Human beings will always hate and fear them, because they are what will replace human beings—unless human beings manage to kill all the mutants first. Their only hope of survival, he says, is a preemptive strike: either the mutants die...or the humans do.

Magneto, a concentration camp survivor, calls his organization the Brotherhood, a name with deliberate religious connotations. Professor X believes humans can learn from history; it's why he runs a school. Magneto, however, believes that history always repeats itself—and while religious persecution is a recurring theme throughout history, religions have also demonstrated the tenacity needed to survive and thrive under adverse conditions.

Conditions like the desert. Why is it that one of the harshest climates on the planet is the homeland of so many faiths? Is it that the very hostility of the environment strips the soul down to its basics, that the wind and the dust and the heat somehow scour away everything but spirit itself? Or is it simply that you have to be insane to try to live under such conditions in the first place?

I don't know, but the Black Rock Desert seems to attract as many of the faithful as the Middle East. Sanctuary Village, the Akashic Depot, Goddess Camp and Goddess Wish Camp, the Black Rock City Jewish Community Center, Zenplicity, Ascension Tribe, the Spirit Dream Interpretation Café—these are only a few of the theme camps based on exploring, sharing and celebrating spirituality. On the other side of the coin, we have Crazy Dante's Used Soul Emporium, the God Box, Loose Monks and Ganesh Hanky Camp, all taking a much less serious approach. But whether you come to pray or play, ritual behavior is as much a part of Burning Man as the unpredictability and ever-changing nature of its art.

The more extreme the mutation, the stronger the underlying organism has to be—because extremism produces more than just mutants.

It produces monsters.

The direction evolution takes is visible—at least when looking back at it. We've all seen those diagrams that start with a fish and gradually change from iteration to iteration to produce a fully upright *Homo sapiens*. But tracing the evolution of mutants like the X-Men is much harder, because they don't follow a straight line of development. Wings, fur, energy blasts, psionics; anything and everything is possible.

The evolution of mutants as metaphor is somewhat easier, though harder to portray in diagram form. Its starting point is chance; from there, the element of conscious decision-making creeps in, becoming stronger as the metaphor shifts through the gray areas of sexuality and religion, until the dominant factor is no longer the vagaries of DNA but the power of choice.

Hero, or terrorist.

Not all mutations are easy to spot; your neighbor could be one, and you'd never know. Mutants have a tremendous capacity for destruction, and their charismatic leader hates humanity and everything it stands for. He won't be satisfied until the human race is extinct...so really, the government is justified in doing whatever it takes to track them down and eliminate the threat. Right?

In the face of public attitudes like this, mutants have a difficult choice to make. Try to use your abilities for the common good, like the X-Men? Or react violently, like Magneto's Brotherhood? It's not a clear-cut decision; while Magneto's methods are reprehensible, it can still be argued he has a valid point. At heart, he and Professor X want the same thing—the survival of mutants as a race.

I have a suggestion for them both.

There are many parallels between mutants and the citizens of Black Rock City (also known as Burners). Ultimately, the biggest difference seems to be that mutants are born strange, while Burners consciously decide to engage in strange behavior—but as it becomes clear that choice, not chance, is the most important factor in a mutant's life, the two phenomena converge.

Fact and fiction, real life and make-believe, myth and truth have always danced hand in hand at Burning Man. Burners have already learned the lesson the X-Men have yet to figure out—that it's okay to *choose* mutation. People who get tattoos, who have their body pierced or their teeth sharpened, they've made their allegiance clear; they're mutants, and they're proud of it.

That's what Black Rock City is: a celebration of mutanthood. Burners take the everyday and warp it, deform it, force it into new and unusual shapes. We (and yes, I am definitely a Burner) are deviants, in the truest sense of the word. And yes, we live among you; yes, you can't always tell just by looking at us; yes, we espouse radically different views that conflict with that of normal society. We *are* terrorists—cultural terrorists, attacking established modes of conduct and commerce.

So why haven't we been rounded up and arrested?

Because we give birth to the new. And the new is more than just scary, more than just weird or wonderful or unique. It's *necessary*.

There are as many engineers in Black Rock City as there are artists. It's not just a city of ideas, it's a city of *creation*—things aren't merely conceived, they're actually hauled out to the desert and built, and they are staggering in their imagination and scope. Functionality meets beauty in ways both striking and surreal, in everything from the costumes the attendees wear to the structures they live in—and, perhaps most of all, in their transportation.

The licensing arm of the Burning Man organization is known as the DMV: the Department of Mutant Vehicles. They issue permits for full-scale Spanish galleons built on the frames of buses; for giant electric tricycles; for thirty-foot-high floats made of cattle bones; for fire-breathing robot giraffes, brushed aluminum flying saucers, motorized tiki bars and hundreds of other contraptions. And seeing these bizarre, unique creations roll and lurch and glide across the barren, desolate landscape of the playa, you can't escape the feeling you're seeing not just one but dozens of new life-forms emerge—some frightening, some whimsical, some so odd they can't be classified.

But you're glad you got the chance to see them.

To encourage mutation is to encourage creation. This, then, is my advice to mutants everywhere: create. Express yourself. Make something—art, technology, performance—and share it with the world. Transform fear into awe, suspicion into wonder. Use your talents to build, not destroy—after all, who wouldn't want a metal sculpture created by a master of magnetism?

They say the more things change, the more they stay the same. I guess, in the end, what Stan Lee tried to tell us at the very beginning still holds true: the difference between a hero and an outsider is just one of perception.

In Black Rock City, you can't always trust your perceptions. Sometimes the line between real and surreal is hard to see. I've never met a Magneto there...

...but I *have* met a lot of Pyros.

Don DeBrandt's mutant ability is the power to find stuff. Not stuff that's lost, like your keys—the stuff he finds is inevitably weird or ironic or useful. He has been known to find money, clothing, drugs, sex toys and punch lines. One Easter, he even found a dead rabbit—hey, sometimes power is a curse.

From X to Ex

How the Marvel Myth
Parallels the Real Posthuman Future

MAX MORE, PH.D.

I am, by nature, a rather apolitical person. Save for the past six years, where political forces have radicalized and divided this country in a way not seen since the Civil War, I have never really understood the intricacies of the political process and thus feel myself totally unqualified to discuss them. Noted Ph.D. Max More, however, has no such limitations. Here, he speaks to us about the many possibilities of transhumanism and the dangerous consequences thereof.

Two fundamentally opposed forces are assembling and preparing for a world-changing battle. On one side are those who want to protect humanity from a threat to its very nature. On the other side are those who advocate peaceful coexistence between humanity and what might be termed *Homo superior.*

IS THIS A DESCRIPTION of the central conflict in the fictional universe(s) of the X-Men? It easily *could* refer to the struggle between mutants and those who hate and fear them. What I'm referring to, however, is a struggle between the forces of *transhumanism,* who advocate using science and technology to overcome the physical, cognitive and emotional limitations of the human condition, and the forces of *bioconservatism*, who oppose biotechnologies that could modify humans in a way they believe threatens the "natural order." The X-Men mythos considers and dramatizes many of the issues addressed by real-world transhumanism and its critics. Both the fictitious and the factual narratives expect transhumans or posthumans to supersede humans in the imminent future. They differ over the scope and the unfolding of that transition, but it's not hard to find some intriguing parallels between them.

The "X" in "X-Men" neatly signifies the superhuman nature of the mutant heroes; the X marks their crossing of the boundary that defines the human species. The "trans" in transhumanism has essentially the same function, except that it not only *describes* a change, it *recommends* it. Transhumanists are therefore those who favor making the transition from human to posthuman (or, to underscore the parallel, *ex-human*).

The X-Men have sustained numerous comic book series, from the original *X-Men*, through *Uncanny X-Men*, to *Ultimate X-Men*, *New X-Men* and all the offshoots along the way. Something about the mutant supers resonates with the spirit of our times. For decades or even centuries, embryonic forms of transhumanism have pushed up small buds of mutated thinking through the hard pavement of human culture. But only in recent years—almost the same years in which the X-Men have risen from the ashes of almost-canceled comic book to become a massive success—has transhumanism matured into a sophisticated philosophy and plan of action discussed everywhere from popular magazines to presidential councils.

Fueling the simultaneous ascent of X and Ex has been a widespread recognition of the unique nature of our times. The transhumanist goals of vastly extending the human life span, augmenting cognitive abilities and reshaping ourselves physically and emotionally have become much harder to dismiss as new technologies—genetics, nanotechnology, biotechnology, intelligence augmentation, artificial intelligence and human-machine interfaces—have emerged and increasingly demonstrated their capabilities and potential.

X AND EX

The deliberate, conscious remaking of the biological, genetic and neurological bases of human nature differs from the accidental mutations that gave birth to the X-Men, but the possible outcomes are hardly less remarkable. The transhumanist agenda includes super-longevity (the removal of natural limits to our life span), technologically augmenting our perceptual range and intellectual capabilities, refining and sculpting our motivational patterns and emotional responses, and mastering our genes to achieve complete choice over bodily form and function and integrating technology into ourselves so as to go beyond biological limitations. On a philosophical level, the core values of transhumanism include perpetual progress, self-transformation, practical optimism, intelligent technology, open society, self-direction and rational thinking.

Superhuman mutants could also be described as posthumans, although in most cases they are still human in all respects other than their particular mutation. I will occasionally use the term "Ex" to refer to "ex-humans," that is, humans who have become transhuman or posthuman. "Ex" not only stands for ex-humans and parallels with "X-Men," but is also the prefix for the main system of transhumanist thought, my philosophy of extropy. *Extropy* isn't a technical term but a metaphor for the increasingly more complex and advanced products of evolution, whether the technologically enabled posthumans or the natural mutations that gave rise to humans and, fictitiously, to the X-Men.

The term "transhumanism" has been independently coined several times through the centuries, but I coined and defined it in its modern sense, around the same time that I wrote the first transhumanist statement of principles: the Principles of Extropy. The X-Men may well have been one of several sources that influenced my vision of transhumanism: I was a big fan of the X-Men, beginning with Chris Claremont's first run. It's fitting that I, as the founder of the major school of transhumanist thought, always identified most closely with Professor X. I had stopped reading *X-Men* by the time I earned a Ph.D., but I could hardly avoid ironic amusement when some of my students called me "Prof. Max."

The character of Professor Charles Xavier—Prof. X—suggests another significant parallel between the universe of the X-Men and the world of transhumanism—between X and Ex. Xavier means, of course, "savior," the savior of lost, confused and isolated mutants. Prof. X established his school to take in, protect and educate feared and persecuted mutants. He fears that without guidance his young charges will react to the anger and resentment others direct their way by becoming hostile to humans. His school is a haven for gifted misfits and helps them to develop their full potential.

We can see a parallel between Xavier's role in assembling, protecting and educating mutants and the transhumanist philosophy of extropy and its organizational manifestations, from magazines to conferences to online forums. We originally organized in California, not New York, and we have never owned a jet that we store underground (or, if we do, I'm not telling). In essence, however, Xavier's school and transhumanist organizations have performed similar functions, especially in the early days of transhumanism.

In the 1980s and '90s, when we were publishing *Extropy: The Journal of Transhumanist Thought*, I would hear with remarkable frequency from isolated people who thought in ways that diverged radically from those around them. With each new issue, I would hear from more readers like the fellow in Nebraska who longed to chat about advanced technologies, abolishing aging and death, augmenting intelligence and the like. Attempts to discuss these ideas with those around him would cause them to look at him as if he were an alien...or a mutant. Like Xavier, transhumanism has always emphasized self-improvement, benevolence and cooperative, mutually beneficial social arrangements.

Beyond these commonalities, crucial differences *do* exist between the two visions of posthumanity. We will notice the most obvious and significant divergence if we look at the origins of X and Ex. A sudden spurt in the natural process of evolution gave rise to superhuman mutants; posthumans will emerge by the deliberate application of technology to enhance the biological, genetic and neurological structure of humans. Notice a crucial feature of this divergence in origins: *Homo superior* mutants appear all at once, as a race distinct from humanity; posthumanity, by contrast, emerges gradually from humanity as each individual chooses to augment himself or herself one ability or function at a time.

The one-time nature of the mutations that give rise to *Homo superior* in the X-Men universe implies two other contrasts with the transhumanist vision. Aside from some special cases, the superhuman mutants take the form dictated by a *single*, exceptional evolutionary leap. Transhumanists, in contrast, take a view of "mutation" as *perpetual progress*—the continual, technologically enabled self-improvement and self-refinement of the transhuman person. A person could exceed human capabilities so clearly as to be unarguably *post*human without having arrived at a *static* state of being.

Not only do mutants result from a single evolutionary leap, their identities—usually even their *names*—are shaped by the specific powers bestowed by their mutation. Posthumans, as self-transforming creatures, will repeatedly choose their own identities, and shape (or supplant) their genes to reflect those identities, rather than the other way around.

POSTHUMAN POWERS

The X-Men display a stunning array of superhuman abilities, from superstrength, invisibility and intangibility to control of weather, moisture and magnetism to mind-reading and thought control. To what extent might real posthumans match—or even exceed—these capabilities?

Wolverine is an especially plausible mutant from the perspective of speculative science and technology. Technologically augmented posthumans could probably duplicate Logan's powers of strength, speed, sensory acuity, hardened bones (and claws!) and rapid healing. Already, MIT researchers have outlined a way to make robotic, polymer-based muscles that work 1,000 times faster than human muscles.

We will someday be able to replace the human skeletal structure with a system of interconnected nanorobots. If they use artificial diamond as a building material, posthumans will have skulls, spines, arms and legs that are practically unbreakable and uncrushable. If any damage is sustained, these posthuman skeletons will self-repair.

Medical nanorobots will take the form of artificial platelets and speed up bleeding control a thousandfold. DNA repair nanorobots and other nanoscale medical devices may move from the design phase to construction phase in only two or three decades.

Assuming Wolverine's healing factor extends to infections, we could again match the mutant by using "microbivores"—robotic macrophages each two to three microns in size, designed by *Nanomedicine* author Robert Freitas—to replace our white blood cells and attack pathogens more effectively. These will be upgraded via downloadable software to wipe out particular infections hundreds of times more quickly than antibiotics, eliminating the most severe septicemic infections in minutes to hours. Microbivores also beat out our natural biology in that they will work against *all* types of infections—fungal, bacterial and viral—as well as cancers, and will not be slowed by bacteria that have developed multiple drug resistance to antibiotics or other familiar therapies.

Once we've upgraded to posthuman bodies, our energy-production and mobilizing capabilities would make any mutant proud—maybe even envious. Billions or trillions of artificial red blood cells called "respirocytes" will outperform the originals by a factor of hundreds or thousands. Although respirocytes will look like red blood cells, they will function more like miniscule scuba tanks just one micron in diameter and, if made of sapphire, could store large amounts of oxygen compressed up to about 100,000 atmospheres. By vastly expanding your body's oxygen-carrying capacity, these respirocytes will allow you to run all out at Olympic speeds (or swim at full speed underwater) for fifteen minutes without taking a breath. In the absence of such strenuous exertion, respirocytes would allow you to survive without breathing for several hours.

Organs, especially the heart, will certainly be replaced in the future. Going beyond supplementing the blood with nanorobotic blood cells, Freitas has designed a 500 trillion nanorobot system, a "vasculoid," to replace the entire bloodstream. Researchers have already developed early-stage microscale and nanoscale fuel cells. Posthuman bodies may be powered by tiny fuel cells running on hydrogen or our bodies' native ATP.

The lungs are also a good candidate for replacement. During an intermediate phase we will supplement our biological oxygenation system with respirocytes. As we move on to a real posthuman stage, we're likely to eliminate lungs entirely—along with breathing itself—and replace them with nanorobots. Most of our other organs will also be replaced or made unnecessary. In the case of a posthuman, neither a pulse nor breathing will be a reliable sign of life.

This ability to change the form and function of our bodies—what transhumanists often call "morphological freedom"—applies just as well to more prosaic matters. Consider that we don't often see the X-Men *eating*. Of course that's because watching superheroes eat isn't that thrilling; it's not because they don't *need* to. But posthumans really won't need to eat, at least not in any sense we recognize today. In place of food, we will introduce exactly the nutrients we need into our bodies, then metabolic nanorobots, guided by sensors and wireless communication, will transport them precisely where and when they are needed for optimal functioning.

Unbreakable bones, superstrong muscles, an invincible immune and self-repair system—these are all great things to have, but Wolverine wouldn't be Wolverine if not for his enhanced senses. Although popular fiction has often portrayed future humans as entirely cerebral creatures, almost totally devoid of sensory engagement with the world, real posthumans are likely to resemble Weapon X in this regard. Researchers have already developed an "artificial nose" that may have a better sense of smell than a bloodhound. This device uses chemical sensors to sniff out explosives, food contaminants and various other chemicals, and may be able to diagnose certain medical conditions by smell.

We might also use terahertz rays (T-rays)—a curious form of emission found between infrared and microwaves—to see through clothing, plastic and packaging to spot explosives, guns or even biological weapons much more effectively than we could using optical, infrared or x-ray imaging. As we increasingly merge our machines and technologies with the human body, we can expect our existing senses to be sharpened and new senses to be added through interfaces with mechanical sensors.

The technologies emerging over the next few decades will confer on posthumans many other mutant-matching capabilities. The ability to make real-time modifications in our appearance in high-resolution, full-immersion virtual reality will make us comfortable with shape-shifters. That will prepare us for the posthuman ability to change form at will in *physical* reality, once we have fully incorporated nanotech into ourselves. If we convert at least part of our physical embodiment into a swarm of interlocking devices known as "foglets," our physical bodies will be almost as configurable as virtual bodies. Foglets are a form of "programmable matter" that can take almost any form, from soft and permeable to as hard-yet-mutable as Colossus' "organic steel" body.

Posthumans begin to truly outshine mutants in potential if we shift focus from physical enhancements to enhancements in the realms of longevity, psychology and intellect. X-Men seem not to have extended life spans. One of the few clear exceptions is Wolverine, whose regenerative powers have maintained his biological age over decades. One of the major shifts we will experience in the transition from human to posthuman will be the abolition of aging and death. A growing number of scientists think this could happen in the lifetimes of some of now living.

We will achieve something like immortality, not in one great leap forward but in baby steps. What we need to do is stay alive to ride the wave of accelerating longevity. Life expectancy keeps growing and should continue to do so at an ever-faster pace. We will live *indefinitely* once biomedical advances extend our lives by at least one year each year. At that point, we will have reached *longevity escape velocity* (LEV). Three crucial factors underlie the driving forces bringing us closer to forever: the stunning and unceasing success of the scientific method; instruments that see further, deeper and more precisely; and the cross-fertilization of information technology and biotechnology, creating new capabilities in areas like genomics and drug design.

When might we attain LEV? Biogerontologist Aubrey de Grey has mapped out the challenge in detail. He estimates reaching LEV in fifteen to a hundred years, with twenty-five years as his best guess. To move the odds in his favor, de Grey instituted the Methuselah Mouse Prize, an award that may have the same effect on achieving LEV as the Ansari X Prize had on the more familiar kind of escape velocity in the case of private space launches.

MAXIMUM HEADROOM

The mutant universe of the X-Men also lacks any solid evidence of *emotional* evolution. As Sabretooth puts it: "Super-people are supposed to be the next stage in human evolution, and all we do is fight each other." Popular portrayals of superhumans typically play on their incredible physical abilities—usually their *destructive* capabilities. In reality, it might take only a relatively modest genetic mutation (or technologically engineered neurological modification) to give us superhuman emotional responses.

In the human brain, there are plenty of neuronal connections following a path from the amygdala (the emotional center of the brain) to the cortex (the cognitive region). The amygdala's many projections into cortical areas greatly outnumber the pathways from the cortex to the amygdala. The amygdala uses its evolutionarily developed defense networks to influence attention, perception and memory, meaning that, in situations where we believe we are facing danger, emotional arousal can dominate and control thinking. These unbalanced connections in the brain are true of all mammals, and they make it rather hard to consciously and deliberately turn off emotions by shutting down the amygdala.

It turns out, however, that primates have far more cortical connections to the amygdala than do other mammals. It doesn't seem unreasonable to suppose that we might put neurotechnology to work in building new pathways in the other direction, bringing the connections into balance. In posthumans, rather than reason and passion working separately, we might integrate them to achieve a harmonious modulation of emotions. As a result, we might end up altering the emotional responses—even the basic drives—imbued in us by the imperatives of our genes. Real risks exist in messing around with our fundamental makeup, yes, but enormously positive possibilities aren't hard to envision either.

Contrary to stereotyped popular portrayals of future humans as dryly cerebral beings, posthumans will have the means to better integrate their feelings and automatic responses with their conscious values and ideal self-image. Rather than crushing our emotions, we will carve them, making them more mature, reworking undesirable feelings into ones fitting our values and sense of our true self. The mark of the posthuman will not only be an augmented body and brain but more highly evolved emotions.

The means by which we will shape mood and modify personality will include hormonal manipulation, psychoactive drugs, genetic engineering of neural tissue, computerized inner assistants and biochemical implants, all combined with the "soft" technologies of introspection and meditation. We can expect to apply those ubiquitous nanorobots to make direct modifications of brain structure in order to achieve more drastic transformations of our psychological nature, and hardwired neurological modifications (or "mods") might allow us to bring errant desires into line with our deeper values, such as by totally abolishing the desire to engage in a self-destructive habit. They might make it much easier for us to fall into a state of attention rather than distraction, energetic optimism rather than depression, calm confidence rather than anxiety and deep interpersonal awareness rather than self-absorption.

Exotic new emotions and personalities unimaginable to the humans of today will await new posthuman brains capable of thinking thoughts as different from ours as differential calculus or philosophical awe differs from the emotional range of other mammals. As cognitive psychologists have shown, the particular nature of our emotions is shaped by the thoughts underlying them. Strange new emotions will be aroused by strange new thoughts. One path to a posthuman persona might be to deliberately and carefully divide an individual mind into multiple personas or partial personalities, converting the individual into a close-knit community of mind, as Walter Jon Williams envisaged in his novel *Aristoi*.

Another thing almost completely missing in the X-Men version of posthumanity is *cognitive augmentation*. By this I don't mean heightened sensory capabilities, or mentalistic or psychic augmentation; I mean intellectual, conceptual, analytical and creative abilities that exceed the bounds of human possibility. X-Men's really smart mutants seem to be no brighter than the most intelligent *Homo sapiens*. We don't see genuinely superbright mutants for an entirely understandable reason: it's incredibly hard to portray plausibly. How can a sharp but non-genius human writer come up with believable thoughts for a superhumanly intelligent being? He can't. The next best approach is to leave the superbright being in the shadows, its thinking processes shrouded in mystery with only the *effects* being seen.

We should expect cognitive augmentation to be a major goal for posthumans if for no other reason than that it's tremendously advantageous to be hyperintelligent. As Xavier said in *Ultimate X-Men* #13, "Post-human problems require post-human solutions." Some people are already taking early kinds of "smart drugs" (or "nootropics") to sharpen their concentration or memory. It's not too hard to see us using biological, genomic or nanotechnological means to upgrade our intellectual faculties. For instance, we might stimulate growth in the hippocampus in order to expand our "working memory." That would allow us to engage in far more complex chains of reasoning without losing our way.

Software agents and "knowbots" embedded in the brain will help posthumans to gather information, relieving them of tedious work hunting down and managing information. Early-stage artificial retinas and cochlear implants are already in use, and other brain implants using "neuromorphic" designs that learn from nature are in the early stages of development. The Max Planck Institute's "neuron transistor" and other achievements in linking biological neuron to field effect transistors point to a day when our computers will be tightly integrated with our brains, becoming part of us, abolishing barriers to the attainment of posthuman intelligence.

Where lie the ultimate limits to posthuman intelligence? Currently, we're doing all our thinking with a hundred trillion neurons that communicate using sluggish electrochemical processes. Several estimates put the computational power of the human brain at around 10^{14} to 10^{16} calculations per second (cps). Posthuman memory based on nanorobot communication will be millions of times faster, but that still leaves us very far from the ultimate limits for computational power, even allowing for limits imposed by power requirements, error-correction and so on.

How far away? That theoretical limit can be calculated by dividing the total energy of an object by Planck's constant. MIT professor Seth Lloyd has figured that one kilogram of matter (about the amount in a human brain) could support about 5×10^{50} operations per second.

It's rather silly to represent this in words, but for the mathematically challenged, that number translates to five times 100 trillion trillion trillion trillion. If human intelligence can be emulated with 10^{16} cps, that would mean that an object the size of the brain could, at its theoretical ultimate, boast cognitive power equivalent to five trillion trillion human civilizations.

Even if we reduce this estimate conservatively by a factor of 10 million, Ray Kurzweil has calculated that the ultimate computer-brain could "perform the equivalent of all human thought over the last ten thousand years in no more than ten microseconds." Kurzweil has also estimated, based on remarkably stable long-run trends, that we may be able to buy this amount of computing power for $1000 around 2080. Nanotechnology pioneer Eric Drexler has patented a far more modest and conservative computer design using entirely mechanical components. *Even this device* should be able to simulate 100,000 human brains in a cubic centimeter.

What will all this accelerated evolution in physical, intellectual and emotional capabilities mean for the unity of human society? Will only *some* individuals and *some* countries acquire posthuman powers and status while others remain human? Will that lead to a conflict between humans and posthumans akin to that between humans and mutants in the X-Men stories? Or might the conflict be real, but cut across lines differently than in the X-Men universe? Answering those questions takes us into our last comparison of X and Ex.

THE TOMORROW WARS

In the X-Men universe, Magneto is intent on dominating humanity and forcibly replacing the species with himself and favored members of *Homo superior*. At the height of his megalomania, Magneto declared to a frightened planet that in his mutant utopia, humans would become food, fuel or slaves to their new masters. The Master of Magnetism despises and resents human beings, while many humans fear and hate mutants. Charles Xavier has chosen the far more benevolent path of integrating the two species, but despite their radical differences, both leaders share an assumption that may be true in the X-Men universe but will not be true in the real posthuman future.

Xavier and Magneto assume a *sharp distinction* between humans and mutants: either you possess the X-gene or you don't. Even in their world, that division is a little too neat. Some individuals don't fit comfortably in either box. Superpeople *without* the X-gene (such as the Ultimates) form a third group. And what about those such as Tony Stark, who can step into a suit of high-tech armor and become the powerful superhero Iron Man? If Stark were to *internalize* the Iron Man technology through further miniaturization, he would become a true cyborg—one kind of genuine posthuman being.

Fears of conflict arise from this assumption of a radical divide, whether it's between humans and mutants or humans and posthumans. Wars are more difficult to wage when you're not sure who is on which side. Even with the qualifications I've suggested, the sides are clear enough in the X-Men world to make it entirely understandable why anyone who *isn't* a mutant would worry about the evolutionary leap. All the evidence suggests that the transhuman transition will be a different matter. Consider just two points in this respect: the move from human to posthuman will not be an all-or-nothing, us-versus-them affair; and there will be forces other than human and posthuman to complicate the picture.

As I noted in the first section, posthumanity will emerge gradually out of humanity as each of us chooses whether and how to augment ourselves, one function at a time. Instead of a single, world-shaking jump to a new level of being, the transition will consist of a small cognitive upgrade here, a perceptual augmentation there, additional years added to life expectancy and so on. Superhumanity will arrive in small steps.

It seems likely that transhuman enhancements will be widely adopted, with some being almost universal (core cognitive upgrades, for example) and others more limited and specialized (specific perceptual upgrades, environmental toughening). We will see a wide spectrum of posthuman capabilities at varying levels of advancement. Some cultures may even choose to adopt certain enhancements but stand firm against others—just as the Amish allow technologies such as the cell phone that they find compatible with their culture, but don't allow fixed telephones or televisions. We might think of those who upgrade some abilities while refusing to move beyond a certain level on others as the "humanish."

Another factor that makes the picture of human-posthuman conflict implausible is artificial superintelligence. The simple scenario of a two-sided conflict splinters when we consider AI as a third force. At least one of the X-Men writers has noticed this, as indicated by these words spoken in *Ultimate X-Men* #25 by Mr. Seville of the Hellfire Club, in reference to an article handed out by Xavier: "Oh, just some stupid *article* from the London *Times*. It's a piece by Stephen Hawking about mutants being man's last hope against the evolution of *artificial intelligence.*"

We cannot yet be sure whether AI will be friendly, hostile or indifferent toward humans and posthumans—or all three, depending on its manifestation. Further, machine intelligence is likely to often take the form not of an independent AI but of participatory superintelligence—IA (intelligence augmentation) rather than AI. This will be participatory both in the sense that we work together with the thinking technology, and in the sense that anyone will be able to tap into it in order to work together, just as we are doing already with the Internet.

If the future isn't likely to be shaped by a conflict as simple and clear as human versus posthuman, another conflict is more likely. Indeed, it has already begun. This is the ideological and cultural battle we can see developing between pro-posthumans (transhumanists) and anti-posthumans. The Senator Kellys and the William Strykers of the X-Men world seek to stamp out "the mutant menace"—even if that means using dangerous tools such as the Sentinels. Similarly, the anti-posthumans, now known as the bioconservatives, seek to block the transhuman transition—even if that means banning whole lines of technology or prohibiting the pursuit of knowledge.

In "The Red-Green Divide Over Human Enhancement," journalist Jim Pethokoukis notes that "it is surprising how often talk of the X-Men comes up" when he speaks with enhancement advocates such as transhumanists. He no longer thinks such a metaphor is over the top since he heard "bioethicist George Annas, who favors a ban on enhancement technologies like germline engineering, stat[ing] that such laws are needed precisely to prevent 'a group of super individuals who view us as defective from subjecting us to their genetic genocide.'"

Annas is far from alone in this. For its September/October 2004 issue, the editors of *Foreign Policy* posed the following question to eight prominent policy intellectuals: "What ideas, if embraced, would pose the greatest threat to the welfare of humanity?" One of the eight wise men was Francis Fukuyama, who made his name with the book *The End of History* before following up with *Our Posthuman Future: Consequences of the Biotechnology Revolution*. Fukuyama's choice for the world's most dangerous idea was transhumanism, which he identified as "a strange liberation movement" that wants "nothing less than to liberate the human race from its biological constraints." Fukuyama based his view on the threat to "Factor X" (no joke), a term that appears to stand for some idea of the human essence or soul.

The combatants in this brewing battle for the future of the human species will not be familiar, preexisting groups aligned with the usual political factions. This existential-technological-political conflict is already bringing together strange bedfellows on the bioconservative side: precautionary principle-wielding "left" environmentalists are joining forces with religious conservatives; former Sun Microsystems chief scientist Bill Joy has joined longtime technocritic Jeremy Rifkin in attempting to restrict genetic, nano- and robotic technologies; and self-described "liberal" (anticorporate) humanists are marching in step with reactionaries who care little for humanistic heresies.

We transhumanists are not the utopians critics like to accuse us of being. We fully expect the future to be disturbed by challenges, conflicts and troubles—although perhaps on a higher level than those of today's monkey politics. Given the probable nature of emerging post-humanity, however, I think we can expect the struggles of ex-men to be at least as engaging as those of the X-Men. With a little luck and some personal effort to reach longevity escape velocity, many of us may be around to contribute to the plot.

REFERENCES

Austen, Chuck (w), Essad Ribic (p), and Livesay (i). "You Always Remember Your First Love, Part 1." *Ultimate X-Men* No. 13. Marvel Comics, February 2002.

Fukuyama, Francis. "Transhumanism." *Foreign Policy*, September/October

2004. Also available online at http://www.foreignpolicy.com/story/cms. php?story_id=2667.

Millar, Mark (w), Adam Kubert (p), and Danny Miki (i). "Hellfire and Brimstone, Part 5." *Ultimate X-Men* No. 25. Marvel Comics, February 2003.

Max More, Ph.D., is an internationally acclaimed strategic futurist who writes, speaks and organizes events on the fundamental challenges of emerging technologies. Max is concerned that our burgeoning technological capabilities are racing far ahead of our standard ways of thinking about future possibilities. His work aims to improve our ability to anticipate, adapt to and shape the future for the better. Max cofounded and is chairman of Extropy Institute and authored the Principles of Extropy, which form the core of a transhumanist perspective. His most recent project is the Proactionary Principle, a tool for making smarter decisions about advanced technologies.

Best description of why too much "interpretati
is a bad thing.
    ex   over analyzing an English literature story.

Lee, Kirby and Ovid's X-Metamorphoses

or How Not to Read the X-Men,
and then How to Read Them

ADAM ROBERTS

*Here, Adam Roberts takes center stage to argue that we've all been read-
ing the X-Men incorrectly for the past four and a third decades and that,
rather then reading the books with an emphasis on the WHAMs, BAMs
and POWs, we should instead be reading the book in...Latin?*

SEE IF YOU CAN IDENTIFY the odd one out in this list:

- Stan "the Man" Lee (born 1922)
- Jack "the King" Kirby (born 1917)
- Publius Ovidius "the Nose" Naso (born 43 B.C.)

You got it? It's pretty obvious, I know.

The odd one out, of course, is Kirby, because he is a visual artist.[1]
Ovid and Lee are both writers, and writers, moreover, who conceived
and executed a massive continuous work about the adventures of a
large and diverse group of mutants across a world-spanning land-

---

[1] There's a second reason why Kirby is the odd one out in this list, although it's less relevant to this essay. It has to do with nicknames. Stan Lee is, without a sliver of doubt, a man. Naso is indeed the Latin for "nose," a cognomen that tells us that Ovid's family was well known in ancient Rome for their prominent conks. But Kirby, though a truly gifted artist, is not and has never been a king.

139

scape of good and evil, gods and mortals. Lee's epic has gone under various names: *Uncanny X-Men*, *X-Men*, *Giant-Size X-Men*, *Astonishing X-Men* and even, for a while, *New Mutants*. Ovid's has just one name, *Metamorphoses*, a word we might as well translate as "mutations." These two works are actually the same.

Before you go "Huh?" and turn the page, give me a moment to explain why it makes sense to bracket together a 12,000-line poem in Latin hexameters written in ancient Rome between 2 B.C. and 8 A.D. with a mutant-superhero franchise that began in the 1960s as a comic and has now itself mutated into graphic novels, spin-off fiction, animated tales, motion pictures, action figures and various other forms.

I'd like to argue that the *X-Men* series is an extension of Ovid's *Metamorphoses*.

I'd like to suggest that there are different ways of reading "texts," works such as this Latin poem on the one hand, or this collection of comics, graphic novels and movies on the other. One way is to try and get *behind* the book—to decode it, as if it contains within its various meanings a hidden meaning. It means asking: "This story seems, on the surface, to be about good mutants fighting bad mutants whilst humanity rejects them both...but what is it *actually* about?" This is a very popular way of reading *X-Men*, perhaps because it redeems what might otherwise be seen as a sometimes daft triviality into the terms of *seriousness* and *depth* that literary critics prefer. Here's an example of what I mean:

> [1] *X-Men* is *actually* about race—the mutants stand in for those racial groups that have suffered marginalization and persecution at the hands of larger society. They might be seen, for instance, as ciphers for the Jewish experience, or the black experience.

"Professor Xavier," says the invaluable Wikipedia, "has been compared to African American civil rights leader Martin Luther King, Jr., and Magneto to the more militant Malcolm X." Compared by whom? We're not told. Never mind—or hold that thought, anyway. Another example:

[2] *X-Men* is *actually* about the experience of being gay in a predominantly heterosexual and homophobic society.

Here's Wikipedia again:

Comparisons have been made between the mutants' situation, including the concealment of their powers and the age they realize these powers, and homosexuality, as was illustrated in a scene of the X-Men film *X2* (a film by openly gay director Bryan Singer) that had Bobby Drake 'come out' as a mutant to his parents.

These two approaches both represent one way of "reading" *X-Men*: as allegory. But I'm going to suggest that this is the wrong way. In fact, I'm going to spend the rest of this essay arguing that these sorts of approaches are not only wrong-headed but may be actively dangerous. I'm going to argue that, instead of reading *X-Men* as an allegory of race or gay rights, it makes much more sense to read it as a version of a 2,000-year-old poem written in a dead language. And furthermore, if you persevere to the end of the essay, you are going to agree with me.

SO WHAT'S WRONG WITH ALLEGORY?

Well, since you press me, it's hard to argue that there's anything *wrong* with allegory. Plenty of critics read texts as allegories. Sometimes this is because the authors concerned deliberately wrote their books as allegory—for instance, John Bunyan's little novel *The Pilgrim's Progress* (1678), which seems to be telling a story about a man trekking through a fantastical landscape but is in fact the allegorical tale of the progress of the soul through this world and into the Christian heaven of the next.

Reading *The Pilgrim's Progress* as allegory is a logical thing to do. But, more often, this sort of reading is applied to works that were not intended to be allegories, but which critics decide to read in this "decoding" manner anyway. Seeing past the surface meanings of a text to its buried significance can make a person feel clever, insightful and even self-congratulatory. And if you enjoy decoding texts in this manner, then, hey, be my guest. Knock yourself out. But it seems to me a dumb way of doing things, and it may be a dangerous way of doing things.

Why is it dumb? Because (and excuse me for stating the obvious) Charles Xavier is not Martin Luther King, Jr. He's Charles Xavier. There is *one* way in which he resembles the great Dr. King—he has dedicated his life to the peaceful emancipation of his people. But there are myriad ways in which he does *not* resemble King: he is a bald-headed white cripple with tremendous telepathic powers who lives in an enormous mansion in New York State, is in charge of a school for gifted mutant supermen and is an occasional traveler into outer space. It's been a while since my high school classes on twentieth-century American history, but I don't *recall* Martin Luther King, Jr., being any of these things. Concentrating on the one thing these two people have in common to the exclusion of all these points of difference is plain myopic. Here's a similar syllogism: I have two legs. Alexander the Great had two legs. Therefore, I conquered the whole of Greece and most of Asia Minor in a blistering military campaign.

Why is reading *X-Men* as allegory dangerous? For two reasons, one specific to *X-Men* and one more general. The more general point is that a mindset that is constantly itching to see "behind the veil of appearance" can shade very easily into a mindset that is plain paranoid. The habit of ignoring the actual in favor of an imagined "true reality" distorts lived experience—evidence that contradicts the allegorical reading is ignored, and trivial orts and scraps that appear to support it are exaggerated beyond all significance. This is the mindset that insists (despite the fact that for two and a half centuries American governments have meekly come and gone as the electorate has voted them in and out) that the federal powers that be are secretly plotting to enslave the people, and that therefore we should all arm ourselves to the teeth and go live in compounds in Montana. Or, to choose a slightly different example, it's the mindset that can ignore the most patent of realities ("By flying this plane into this building, I am going to kill myself and many innocent people for no purpose at all") in favor of a fancied "truth" behind the allegory of this world ("I'm doing what God wants and will go to paradise"). These are extreme examples, of course, but they're versions of a more common psychological failing. Some people condition themselves *not* to live in the world as it is, and instead retreat into a disconnected fantasy version of that world in their heads. They abandon the reality principle in favor of personal crotchets, and these, in turn, bend their view of the world into peculiar shapes.

And this is the problem I have with reading *X-Men* as an allegory for the civil rights movements. Don't misunderstand me: the major civil rights movements of the last half century, liberating women, African Americans and homosexuals from centuries of actual oppression, are amongst the noblest achievements of modern humanity. But I don't see why the best way to tell their stories is by coding it as the discontinuous adventures of a series of mutant superheroes. Surely the best way to tell the powerful and inspiring story of Martin Luther King, Jr., is to, well, *tell the story of Martin Luther King, Jr*. What King achieved, after all, was not fantasy; it was real, something won not by pseudo-magical superpowers but by human determination and will. My problem is not that fantasizing this story trivializes it, but that it misses the point.

But in case this is all sounds a bit high-handed, let me offer one other reason why allegory is a dumb way to read *X-Men*: because it tends to take the things that make the stories so compelling—the way the characters actually are, the way they interact, the adventures they have, the dazzling artwork, the mind-stretching concepts and, above all, the fantastically varied and sprawling range of stories, the localized particular delights of the text—and squeeze them all into a preformed box marked "race" or "sexuality." That does little to account for the actual, multiform delights of *X-Men*.

I don't believe one person in a thousand picks up an edition of the *X-Men* comics thinking, "Excellent, this will bring me closer to the experience of African American oppression. . . ." Readers of the comic are looking for the *actual intensities* that their reading offers them: the brilliance of the artwork, the interactions of the specific characters, the concepts, the development.

AND THERE'S AN ALTERNATIVE?

Here's another way of reading *X-Men*: we can pay attention to what is actually going on in the text.

This isn't to say that we can't identify patterns, pick out themes and admire the sophistication with which they're handled. Nor is it to say that we can't transfer lessons from the story to the real world—if reading about heroes helps us act more heroically in our lives, then that's all to the good. I'm not suggesting that the business of reading stories is wholly transparent and obvious, or that it can be reduced to simply restating what goes on in the story. If that were the case, there'd be no need for criticism of any kind (and by criticism I mean reviews, articles and fan sites as well as essays like this one), and instead of writing this essay I could just reprint my favorite X-Men story[2] with a "Read this! It's really cool" at the beginning. But that might get me into copyright difficulties. And you don't need a Ph.D. in literature in order to say, "Read this, it's cool!" I spent years writing my Ph.D. thesis. I'd hate to think all that time has been wasted.

What we need to do is ask the question, "What is *X-Men* about?" in a way that pays attention to what the stories are actually doing, not with reference to some theory about what lies *behind* the appearance.

So what are these stories *actually* doing?

Obviously, *X-Men* has a lot in common with other superhero story arcs that originated in Marvel comics in the 1960s, stories written for *Fantastic Four*, *The Incredible Hulk*, *Spider-Man* and others. *X-Men* presents the world as a battleground in which good fights with evil. Like Superman or Batman, the X-Men use their more-than-human powers in the service of good; and, like Superman or Batman, their success has meant that they have become, in effect, modern myths.

A myth is not an allegory; it is not something to be decoded to get at the hidden truth that lies behind. It is what it seems to be: a story, a set of characters, that captures something crucial about the human condition and expresses it directly, not in a furtive or secretive manner. Myths have been part of the human diet of stories for as long as there have been humans interested in stories. Some of these myths have been religious, but by no means all of them. Of the myths of ancient Greece, for instance, something like a tenth relate to specific

---

[2] It is Chris Claremont and Brent Anderson's "God Loves, Man Kills" (Marvel's Graphic Novels #5) from 1982, since you ask.

religious practice—the gods and goddesses worshipped in temples, the various cults. The rest elaborate more general human concerns, dilemmas and experiences.[3] Most of these myths are about men and women who are faced with mountainous difficulties, and overcome them. About heroes and heroines.

Modern myths function in very similar ways. It makes sense to think of *The Lord of the Rings* as a modern myth: not as an allegory of the Christian religion (Tolkien always insisted that he "cordially disliked" allegory), but as a story to be taken on its own terms as an illumination of, or account of, or perhaps even a guide to, the way we live in the world.

X-Men has an interestingly different emphasis than Superman or Batman. Superman is a superhero because he's born on an alien world. Batman is an ordinary man with extraordinary martial-art skills and plenty of cool gadgets. Neither of them are *mutants*. But in *X-Men*, not only are the protagonists humans who have mutated into something else, but the major emphasis of the whole franchise is precisely on this process of mutation—on, in other words, *change*. This, if you want it reduced to a single world, is what the X-Men are about: change.

CH-CH-CH-CHANGE

Change is the human condition. We may yearn to keep certain things frozen forever (youth, love, joy), but it can't be done. I'm sorry to be the one to bring you this bad news, but it's inescapable.

Actually, I think that kids, and especially teenagers, already understand this truth, and understand it better than adults, because they are living every day through the experience of changing, radically and completely. This, I think, is why *X-Men* has enjoyed its very great success. More than other comics, it dramatizes this process of change; it elaborates upon it, gives us eloquently extreme versions of it and works through the implications of what this change means. The very word "mutation," of course, means "change."

The mutations that define individual X-Men manifest themselves

---

[3] I get the figure of "one-tenth" from Robert Graves, who tabulates and retells all *The Greek Myths* in his book, called, unsurprisingly, *The Greek Myths* (1955).

during puberty. We, as readers, understand the *rightness* of this fact, because puberty is when we changed the most, and the most rapidly.

The world represented in the *X-Men* comics is one in a process of radical change: a new species has come into being. The drama of the series is the battle between those who accept this change and those amongst old humanity, which refuses to accept it.

On another level of interpretation, *X-Men* taken as a whole is *a text in a continual process of change*. To follow the *X-Men* "megatext" through its incarnations in all its different media is inevitably to be struck by how restless and mutable a work it is. Nothing is stable. Characters die off but then are resurrected, either in changed form (so, for instance, Jean Grey reemerges as Phoenix) or as clones of themselves. Sometimes they just come back to life. Other characters switch allegiance—Magneto, for instance, began as an evil figure, but in the late 1980s he changed sides and even took Xavier's place as the leader of the X-Men (although he didn't stay on the side of "good" for very long). Characters fall in love, as did Cyclops and Jean Grey; but this love becomes mutable (in the Grant Morrison years, Cyclops had a sort-of affair with Emma Frost behind his beloved's back). Whole story lines are set in "alternate realities" in which all the assumptions of the standard X-Men universe can be changed. The characters change their physical appearance from artist to artist; they change their costumes; they change their location (to Australia, to the moon). They change the medium in which they are figured: comic, novel, animated TV, film. The one thing they never do is remain static.

For some, this sheer restless mutability has begun to undermine the appeal of the whole. Fans like to know where they stand with their favorite stories, after all. But this is to ignore what makes *X-Men* special. Change is the *point* of *X-Men*; it is the insight into the human condition that the series most eloquently and elaborately expresses.

OVID

The classical world had a more direct access to this truth than many other civilizations. Do you know what the oldest surviving philosophical insight to have survived from the classical world is? Not "know thyself"; not "the golden mean"; not even "What's a Greek urn? About a hundred drachma a week." It's the wise old saw attributed to the sixth-century B.C. philosopher Heraclitus: "Everything changes; nothing remains the same."

The great classical masterpiece in this idiom is Ovid's great poem. In fact, there are some critics who argue that *Metamorphoses* is the most influential work in the whole tradition of Western literature. Not only was it enormously successful in its day, it provided pretty much the whole of late medieval and Renaissance Europe with its version of classical myth. When Shakespeare dramatizes classical myth, or makes reference to it, everything he knows comes from Ovid. Almost every poet of note who has written in English, from Chaucer to Keats to Ted Hughes, has been besotted with Ovid.

Ovid's ambition in this poem was not small. He set out to tell the whole story of the world, from its creation out of Chaos up to the Roman present day. What this meant in practice was that he provided versions of just about every myth and legend he knew, from Deucalion's flood to the apotheosis of Julius Caesar. Some of these retellings are short, a dozen lines or so; some are long, running to many hundreds of lines of perfectly formed verse. *Metamorphoses* is a huge compendium of pretty much all the myths of the classical world.

In a similar way, it has always seemed to me, comic books are a huge compendium of pretty much all the myths of the *modern* world. That looks like a pretty big claim, so I'd better unpack it a little bit. By myths, I mean those stories we hold in common, that have perhaps even become clichés. In the classical world, myths were often the medium of religious revelation, but in our day and age, people (*some* people) get antsy when they hear it suggested that Christ's crucifixion, death and resurrection are "myths," so let's leave that behind. Let's instead mention some of the parallels between classical myth and comics.

Classical myths were often about heroes like Hercules, Theseus, Achilles; when we look for modern-day stories of heroes, we find them most powerfully embodied as superheroes in the pages of comics. Batman and Spider-Man, Wolverine and Night Owl are all ordinary people raised to the level of hero by some key change within them. Classical myths also concerned the gods and goddesses of the

Olympian pantheon, beings with supernatural powers, strength and resilience, yet not divine in the omnipotent sense that Yahweh, the Christian God or Allah are considered divine today. The Greek and Roman gods, for instance, could die (the god Pan was the first god to die in our time), or could be overthrown and imprisoned in eternal confinement (as were the Titans). In this respect, the Greek and Roman gods have much more in common with figures such as Superman, the Silver Surfer, Swamp Thing or Neil Gaiman's Sandman. Indeed, I'd go further and say that there isn't anything else in contemporary culture as true to the spirit of the classical pantheon of gods as those figures. The adventures and misadventures of heroes and gods, the stories of their birth, travels, battles and triumphs, and occasionally their deaths—this is what constitutes almost all classical myth. And this is what I mean when I say that, when we look to see where those myths are today—outside the academies that study them, I mean; where they are in a living sense—then we find them in comics. Just as *Metamorphoses* is the great anthology of the myths of the ancient gods and heroes, so comic books today, taken together, are the great anthology of the myths of modern gods and heroes.

There's another way in which Ovid's book anticipates modern comics. When it was reprinted in the Renaissance—as it was, hundreds of times—it was almost always illustrated with anything from dozens to hundreds of pictorial versions of the book's myths. Given that these illustrations were usually aimed at the *hoi polloi*,[4] they were often rather crude, "cartoony" in a slightly stiff, Renaissance manner. This, for instance, is an illustration of the myth in which the goddess Venus cheats on her husband (the lame smith, Vulcan) with Mars, handsome god of war, and Vulcan catches them at it in a metal net he has specially made. It's from a 1497 edition of Ovid.

It's not exactly King Kirby quality, I know. But it has at least *some* of the immediacy of comic book visuals, and it concerns a love triangle involving individuals with godlike powers (we could compare Wolverine, Cyclops and Jean Grey...).

But *Metamorphoses* is much more than merely a grab bag of myriad mythic stories. The one feature that Ovid saw in all the myths

---

[4] Greek for "the masses."

he gathered together and retold was—change. Mutation. Alteration from human to something other than human. In book one, he tells the story of how the god Apollo fell in love with the beautiful nymph Daphne and pursued her, but she evaded his advances by transforming into a laurel tree (the Latin *daphne* means "laurel tree"). Lycaon was an early king whose evil nature prompted him to cannibalism; he mutated into a wolf (once again, the clue is in the name if you know your Latin). Later in the poem, the mortal strongman-cum-action-hero Hercules mutates into a being with supernatural powers who flies up into the sky (he is so weighty a muscleman, incidentally, that Ovid says this makes the sky notably heavier). In all these cases, the poem is describing not situations that are *like* the stories of the X-Men; they are, I think, further examples of *exactly the same thing*. In both works, the world is seen in terms of its mutability.

What I mean by this is more than just the observation that "people change," for example growing up, or growing old, changing from small to big or from live to dead. The changes involved are more profound than that, and more extraordinary, as well. People change in themselves, but they also sometimes change *out of* themselves into things that are quite different. Sometimes people become animals, or gods.

Now of course, not everybody undergoes such radical changes as "human to animal" ("Canadian soldier to wolf," say, or "U.S. senator to jellyfish")—or even more radically, as "human to god" (Jean Grey to Phoenix). Most of humanity continues its mundane existence. But those beings who survive the change become heroes, whose destiny ties them to a greater struggle than day-to-day ordinariness. They must choose their sides; they must decide whether to defend humanity or prey upon it. Not everybody lives through the trauma of mutations: Actaeon, for instance, turns into a stag—but the mutation happens whilst he is out hunting, and before he can put his new-found swiftness and enhanced reflexes to use he is torn to death by his own hounds. But, as with the *X-Men* text, most of those who do survive go on to fight as warriors. Book nine of *Metamorphoses* describes how some of the fiercest warriors of ancient Greece, the Myrmidons, came into being. ("Myrmex" being the Greek for "ant," you don't need me to tell you from which sort of animal they mutated.)

This, in turn, connects with a deeper insight into the nature of things. Sometimes we think of change as something we have to endure, to get out of the way so we can get on with our lives. A kid might think to himself, "I can't wait until I'm grown up, then I'm really going to have fun." The truth is different; any adult will tell you that there's never a place you reach where you can say, "That's it! I've arrived—I'm *grown up* now." The fact is that all of you—your rational mind, your emotions, your body—it all changes continually; you get better and worse, you grow more sophisticated or become dulled by habit, you change your work, your friends, your beliefs, your tastes in music. It's a process that never stops. This is what the philosopher meant; everything changes, nothing stays the same. This is what "mutability" means. Of course, in the real world we don't *literally* turn into wolves or stags. But these myths work as well as they do precisely because they exaggerate the truth for dramatic effect. The heart of the *X-Men* stories is not just the mutations the characters undergo; it's the way they cope with those changes. And that's the heart of our stories, too.

In other words, *X-Men* is a continuation by other means of one of the greatest projects of classical literature: Ovid's epic *Metamorphoses*. It seems like a strange link to make, but perhaps that's only because nowadays a) so few people learn Latin, b) so few people read epic poetry of any kind, and c) so few people, I'm sorry to say, are familiar with Ovid's work. But you (yes, I'm talking to *you*): you shouldn't let your own ignorance blind you. There's no shame in being ignorant—it is the condition into which everybody is blamelessly born, after all. The shame is in *staying* ignorant. Ovid's poem exercised an enormous influence over Western literature throughout much of the last millennium. I don't see any evidence that this influence is fading. Since people nowadays are less interested in epic-length hexameter poems, the Ovidian project is being continued by new writers in new media—the genre pulp, the graphic novel, film—writers who may well not even be aware that the tradition to which they belong goes back at least to the switchover from B.C. to A.D. And what is that tradition? What makes Ovid's poem so enduring? It is his eloquent and multifaceted insight into the fact that the human condition is defined by change, and that a collection of disparate but linked stories about individuals caught up in the sharp end of that change—mutants, in a word—is the best way to speak to human concerns, human anxieties and fascinations, human passions and human life.

REFERENCES

Claremont, Chris (w), and Brent Anderson (a). "God Loves, Man Kills." *Marvel Graphic Novel* No. 5. Marvel Entertainment Group, 1994. (Originally published 1982).

Graves, Robert. *The White Goddess: A Historical Grammar of Poetic Myth.* London: Faber, 1961.

Adam Roberts took an M.A. in English and classics from Aberdeen University and a Ph.D. in the same field from Cambridge ("took" in the sense of "studied for and paid all the fees"; not "stole"—*that* would be morally wrong). Now he works as a writer of science fiction and sometimes teaches at the University of London ("teaches" in the sense of "participates in a cartoony battle of good against evil through the medium of lectures and seminars").

Growing Up Mutant

L A W R E N C E   W A T T - E V A N S

Everybody has one: that moment in our childhood where some event, sometimes so small it seemed insignificant at the time, changed the course of our life forever. For Lawrence Watt-Evans, it happened one quiet afternoon in Bedford, Massachusetts, in the summer of 1963, when he walked into Dunham's Bookstore and... Well, why don't we let Lawrence tell it himself? After all, he was there.

BEDFORD, MASSACHUSETTS, in the summer of 1963—I was eight years old, about to turn nine, a skinny blond kid with four sisters and a brother, living in a big old Victorian house a block from the town common. I got a dime allowance every Sunday—or possibly I'd just gotten a raise to twenty cents, I'm not entirely sure, but it doesn't matter—either way, it wasn't very much, and I tried to stretch it as far as I could. Most weeks I would walk up to the corner, where there was a tiny block of stores too small to be called a shopping center, to spend it.

At the north end of the shops was the Bedford Tailor, which I have never set foot in to this day. At the south end was Harry Silverman's little grocery, usually referred to simply as "the corner store," where my sisters and I bought penny candy. It really cost a penny back then, and certain varieties could be had for less, such as these two-for-a-penny strange green squares called "mint juleps" that you had to soak in your mouth for a minute before they got soft enough to chew, and Chum Gum, the world's cheapest chewing gum, which came three sticks to the two-cent pack.

I'd usually spend a nickel at Harry's, mostly on mint juleps and Chum Gum just because that meant I got more for my money.

But the rest of my allowance I saved for the middle of the three-store block. That was Dunham's Used Books, which was jammed full of marvels—stacks and stacks of science fiction paperbacks along one wall, shelf after shelf of strange old books filling most of the shop, hundreds of books dating back as far as the middle of the nineteenth century. One long shelf held dozens of yellow-bound volumes of the adventures of Tom Swift, Jr., many of which eventually found their way into my possession.

Behind the counter at the front was Mr. Dunham—or, more rarely, Mrs. Dunham—who was invariably reading, interrupting his current book occasionally to glance at his customers and make sure we weren't doing any damage.

And on one side of the counter were two or three big stacks of old comic books in various states of disrepair. The intact ones cost a nickel apiece; the ones missing the cover or inside pages were two for a nickel. Even when the cover price for new comics had gone from a dime to twelve cents a couple of years earlier, the Dunhams had held the line at a nickel.

This is where we bought most of our comics, my sisters and I. Marian, the oldest, would look for anything with horses in it, which mostly meant old Dell westerns featuring the Lone Ranger and Tonto, but she also bought *Tarzan* and sometimes a few superhero titles. Jody, the next-oldest, was a big Superboy fan. Me, I liked anything with spaceships or monsters. I don't think the younger two were buying any of their own comics yet in '63, but they'd look at our purchases when we got them home and passed them around.

None of us bought Marvel comics much; the Dunhams didn't get very many in. The local outlets for new comics in Bedford, the racks in the drugstores and five-and-dime stores, didn't usually carry any Marvels that I saw; I think it must have been a local distribution problem. And also, I think even then a lot of Marvel readers *kept* their comics rather than selling them to the Dunhams.

The store did get a few, though, and we'd thumbed through battered copies of *Strange Tales* and *Tales of Suspense* and *The Incredible Hulk*, but we didn't generally buy them. They seemed weird and, frankly, sometimes a bit stupid—the Hulk and the Thing never did anything clever, they just kept hitting the bad guys until they fell down, and didn't the Human Torch set a lot of things ablaze throwing those fireballs around? Iron Man always seemed to have exactly the gadget he needed, and Dr. Strange didn't make any sense at all. The colors all seemed muddy. My eight-year-old self didn't appreciate these now-classic issues, and my sisters despised them.

But then one day I dug through the pile of comics at Dunham's and found a comic book that didn't look quite like anything I'd ever seen before. The title was *X-Men*. I'd never heard of it—which wasn't surprising, since what I'd found was the first issue, and it was only a couple of months old at that point. The cover image of the five strange-looking heroes confronting the bizarrely garbed Magneto caught my fancy; I handed Mr. Dunham my nickel and took my prize home, where I curled up in the big yellow chair in the living room and started reading.

And I was captivated immediately.

The first element that grabbed me was that these weren't grown men battling criminals in the streets of some imaginary city; these were teenagers at a boarding school in Westchester County. I knew where that was; I knew about boarding schools. And these characters *acted* like teenagers, more or less, playing jokes on each other, mooning over silly crushes and so on.

We were introduced to them one by one—Iceman, Beast, Angel, Marvel Girl, Cyclops and the headmaster, Professor X. And I thought they were *all* unbelievably cool.

For one thing, none of them were called "Lad" or "Lass."

For another, they had personalities. I don't remember much of the plot after all these years, but I still remember Iceman pulling on boots and a hat and sticking a carrot on his nose to look like a snowman, I remember the Beast hanging upside down from the ceiling while reading a book, I remember Marvel Girl trying hard to please the Professor by strengthening her telekinesis with practice, I remember Angel shyly turning away as he unstrapped the wings he'd hidden under his clothes.

And their powers, while fantastic, seemed somehow more realistic than those of most of the superheroes I'd seen. No one here was invulnerable, or able to fly or run faster than light, or stretch himself like Silly Putty. These weren't aliens or super-scientists or magicians.

They were mutants. I knew about mutants. I suspected I *was* a mutant.

Seriously, I did. My parents had worked on the Manhattan Project, building atomic bombs, during the Second World War—who could say I *wasn't* a mutant? It wasn't as if I fit in very well with the other kids at school or anything. I was brighter than most of them, and not very athletic, and sometimes felt as if I was missing social skills the others took for granted. It didn't occur to me until years later that maybe my father's being the only college professor in town might have something to do with it—most of the other kids had parents working for the same handful of companies right there in town instead of commuting to Somerville. Their families all knew each other; my parents' social contacts were elsewhere.

I never considered the fact that neither of my parents was from New England originally, either, and I therefore spoke with a different accent than the other kids. (And any time I *did* start to talk like a New Englander, my father would "correct" me until I stopped. The only thing he never got used to about living in Massachusetts was what the natives did to innocent "r" sounds.)

The possibility that *most* kids sometimes feel left out I would never have believed for a second.

No, when I was eight, atomic mutation seemed a much more likely reason why I didn't feel completely at ease with my peers than any of those others.

And here was a comic book about a bunch of young mutants who had been collected together to defend *all* us mutants from the fear and hatred of normal people. You *bet* I latched on to that.

Of course, I didn't have wings or shoot energy beams from my eyes; the closest thing I had to a superpower was double-jointed thumbs. Still, we were all mutants together, I was sure of it.

So I devoured *X-Men* #1, then passed it on to my sisters, as family rules required—but when everyone had read it, I got it back and made sure it did *not* go up to the rainy-day box in the attic with all the other comic books. I kept it and read it again and again. The main plot was something about Magneto taking over a military base and our greatly overmatched quintet of teenagers finding some clever means of driving him away, and that was all very well, but it was the stuff at Xavier's school that I really cared about.

Man, if I *wasn't* a mutant, I sure *wanted* to be! At least, if it meant I'd get to go to a cool school like that....

Oh, I knew it was all fantasy, but it was a much more attractive fantasy than I'd ever seen in comics before. Most superheroes—well, who'd want to be Batman, really? Not only is he an orphan, but he's spent his entire life working and training and exercising. Superman's too alien to really identify with. And all those guys were adults, anyway.

Nor did kid sidekicks really work for me. I never saw myself as anyone's sidekick—and I wasn't anyone's ward, whatever the heck that meant. It seemed vaguely creepy.

And the whole crime-fighting thing just seemed so unrelated to the world I lived in. The worst crime I had ever encountered in Bedford was bicycle theft.

But boarding school I understood. Playing jokes on your classmates I understood. Having a crush on the cute girl in your class I understood. And a school where *everyone's* weird—well, as Syndrome points out in *The Incredibles*, when everyone's special, no one is, and at that age I didn't *like* standing out.

I liked that even though they were kids, they were the X-*Men*, not the X-*Teens*. It seemed as if they were getting respect with that name.

And ganging up to fight a supervillain with the wholehearted approval of the headmaster was just too frickin' cool for words.

I loved *X-Men* #1. Loved it.

But I didn't see #2. It never showed up at Dunham's. Neither did #3 or #4. And the local drug store or Woolworth's still didn't have any Marvel comics that I could see, just DC and Gold Key and Archie and Harvey. (They didn't carry ACG, either—I never in my life saw an ACG comic for sale new, but Dunham's used to get stacks of them. I could never figure that out.)

After a while, I decided that *X-Men* #1 must have been a one-shot; I never saw any more in the stores, never heard anyone mention the series. It's probably hard to realize nowadays just how little information was available to a comics-reading kid back then, with no comics shops, no Internet, no *Previews*, no *Wizard*. I had no way of knowing *X-Men* was still going.

I never forgot that first issue, though; I would fantasize about attending a school for mutants, about discovering that I *did* have a mutant power more significant than thumbs that bent backward.

And then finally, years later when I was in my teens, I came across more issues of *X-Men*. I don't remember exactly which issues they were; something from late in the original run. I was flabbergasted— the series hadn't been canceled! It was still going! I bought the two or three issues eagerly and took them home and read them.

I was so disappointed!

Because these weren't the X-Men I remembered, the teenaged students at a special boarding school; oh, they were the same characters, but somewhere in there they'd grown up and become just another bunch of superheroes. What fun was *that*? Almost everything I'd loved about the first issue was gone. They still had cool mutant abilities, but so what?

I dug out my tattered copy of #1 and reread it, and yes, it was just as good as I remembered it—but they'd taken all the good stuff out somewhere between issues #2 and #60.

So I didn't look for any more; I didn't buy them when I came across them.

And then in 1975 I came across *X-Men* #95—I'd missed the first couple of appearances of the new team, but I saw that one and bought it.

I was twenty-one, reading comics again after a hiatus; my mother had given my copy of *X-Men* #1 to a church rummage sale while I was at college, but I still remembered it fondly, so I picked up #95.

It was still a superhero team, not the *real* X-Men—to me, the real X-Men were teenage mutants, not adults—but it was pretty good, so I started buying the title again.

There was *some* semblance of the original concept: Professor X was collecting and training mutants. But it was mostly superhero stuff, and they were adults.

When Kitty Pryde was introduced my hopes rose; someone had remembered that Xavier was running a *school*, not a superhero club! But the focus was still on the superheroics.

Over the years, these glimpses of the original concept kept appearing. The New Mutants started out as an attempt to get back to the roots, but almost immediately became another superhero team: teenagers, yes; inexperienced, yes; but they were spending more time in Brazil and Ireland than in classrooms in Westchester. More young mutants appeared over the years, but somehow the stories almost always seemed to focus on the adults, on superheroing, rather than on what I had loved back in 1963 and still desperately wanted to see—stories about growing up mutant and about attending a *school* for mutants. Not a school for superheroes; a school for mutants. A school where everyone accepted that yes, you're different, and that's okay, we'll teach you to handle it.

And looking back forty years, I realize that what I saw in that first issue and wanted more of was the same thing that modern kids are getting from the adventures of Harry Potter. Sure, the conflict with Voldemort keeps the plot moving, but what the readers really love is Hogwarts. Rowling knows that, and keeps the focus on the school, on Harry's classes and teachers and classmates and sports, as much as on the larger adventures.

Alas, Marvel has never managed to maintain that focus: over and over, writers have recognized the appeal of the school setting and tried to drag the stories back to Xavier's School for Gifted Youngsters, but time after time they have slipped away again, to New York and Genosha and a thousand other places, chronicling the struggles of mutant against mutant and mutant against human. The X-Men have not just been another bunch of superheroes, I'll grant them that; they've served as a metaphor for discrimination and oppression of every kind, and that's a good thing.

But it isn't what I found in the first issue. I wasn't black or gay or Jewish, I wasn't oppressed or discriminated against, but I still sometimes felt like an outcast, a weirdo, a mutant. I didn't particularly want to be a hero or save the world; I just wanted to be accepted, despite being who I was.

And Xavier's school was initially, for me, a fantasy of a place where everyone, no matter how weird, was accepted for who they were. No one tried to make them normal. No one pretended they were all alike. The students were all pushed to perform to the best of their abilities, no matter how bizarre those abilities might be.

And I wonder whether that might explain the curious sales history of the *X-Men* titles.

X-Men was not a hit in its original incarnation. When Stan Lee recreated Marvel Comics in the 1960s, he threw a lot of ideas out into the market; some clicked, like Spider-Man and the Fantastic Four, and some didn't, like Ant-Man and Captain Marvel. Hard as it may be to believe now, the X-Men were one of the less-successful creations; they didn't have anything close to the sales figures of the FF or ol' Webhead. The title struggled on for a few years, then went to reprints for a few more, before being reinvented and relaunched in the mid-1970s.

But once it *was* relaunched, it quickly became a hit, and by the mid-eighties was Marvel's top-selling title by a fairly wide margin; it made up such a large part of the business that some comic book shops considered *Uncanny X-Men* (as it had been re-titled) to be the difference between profitability and bankruptcy. What had changed in there? Why was the concept a flop in 1963 and a major hit in 1975?

Oh, there were changes in the comic itself—the addition of Wolverine and Nightcrawler and Storm certainly didn't hurt, as they're great characters. The art, especially during the Byrne/Cockrum period, was better than it had been for most of the early issues. I don't think that really accounts for it, though. What had changed was the rest of the world.

In the summer of 1963, the 1950s were still lingering. Kennedy hadn't been assassinated yet; the Beatles weren't yet on the charts; the Vietnam War was a matter of a few military advisors in a country most Americans still hadn't even heard of. People trusted the government—after all, our leaders had seen us safely through World War II and were fighting the Cold War to protect us all from Communist tyranny. Conformity was seen as one's patriotic duty. And most kids read comic books—those stacks at Dunham's turned over pretty quickly, and every kid I knew had a few comics at home, even if they were just *Archie* or *Richie Rich* titles.

A comic book where the heroes were mutant weirdos did not suit the temper of the times, to say the least. Remembering those days, I think most kids probably found the X-Men to be pretty creepy. *I* didn't, I loved them—but I was an oddball, a suspected mutant.

There were enough oddballs like me to keep the book going, but not enough to make it a success.

But then the phenomenon known as "the sixties" happened. The counterculture began setting its own standards, with *Zap Comix* existing alongside the mainstream fare like *Gilligan's Island*. Long-haired kids took pride in being called "freaks."

And except for a temporary surge during the "camp" craze triggered by the *Batman* TV show, comic book sales plummeted. When I started reading comics in 1959, *every* kid read them; by the time *X-Men* sales peaked in the 1980s, if I mentioned that I collected comics I would sometimes be asked, "Are they still publishing those?"

Comics went from being a mass medium to being a specialized taste: by 1975 reading comics marked a kid as something of an oddball.

And the natural audience for the X-Men has always been oddballs and misfits.

Furthermore, the counterculture had spread the idea that conformity was a trap; the Vietnam War had destroyed faith in authority. More people were admitting their differences, rather than trying to suppress them. People who were different from the norm were no longer automatically seen as creepy and threatening.

That comic book I fell in love with in 1963 had just been a dozen years ahead of its time. The world caught up with it eventually, but *X-Men* was there first.

And I'm glad it was, because when I was eight going on nine, reading about the Beast and the Angel and Iceman and Cyclops and Marvel Girl, I took great comfort in its existence—in knowing, because this comic book was being published, that I wasn't the only kid in America who felt as if he was growing up mutant.

Lawrence Watt-Evans is the author of some three dozen novels and over a hundred short stories, mostly in the fields of fantasy, science fiction and horror. He won the Hugo Award for short story in 1988 for "Why I Left Harry's All-Night Hamburgers," served as president of the Horror Writers Association from 1994 to 1996 and treasurer of SFWA from 2003 to 2004, and lives in Maryland. He has two kids in college and shares his home with Chanel, the obligatory writer's cat.

New Mutant Message from the Underaged

My Life, or Lack Thereof, in Comics

NICK MAMATAS

As I mentioned way back in my introduction, the X-Men has spawned an inordinate number of spin-offs over the past three decades. As well as the original title, we've had Uncanny X-Men, Ultimate X-Men, Astonishing X-Men, New X-Men, Mutant X, District X, Excaliber, X-Force, Xmas *(wait, scratch that last one) and more other X-titles than I can think of at the moment. In the following, Nick Mamatas shares his memories of the first X-spin-off and of how* The New Mutants *reflected his own teen experience.*

YOU KNOW WHAT? Screw Robin. Screw Robin and the little orange motorcycle he rode in on. Of course, I say that now because I'm thirty-three years old, own a half-wild dog and currently live in a state where you don't even need a permit to carry a concealed handgun. Plus, Robin isn't even real. But I always said "Screw Robin," albeit *sotto voce*, because I knew that Robin was a prick. Underage stunt driver, millionaire's kid, athletic nearly to the point of the preternatural—if not for his crime-fighting career, Dick Grayson would have been jacking kids like me up for lunch money and a chance to impress the gum-cracking cheerleaders over by the lockers. The rest of the Teen Titans were just sniggering Socs in a spandex version of *The Outsiders*, as well.

And most of the other teenage heroes were no better. Superboy was clearly a deranged Eagle Scout, waiting patiently for the chance to go on some sort of Space Mormon door-to-door mission in decadent and sinful Metropolis. Captain Marvel? Don't even get me started.

DC was always hokey, but Marvel was little better. Peter Parker's high school years were before my time as a reader; when I got my first issue of *Amazing Spider-Man*, Spidey was already struggling to pay the rent and eating saltines and peanut butter for dinner. I was to follow him into that lifestyle soon enough. The X-Men had Kitty Pryde, of course, but she was a snot, too—the sort of girl who'd brag about her older cousins or some college boyfriend sneaking her into clubs and the like. Rogue was supposed to be a teen, but she was built like she got a boob job for her sixteenth birthday and acted like she was forty.

The New Mutants, however, were different. Cannonball, Psyche (later Mirage), Wolfsbane, Sunspot, Magma, Magik and Cypher, they were the first real teenagers in superhero comic books. Mutation has always been a stand-in for the physical changes of puberty and the identity crises that teens face (among other things), but getting teens right is a lot trickier than that. Chris Claremont's use of the boarding school setting and the already-proven gimmick of an international cast helped move the comic and its denizens from the realm of cliché to characters. Let's hit some of the high points.

Sam Guthrie, Cannonball. A writer to the *New Mutants* letter column once asked something along the lines of "Is Sam Guthrie the strong silent type, or just awkward?" The answer was, cleverly, "Sam's the awkward, shy, strong, silent type—and we like him just the way he is!" (*New Mutants* #7) Sam was a miner's son and the oldest child of a huge Kentucky family who escaped his father's fate (decades of misery, years of the black lung) both literally and figuratively because of his powers. He "cannonballed" his way out of a collapsing mine and then found himself the recipient of a world-class education at Xavier's, in tony Westchester County, New York.

He could have been written as a yokel or as a generic all-American do-gooder, but he wasn't. Sam was eager enough to do well and smart enough to pay attention, but also foolish enough to brag, during a seemingly lost-cause battle, that his ancestors had fought for the Confederacy...in front of his Native American and black teammates (*New Mutants* #74). Accused of slumming by local high schoolers when the New Mutants attended one of their mixers in the guise of wealthy boarding school brats, Sam could only silently sulk, the crosshatching on his shoulders and his woebegone face telling the tale. He knew he wasn't rich—heck, the Westchester public school kids could probably buy and sell his whole family— but he also knew that he didn't dare speak up (*New Mutants* #45).

Rahne Sinclair, the Scottish fundamentalist Christian of the group, could have been very easily reduced to a simple church mouse stereotype. She even had to consort with spirits and demons, but she was just as worried about the state of her soul when the other girls at a slumber party broke out the Ouija board (*New Mutants* #21). And Rahne lusted: she wanted Sam, she wanted Roberto DaCosta, and her feelings were even a greater challenge to master than her lycanthropic powers. Rahne never hated who she was, but did hate who she might become, and I don't mean a wolfgirl. It's a rare thing to see a religious character, and a fundamentally intolerant person, nonetheless depicted with kindness, struggle and a dash of hypocrisy. In the 1980s, in the Marvel Universe, Rahne was utterly unique for it.

And Roberto? Sunspot was filthy rich, thanks to his father and their millions back in Brazil. He was also black, and the immense racism of Brazilian society reared its head within half a dozen panels of Sunspot's debut. His flinging of a racist abuser across a soccer field was just the sort of aspirational wish-fulfillment readers were hungry for, but soon Sunspot was also used to show what it means to be an overconfident pill (*New Mutants Special Edition* #4). Sunspot was strong but not invulnerable, and was much weaker than the usual superteam strongman. Sealing a hospital door against intruders with his solar-powered muscles, Sunspot declared that no force on Earth short of the Incredible Hulk would be able to open the door. "Ain't worried about the Hulk, Bobby, only the nurse" was the reply (*New Mutants* #19). The shame-filled side of Bobby's Latin machismo was depicted as well too, when he accidentally injured Sam and ran away to New York, where his ruling-class income, Third World sophistication and superpowers weren't enough to keep him from sleeping in an alley with tears in his eyes. He was a kid, just like I was, regardless of his mutant genes.

Danielle Moonstar, the Native American Psyche (her hero name was later changed, without comment, to Mirage) was my favorite character. She hated white people. Just didn't like 'em. And the best part about her attitude was this: she wasn't *wrong*. There was no "very special issue" of *New Mutants* where she learned that people are all the same under the skin, despite the fact that this is an ongoing theme of Marvel's X-books. She wasn't forced to challenge her beliefs in order to save herself or her teammates. She just matured a bit, and the fiery extremism of an angry youth was tempered by a bit of experience. She still couldn't watch John Wayne movies with the rest of the team without wincing, but there were no big blowups amongst friends because of it. Her upbringing made Danielle a bit more mature than the rest; she wasn't just another middle-class kid with middle-class values.

Magik was a favorite as well. Illyana Rasputin was such a compelling character that well into the twenty-first century I've met adults who admit that she was their first object of sexual desire. She wasn't drawn in a prurient fashion—the female New Mutants were generally drawn as still developing, rather than as anatomical impossibilities designed for the dateless—but there was something about her. At age seven, Illyana was sucked into Limbo and raised by the demon Belasco, who gave her magical powers to match her mutant ones. Seven years passed in Limbo, but she appeared to change from child to young adult in only moments in the Marvel timeline. The greatest shock she faced when she returned was that none of her favorite clothes fit her anymore.

Illyana had a dark side, just like all kids who read comics do. Adolescence is when we experiment with deviance, and discover the temptations of sex and the severe limits of our personal freedom. Identity is ours for the taking. Hearing the Golden Rule from Superman is meaningless, and even Spider-Man's endless angsting about poor ol' Aunt May gets tired after a while. We don't want to sullenly accept our responsibilities—we want to feel the rage of wronged youth and the hope of freedom. And we know it's a tough road ahead; there was nothing to aspire to in the manipulative and sometimes haughty Magik, but there was much to relate to.

The other characters who rounded out the team were fairly well-drawn, too. Doug Ramsey, Cypher, was a nerd. Even his power, the ability to instantly understand and communicate in any language, was nerdy (and led to a number of contrived plots where only he could save the day by reading the label under some alien self-destruct button). And he knew it. Like a fair number of nerds, he drifted toward the other social outcast of the group, the alien techno-being named Warlock. Warlock was the ultimate foreign exchange student, and early on was used as comic relief, but after Cypher's death he became far more tragic—even going so far as to animate Cypher's corpse in a misguided attempt to cheer up his surviving friends. When was the last time *That '70s Show* admitted that Fez had actual feelings, and a heart? Then there was Magma, a mutant from a long-lost ancient Roman outpost in Brazil. She was blonde, beautiful and aristocratic. Rahne was jealous of her smarts and beauty, Sam was head-over-heels for her, and Magma was oblivious to it all. Like many of the popular girls truly are.

So the characters were good. Big deal, right? We're still not talking Tolstoy here. Indeed no. What we are talking about is a missed opportunity. Teens grow up, but intellectual property with the potential to be licensed to cross-platform media experiences are never allowed to. They can change, and change plenty, but after Claremont's initial run on *New Mutants* ended, the characters were left to the whims of hacks and crossover junkies.

Magma was revealed as a British citizen. All of Nova Roma was simply the result of magical brainwashing. Then that was all revealed to be false as well. Mirage's ability to create mental images of one's fears or desires was turned into the power to control reality itself. Oh, and she had already become a Norse Valkyrie.[1] Then her powers were altered again, and her politics radicalized. Now she's back to where she was in 1983. Magik, the most retroactively rewritten New Mutant, has had too many revisions of character, personality, age and power to even keep track of, and that's without even listing all the alternative universes within the Marvel continuity that have showcased her. The characters hardly matter in a corporate environment;

---

[1] Dani's powers were altered in New Mutants Annual #4. She became a Valkyrie in New Mutants Special Edition #1.

what's important is the number of action figures that can be created from a single template and trademarked name and image. Magma is an American girl in an X-Men video game, a modern Latin Brazilian (who nonetheless is new to things like light switches) in the most recent TV show, and God knows what she'll be like next time she shows up in a comic. As long as corporate copyrights are in danger of ever expiring, I'm sure Marvel will hang the name on some dubious concept or other.

For a time there, it seemed that *New Mutants* was immune from the synergy experiments of the 1980s comics boom. With Bill Sienkiewicz installed as the interior artist after a brief run by Sal Buscema, the character depictions literally defied the toy industry. At first, I joined with every other eleven-year-old I knew in my hatred of the new artist. The panels hardly made any sense; topology was topsy-turvy, and the art was often expressionistic and defied the commitment to realistic depictions and anatomy that most Marvel Comics artists held to at the time. The cover to *New Mutants* #26 is a classic example: It is painted and shows a near-featureless face blending into a reddish sky or landscape. In the foreground, a black-and-white photo of a grim-faced young man is torn in three, and the pieces linked (but not taped or held together) with scotch tape. The image is not realistic, but it is representative. The story line involved Legion, Charles Xavier's insane mutant son. He had three personalities, one for every one of his psychic powers, but we didn't know that until we got past the arrested, unsettling image. The personalities included a nihilistic young girl (a challenge to sexual/gender notions, and heavy stuff for a young kid to absorb) and a B-movie hero sort whom even Professor X was suckered into admiring. There was no room for aspirational daydreaming in Sienkiewicz's dark vision for the comic, and there was no way to make a toy out of his haphazard lines and free-flowing rivers of muted color. Sienkiewicz's run on *New Mutants* was not only my "gateway drug" to alternative comics, but to an appreciation of modern art in general. The art had as great an impact on my growing up as did the writing. Twenty years later, I can still remember entire issues of the run, panel by panel, even though I haven't so much as flipped through a copy in ten years.

I remember too, not daydreaming about being a New Mutant, but literally dreaming of the landscapes of *New Mutants*. The Legion story line took place within a mindscape that jigsawed Paris and war-torn Beirut, and I spent many a night picking my way through it. When I think of the word "cold," one of the first images that comes to mind is of the few lines that make up the lithe body of Danielle Moonstar, in profile, pushing her way through a blizzard to confront the Demon Bear who had long ago captured her parents. (A few issues later, Dani's parents were back to correcting her grammar while speaking to her on the phone; kids don't get no respect.) And when I woke up to life in Brooklyn in a crumbling old apartment over a florist, to schools where crack had even percolated down to the eighth grade and where I sealed a stab wound with Krazy Glue so I wouldn't have to tell my parents, I only wished for the opportunity to take my chances in Limbo, and maybe meet some friends who were as flawed and hopeful as I was then.

REFERENCES

Claremont, Chris (w), Arthur Adams (p), and Christie Scheele (i). "Home Is Where the Heart Is." *New Mutants Special Edition* No. 1. Marvel Comics, 1986.

Claremont, Chris (w), Sal Buscema (p), and Bob McLeod (i). "Flying Down to Rio!" *New Mutants* No. 7. Marvel Comics, September 1983.

Claremont, Chris (w), Jackson Guice (p), and Kyle Baker (i). "My Heart for the Highlands." *New Mutants* No. 74. Marvel Comics, January 1987.

———. "We Were Only Foolin'." *New Mutants* No. 45. Marvel Comics, November 1986.

Claremont, Chris (w), Bob McLeod (p), and Glynis Wein (i). *New Mutants Special Edition* No. 4. Marvel Comics, 1982.

Claremont, Chris (w), and Bill Sienkiewicz (p, i). "Legion." *New Mutants* No. 26. Marvel Comics, April 1985.

———. "Siege." *New Mutants* No. 19. Marvel Comics, September 1984.

———. "The Shadow Within." *New Mutants* No. 22. Marvel Comics, December 1984.

———. "Slumber Party!" *New Mutants* No. 21. Marvel Comics, November 1984.

Simonson, Louis (w), June Brigman (p), and Glynis Oliver (i). "Mind Games." *New Mutants Annual* No. 4. Marvel Comics, 1988.

Nick Mamatas is the author of the Lovecraftian Beat road novel *Move Under Ground* (Night Shade Books, 2004) and the Marxist Civil War ghost story *Northern Gothic* (Soft Skull Press, 2001), both of which were nominated for the Bram Stoker Award for dark fiction. He's published over 200 articles and essays in the *Village Voice*, the men's magazine *Razor*, *In These Times*, *Clamor*, *Poets & Writers Magazine*, *Silicon Alley Reporter*, *Artbytes*, the *U.K. Guardian*, five Disinformation Books anthologies and many other venues, and over forty short stories and comic strips in magazines including *Razor*, *Strange Horizons*, *Chi-Zine*, *Polyphony* and others. Some of his short pieces were collected in *3000 MPH in Every Direction at Once: Stories and Essays* (Prime Books, 2003). A native New Yorker, Nick now splits his time between NYC and Vermont.

Why I Didn't Grow Up to Be Marvel Girl

CHRISTY MARX

Truth to tell, I have absolutely no idea how my dear friend Christy Marx feels about asparagus but, boy, does she love Jean Grey. A fan of the erstwhile Marvel Girl from the X-Men's very first issue, she here takes issue with the cavalier way in which the character has often been treated, lo, these past four decades. From Jean Grey to Marvel Girl to Phoenix to Dark Phoenix and back again to Jean Grey, Christy has followed Marvel's talented telekinetic through all of her incredible highs and embarrassing lows. What follows is her report.

BEFORE THE X-MEN CAME ALONG, I wanted to grow up to be the Batman. I was devouring DC Comics at the time, the only large publisher around. My parents worried about me. It was the era of Fredric Wertham and his anti-comics crusade, the original blame-the-*fillinthemediahere* scapegoater. Worse yet, I was a girl, a little Midwestern girl in an average Midwestern town in an average middle-class family, and I had this . . . *obsession*.

I was obsessed with comic books. Not only comics, actually, but the entire sequential storytelling medium, a big name for what I only knew as comics and which included newspaper strips like *Brenda Starr* and *Captain Easy*. If it had a serious, continuous story, it was irresistible. Then I found an issue of *The Brave and the Bold* in my desk in elementary school and the fix was in. I was hooked. I had to have more. And *more*. I knew the location of every magazine and spinner rack in my town. I would ride my bicycle for miles in search of those four-color dreams.

Is it a genetic thing? Are some of us born with a love for sequential storytelling, with a passion for the visual story laid out in panels with these funky white balloons popping out of people's mouths? I don't know, but if you're reading this, you're one of us. We're mutants, though I would have preferred a better power.

My parents tried to make me stop. I was forbidden to buy more comics. I would smuggle them in under my clothes or slip them through the screen of my bedroom window. They gave up.

So I wanted to be the Batman, possibly because the Batman seemed at least, y'know, doable. My dream fell apart for two big reasons. First, I quickly realized I was never going to be a superior gymnast. Nor a mediocre one. Nor any kind of one.

Secondly, when I began to read up on criminology, it was not about X-Men, but about G-men, with heavy emphasis on the "men." When I was a young girl, it was strictly a man's world. There were G-men, and there were their secretaries. These books made it clear which position I had a chance to fill. So much for being a great detective.

When I wrote to DC and asked how I could get a job making comics, the return letter began with "Dear **Mr.** Christy Marx...." I was reduced to drawing long hair, boobies and a skirt on Robin with a ballpoint pen, thereby creating the first transgendered comic book hero. Not that there weren't female superheroes, but most of them felt secondary, like shadows cast off the primary male characters. Hawkman, meet Hawkgirl. Batman, meet Batwoman. Even the villains did it. Catman, meet Catwoman, who will incidentally outlast you forever, hah!

And don't even get me started on Lois Lane. I loved Lois, but the poor broad was totally schizo, depending on which middle-aged New York white male happened to be writing her at the time. She could be the intrepid reporter one minute and the scheming, jealous, marriage-crazed girlfriend the next. After all, she was billed (back then) as Superman's *girlfriend*. That was her primary role. The career was just a handy way to get her into trouble and give grief to Clark.

One day I walked up to the spinner rack in the local grocery store and there was something new. It was a brand called Marvel. My eyes fell upon *X-Men* #1 with a red-haired female team member on the cover. I took it home, read it ten zillion times and began a love affair that has endured for more decades than I care to admit to in print. You can do the math.

I never questioned that the title was *X-Men*. It was what you accepted at the time and besides, X-People doesn't have the same zing. What mattered was that the original X-Men had Jean Grey and Jean Grey was cool. Stan had his faults as a writer, but he wasn't afraid to let women be women, while making them smart, tough, brave and independent. He also knew how to sneak in the soap opera elements without detracting from the superhero action. Jean Grey in *X-Men* and Susan Storm in *Fantastic Four* were women who held their own. They were full-fledged members of their teams, not anybody's sidekick or girlfriend. They were also women who became progressively stronger and developed new aspects to their powers.

Plus there was Jack Kirby, who wasn't afraid to draw lush, sturdy female characters without necessarily overaccentuating their female assets. It was a book and a group that could easily appeal to me as a girl reader. I could feel included without needing my transgendering pen.

Then three things happened: the role of girls and women advanced dramatically as I grew up; those of us who grew up reading comics became old enough to start writing and drawing them and having an impact on what comics would become; and comic characters were transformed into multi-platform, corporate franchises.

My experiences are representative rather than universal, but the changes are no less real. At the time I began reading *X-Men*, I faced a culture where I was expected to be a housewife and mother, but if I simply had to have a career, I could be a secretary, a teacher, a nurse, a librarian or—getting really glamorous and daring here—a model or a stewardess. I rejected those stereotypes from an early age. I wanted to write and draw comics. By the time I was a teenager, I had created easily a hundred of my own strong, independent female characters.

I went into the world, supported myself, worked toward my goals and became a writer. My progress followed the march of women's rights, increased opportunities in work for women, the fight for equal treatment and a whole new world of possibilities for girls.

Comics mirrored these and other changes in society. We finally threw off the shackles of the Comics Code Authority and as a result comics could actually become relevant and deal with real-world issues. Alternative publishers could experiment and push in whole new directions. And by the time I was able to write comics, I had the wonderful option of writing a book specifically for an adult audience.

Likewise, I watched the X-Men and especially Jean Grey as they grew and developed in the changing world. The Jean-Scott relationship was allowed to deepen and actually go somewhere. Wonderful new female characters were introduced—Ororo and Kitty Pryde were two that I felt had tremendous potential.

Along with other X-Men fans, I was awed by the development of the Dark Phoenix. I was moved, stunned and angered by the death...ahem, the *first* death...of Jean Grey. One of my favorite characters and they offed her! At least it was done with purpose and nobility, even if it was a result of Jim Shooter decreeing that a hero cannot murder billions of sentient beings without paying a serious price for it, since this was back in the day when heroes didn't kill people.

I didn't want Jean Grey dead, but considering what's happened to her and the X-Men since...it would have been better to leave it there.

Were comics treated as a genuine form of art and literature, she could have stayed dead. But even then, and now more than ever, comics serve as a commercial medium to create franchisable characters. In the down-and-dirty world of the economic struggle to survive, comics have been forced to resort to building franchises around their most popular characters, while death has become a marketing ploy.

I mean, c'mon, you didn't really think *Superman* would stay dead, did you? That had to be the height of the cynical use of death as a marketing ploy, but DC was hardly alone in realizing that killing off a major character would up the sales.

While that wasn't behind the reason for Jean Grey's original death, it was easy to see that death and the inevitable resurrection had an impact on the sale of books. The odds that Jean Grey would fail to come back were miniscule. She was too pivotal and too popular to vanish from the X-Men forever.

Jean Grey *did* come back. And she kept dying. And dying. And dying. "What'll we do with Jean Grey this week? I know, let's kill her off again. We haven't done that for, oh, months."

Writers twisted themselves into pretzels to bring back Jean Grey or her clone or whatever bizarre construct would work. It was a given that Jean Grey needed to return; it was just a matter of how it was accomplished.

None of which served any real purpose except as a marketing ploy. It didn't advance the character. It didn't make Jean Grey better or stronger or more interesting. It has become instead a joke. Death has been degraded to the level where it ceases to have real meaning. The only thing left for the X-characters to do is joke about it on the pages of the book itself.

"O Death, where is thy sting?" About two hundred issues back, dude.

As I grew old enough to write comics, I watched other generations of readers also grow up to take the reins of various books, including *X-Men*. Marvel comics in particular, and *X-Men* as an example of it, became more complex, downright labyrinthine, and were aimed for an older audience, with a darker, harsher tone.

I can understand this. We were invested in these characters, in the entire storytelling form, and just as we had become complex adults, so we wanted the books we loved to become complex and adult. The problem is that I saw it taken to extremes of absurdity with any hope of a rational continuity thrown out the window.

It comes back to the commercial nature of comics. They're a product, forged by the directions and desires of the current team of creators who do as they wish until superseded by the next team—who must then either live with what has been done or go to extremes to undo it or revise it. That lack of continuous or coherent creative vision is the largest inherent flaw in mainstream comics, but it's a flaw that can't be resolved. It can't be resolved because *X-Men* (and other such comics) are part of a corporate franchise, and a corporate franchise is destined to live forever. Mickey Mouse is seventy-seven going on immortal.

This is not to lay blame on the writers and artists. I've spent the majority of my career writing franchise characters. There are inherent limitations to what can be done with and to such characters. There is somewhat more freedom in the world of comics than in television series or tie-in novels, but only up to a point. The characters can undergo certain kinds of changes, but not to the point where they are no longer recognizable.

The franchise must be protected. Thus we end up with progressions that are not so much linear as cyclical. We end up with characters being "reinvented" and recast in alternate realities or whatever else we can do to achieve novelty without true change. You can stretch the rubber band to the breaking point, but not beyond. Sooner or later, it has to snap back.

Within this structure, those of us who write and draw franchise characters do it with love and our best craft. We aren't hacks who churn out this material purely for the money. We bring our best creative vision to it with the full understanding that we don't own these characters and cannot control their ultimate destiny. We are momentary caretakers who must, inevitably, pass the torch to the next.

And so there were writers and artists who continued to create stories for the X-Men that I enjoyed and the series maintained a roster of worthwhile female characters. Jean Grey was back, albeit in a strange and convoluted manner, but she was back. But there were at times changes that felt like they were made purely for the sake of shaking up the books, rather than staying true to the characters. Why does a female character, such as Storm, need to sport a Mohawk and black leather and get vicious in order to show her becoming a "stronger" woman? Kitty, who I liked as a slim, endearing Jewish girl, was similarly hardened and her body filled out to the point where she could have been any other overemphasized Marvel woman. I began to feel there was this notion that the only way a woman could be "tough" was to make herself into either a dominatrix or something more akin to a man.

It was around the early 2000s that I really began to feel a decline in the nature of the X-Men and a change in the tone of the X-titles, as well as other comics. What I saw were comics that had fallen into the same unfortunate pit as video games in deciding that boys and males were its dominant audience and that was just the way it was going to be. Mostly this comes from boys growing up on the medium to become young men who set out to create product for themselves rather than a wide spectrum audience. Some of these men are apparently oblivious that how they depict female characters can be offensive and demeaning. And I doubt they would care, if they could even be convinced their work was offensive to begin with (though I would love to be proved wrong).

As with video games, I saw the artwork for female characters become hypersexualized. Sheri Graner Ray has researched this extensively for the video game field, but what she found there applies equally well to comics. In her book, *Gender Inclusive Game Design: Expanding the Market*, she notes that it's common for us to want our heroes to be young, strong and fertile/virile. She lists the physical traits for men as having large shoulders, broad chest, slim waist and hips, large legs and long, thick hair. For females, that list is large breasts placed high on the chest, slim waist, round rear end and long, thick hair.

One might argue these days with the long, thick hair part of it, given the bald look, but essentially the traits hold true. It's a cliché of comic book art that the anatomy of the characters is exaggerated, both for the males and the females. But there's one significant difference, one that Ray notes in her book. This key difference is that the traits that are the most exaggerated in the female characters indicate "sexual receptivity, i.e., those physical traits that say, 'I'm ready for sex *right now*.'"

Ray lists those traits as full, darkened red lips, heavy-lidded "bedroom" eyes, flush on the cheeks, open mouth (to indicate the increased respiration that comes with sexual arousal) and erect nipples.

Finally, Ray points out that the real kicker is that these sexual signal traits are the same for men and women with, of course, one obvious addition. If an artist were to draw male characters with the same level of sexual receptivity, those characters would also be walking around with permanent erections. Funny, we never see *that* in the comics.

This female hypersexualization is what I began to see creeping into the X-Men of the 1990s and 2000s. Women were posed more and more provocatively, sometimes with body positions that twisted them around like a Möbius strip so as to please both the tit man and the ass man simultaneously. Breasts became enormous. Butts jutted out in a way that makes my back hurt just looking at them. Women were posed on covers with virtual labia shots, ready for the gynecologist. The worst of these covers were from *New X-Men*. There's Jean Grey with her legs spread on the cover of #139, next to Emma Frost in her dominatrix outfit. There's the ridiculous excess of the Emma Frost cover #116 which took meaningless costumes to a whole new level while making her look like Lolita. The final panel of #128 managed to sink to the lowest level of smut yet, with Emma Frost in a pose that was lasciviously pornographic…and meant to be. On the cover of #122, we have the Shi'ar Empress with spray-on armor, who had been given a coyly disguised cloth labia right there where it ought to've been.

Hey, I was married to a comics artist. I know all of these tricks because he was exactly the kind of male artist who loved to indulge in as much sexual imagery as he could manage, the more overt the better. He would sneak in whatever he could get away with. When he could do whatever he wanted without being reined in, his work was as pornographic as that panel of Emma Frost. The mindset is akin to the story of how artist Wally Wood, in inking over Ric Estrada's pencils on *Power Girl* (for DC), kept making Power Girl's boobs bigger and bigger just to see what he could get away with and, consequently, the trend for that poor character was set. She has boobs the size of Mount Everest.

I like well-done pinup art as much as anybody, don't get me wrong. A beautifully illustrated, sexy male or female body can be a delightful thing. I didn't shy away from sexuality when I had the chance to create my own adult-market series, *The Sisterhood of Steel*. My warrior-women came in all sizes and shapes, dressed for combat in realistic clothing instead of steel bikinis, had power struggles, were strong and independent, formed powerful bonds that could include female love, and they also got naked and had sex with men. None of this was designed to titillate the reader. It was about writing complex, interesting, real female characters who didn't have to wear spray-on latex clothing, or pose with a protruding butt or display vast acres of cleavage in order to attract a readership—or a relationship. There's a significant line between sexy and sleazy. And if I have to explain it, there's no point bothering to.

And sleazy is where I saw the *X-Men* books heading, a direction that I found deeply dissatisfying as a female reader. To some degree, Jean Grey managed to avoid the worst of this visually, but the phenomenon wasn't limited to the art. One of the nadirs for me was a story line involving a mysterious character called Fantomex in #130 of *New X-Men*. Fantomex uttered a line that he could tell Jean Grey was attracted to him by the tilt of her pelvis. I actually ground to a stop at that line, one that could only have been written by a man. A woman would have been too busy laughing her ass off. I was torn at the time between hysterical laughter and being thoroughly disgusted by the reduction of strong, independent Jean Grey to an absurdity like pelvic tilt. Good old pelvic tilt, it gives us away every time.

Spare me.

I very nearly gave up reading *X-Men* around that time. It was such an ingrained habit, and I remain so much the optimist, that I continued to buy the books in spite of my growing dissatisfaction.

Then came the final straw of straws in the decline of the X-Men. Not only did Jean Grey die—*again*—but Scott Summers dumped her for a slut.

Let's be honest about it now. Emma Frost was created to be a slut. She certainly has nothing to offer a girl reader, or any reader looking for something other than a fanboy fantasy. There is an odd disconnect between the elements of male adolescent fantasy in how female characters are treated, on the one hand, and the writers' attempts to make the books excruciatingly adult, modern and hard-edged, on the other. There's an attempt to give Emma a complex, adult backstory to explain how she became what she was, but she otherwise remained exactly the same—an amoral temptress in a skimpy costume who provides fanboy eye candy.

Scott's dumping Jean for Emma Frost was an insult to the characters, change for the sake of change, to shake up the books and do something titillating, but it sure didn't arise organically from the character development of the Jean and Scott I had known for decades. It felt more as though the writer found healthy, normal love between characters to be boring and decided to sleaze it up with some seduction and adultery. When it became inconvenient to have Jean Grey around, she got offed. But only after she told her husband, the love of her life, to go ahead and have fun with Emma be-cause...well, she's more *fun*, isn't she?

I don't ask for much. Simply that a strong, independent, intelligent and worthwhile character like Jean Grey might actually be treated with some respect instead of becoming martyr-of-the-day and tossed aside in yet another convoluted "death."

So what's going on here, and why am I being so bitchy about it?

Because, damn it, I love comics and I want female characters who are more than a teenage boy's drool-fantasy.

When you look around at other media, you see that film, televi-sion, novels and music aren't afraid to have material that is either aimed at a female audience or designed with the goal of at least *in-cluding* the female audience. The two forms of media that have mis-erably failed to reach for the female audience are comics and video games. They both suffer from the same internal problem—they are primarily created by males for males.

As comics developed a new look under a new generation of art-ists, much of it was excellent and exciting, but much of it was also directed very much toward a male audience; new directions were taken by new writers, but almost all of them were male, writing al-most exclusively for a male audience. In the entire history of the X-Men, there has been only one major female writer of note, Louise Simonson, and she wrote for spin-off books. There were bits and pieces of work done by Mary Jo Duffy and Anne Nocenti, but other than the rare women writers who pop up here and there, the vast ma-jority of the X-Men universe has been produced by men.

It's not like I'm accusing the publisher or editors of sitting down and saying, "Let's make sure we don't hire any female writers or art-ists. This is a *man's* book." Of course not. The reality is that I was al-ways a rare bird as woman who read and loved comics, and there are a ton more men in the field than women. It shouldn't be that way—I don't for one minute believe that more boys are born with the comic-book-reading gene than girls—but it is.

I don't have an easy explanation for why comics became so male-oriented in the first place. My best guess is that it goes back to the cultural limitations placed on girls in earlier decades, back in the days when G-men were men (except when J. Edgar Hoover was wearing a dress). Writing and drawing comics simply didn't fall into the small number of careers considered acceptable for women. It was barely considered acceptable for men, and I've read stories of how those early artists would put on a suit and tie, carry a briefcase and pretend to be going off to a "real" office job.

I was part of the early wave of girls who saw no reason why I couldn't do it, but had no path in front of me that I could follow. I can think of plenty of other women now who are making their way in comics, but the majority of mainstream comics, especially the usual superhero stuff, remains male-oriented. Unfortunately, there seems to be the same inertia in comics marketing as in video games marketing, where everyone is convinced that the books and games must fall within limited categories and hit the male audience, the so-called "target" audience.

It's a self-fulfilling prophecy. Male creators put out a book or game that is male-oriented with titillating art or drool-fantasy women and of course it's going to attract male rather than female readers or players. If you ignore, intimidate or insult fifty percent of your prospective audience, what do you expect? If you make more of the same, you get more of the same. Catch-22. While the doors are certainly open for female creators, there is very little done by the main publishers to encourage creators, male or female, to create books for female readers. This is in direct contrast to the vibrant, thriving condition of manga (Japanese comics). The manga publishing field has an entire cadre of acknowledged and respected women creators. Manga doesn't fear putting out books for the entire range of a reading audience, from child to adult, male to female, in every variation of genre imaginable, and it's already making huge inroads in this country among both males and females, indicating a considerable untapped American female audience—one that could be reached with a new era of female participation in creating comics.

Meanwhile, a new cycle of creation has come around for the X-Men. I am greatly heartened to see writers such as Chris Claremont and Joss Whedon—who know how to treat a female character—at the helm of some X-titles. The artists have either pulled back from earlier excesses or they're reflecting the creative sensibilities of the writers. Either way, I'm feeling better about the female role models

I'm seeing. There's even some interesting "rehabilitation" of Emma Frost in which her leadership role, growing sense of responsibility and relationship with Scott Summers seems to be morphing her into what I would call the R-rated version of Jean Grey. She fills roughly the same niche that Jean did, but without giving up the hard-edged personality or the eye-candy costume.

And sooner or later, Jean Grey will be back. I can only hope she is given the chance to do something she hasn't been allowed in a lot of years—live for a while. I would love to see the return of the Jean Grey I loved for so long: strong-willed, cheeky, independent, responsible, outspoken, willing to take a stand for what she believes in....

Hey, wait. Maybe I did grow up to be Marvel Girl after all.

REFERENCES

Morrison, Grant (w), Phil Jimenez (p), and Andy Lanning (i). "Shattered." *New X-Men* No. 139. Marvel Comics, June 2003.

Morrison, Grant (w), and Igor Kordey (p, i). "New Worlds." *New X-Men* No. 128. Marvel Comics, August 2002.

———. "Weapon Twelve." *New X-Men* No. 130. Marvel Comics, October 2002.

Morrison, Grant (w), Frank Quitely (p), Mark Morales, and Dan Green (i). "E is for Extinction." *New X-Men* No. 116. Marvel Comics, September 2001.

Morrison, Grant (w), Frank Quitely (p), Tim Townsend with Perrotta and Florea (i). "Imperial." *New X-Men* No. 122. Marvel Comics, March 2002.

Christy Marx has had a long and eclectic career as a writer, TV series developer, comics creator, story editor and game designer. She has worked on comics, graphic novels, manga, live-action television, film, animation, computer games, console games and online games, and nonfiction books. In 2000, Christy Marx was awarded the Writers Guild of America/Animation Writers Caucus Award for contributions to the field of animation. Her credits include: *Babylon 5, The Twilight Zone, Spider-Man, G.I. Joe, Jem and the Holograms, ReBoot, Conan, Beast Wars, X-Men: Evolution, Stargate: Infinity, He-Man* and numerous games. Full credits available at www.christymarx.com.

Leading by Example

The Tao of Women in the X-Men World

CAROL COOPER

In 1963, Betty Friedan's The Feminine Mystique *helped change the world's perception of the place and role of women in today's society. Also in 1963, Stan Lee and Jack Kirby's* X-Men *helped change the perception of the role of superpowered mutants in today's society. Now, Carol Cooper attempts to reconcile these two perceptions in the face of a world that keeps evolving faster than either Charles Xavier or Erik Lehnsherr could ever have imagined.*

ALTHOUGH DIRECTOR BRYAN SINGER opted not to helm the third episode in the hit *X-Men* film series (launched by 20th Century Fox with the eponymous *X-Men* in 2000), it was Singer's youthful intelligence that brought exactly the right tone to the first two installments of Marvel's top-selling franchise. A science fiction fan still in his mid-twenties when the project began in 1996, Singer was a product of the post-*Alien*, post-*Terminator* school of action/adventure casting and, as such, was easily able to cope with the dominance of strong female leads in the X-Men universe. A good thing, too, because after racial tolerance and multicultural representation, the normalization of female dominance is the thing X-Men books became most famous for once Marvel put Chris Claremont in charge of scripting stories for this team of genetic mutants in 1975.

One of my favorite moments in director Bryan Singer's *X2: X-Men United* (2003) is the scene where team members Storm and Jean Grey are sent to an abandoned church in Boston to capture a renegade mutant under suspicion of having just tried to assassinate the president. Two beautiful women, one a black "weather witch" and the other a white telepathic telekinetic, face down a blue-skinned male teleport who tries to scare them away by materializing in and out of view while making incoherent threats in German. Jean and Storm watch the show for a minute before Jean deadpans: "Are you bored yet?" "Oh yeah," sighs Storm, as she lobs a low-watt charge of lightning up Nightcrawler's butt and Jean telekinetically lowers the stunned acrobat down from the chapel's nave. No fuss, no muss, no moustache twirling braggadocio for these superheroines. Unlike so many of their male peers—whether on-screen or in print—the female leads of the X-Men saga don't preen and make speeches; they simply get the job done.

As Singer skillfully brings across throughout his two X-Men films, the world of the X-Men is one in which all the best goals of second-wave feminism (and more than a few elements of Dr. King's dream of racial equality) are gloriously fulfilled. Not only are the female mutants smart and self-confident in leadership positions, they are also shown as physically equal if not superior to their male counterparts in every meaningful way. Furthermore, they accomplish this gender parity without any suggestion that they would rather be men or don't appreciate men as potential mates, which is possibly why Singer's male characters don't appear the least bit uncomfortable being surrounded by strong female allies.

A lot of the credit for this pioneering view of gender equality can be given to writer Chris Claremont, hired by Marvel Comics fresh from college in 1969. After starting with other titles like *Iron Fist*, he created story arcs for the X-Men that incorporated the social changes and issues most important to him through the '70s and '80s, maintaining a multicultural team of X-Men for seventeen straight years. The son of British survivors of WWII, Claremont was disinclined to write weak or subordinate females, as his own mother had been a radar operator for the Royal Air Force and further asserted her natural skills and ambitions years later by earning an aircraft pilot's license. Chris himself spent two months laboring alongside combat-ready female communards in an Israeli kibbutz in 1970, so he arrived at the Marvel bullpen with a very international perspective and a healthy appreciation for all-around female competence.

The superhero team book Chris inherited had been launched by Stan Lee and Jack Kirby in 1963, in part to reflect young collegiate concerns of the early '60s. Professor Charles Xavier's original five "gifted students" were all white with only one female, who was immediately cast as the love interest of the shy, introverted group leader, Scott "Cyclops" Summers. 1963 was also the year America watched police dogs and fire hoses turned on nonviolent civil rights demonstrators in Alabama, as well as massive crowds gathering for the Reverend Dr. Martin Luther King, Jr.'s first March on Washington. The idea of mutants being feared and fought against for being "different" had profound social resonance from the series' first issue onward and quickly became a pivotal element in X-Men story lines.

Since Singer's X-Men had to compress years of sequential backstory into a few hours, he quickly telegraphed the first film's stance against bigotry by showing Erik "Magneto" Lehnsherr losing his parents to a Nazi death camp as a child. But during the 1960s, the immediate real-life reference point for the X-Men was the violent turbulence of the civil rights era. Ranking right alongside this racial context was the rapidly changing role of the American woman. The new sexual freedom granted by easier access to effective contraception allowed for new definitions of femininity, which were slowly being incorporated into popular entertainments like Marvel comic books. New York City has always enjoyed a particularly diverse female population; thus, the streetwise, bohemian, Gotham-based writers and artists who worked at Marvel had no problem incorporating the sassy banter of urban barmaids and coeds, the smart, spooky allure of Beatnik chicks and the gritty, working-class pragmatism of aspiring career girls into Marvel's adolescent power fantasies.

Then we have what I call the "Jackie O" factor. Look carefully through *X-Men* #1, and you'll notice a striking physical resemblance between the well-dressed young Jean Grey and our former first lady.

JFK's assassination in '63 led to a televised state funeral wherein the already acknowledged strength, poise, beauty and intelligence of Jacqueline Kennedy was fully revealed, further establishing her image in the public's mind as the ideal modern woman. Cultured, genteel, but resilient and tough as nails when she had to be, Jackie proved a woman can be a lady without being a wimp. In my opinion, the template for female dominance in the X-Men books begins there.

Originally, Jean Grey's costumed *nom de guerre* was "Marvel Girl," much like Invisible Girl, Hawkgirl, Supergirl and Bat-Girl before her. The reluctance of mainstream comics creators to call girls "women" was partially linguistic (let's face it, "Supergirl" rolls of the tongue more quickly than "Superwoman" does) and partially a reflection of the implied support role of female superheroes as wives, girlfriends, sidekicks and surrogate baby sisters. Even though women like Sue Storm of the Fantastic Four gave as good as they got in battles against supervillains, Sue and Marvel Girl were still expected to use their softer, less flashy powers in more defensive strategies than their male teammates. Female villains might be allowed to "fight dirty," as it were, but such unladylike behavior was presumed evil, and, as such, couldn't be part of the superheroine's repertoire.

In 1963, Betty Friedan questioned such stereotypes by publishing *The Feminine Mystique*. Three years later, when Friedan formed the National Organization for Women to fight for equal job and salary opportunities for females in the American workplace, the Pill was further liberating women from passive and restrictive concepts of femininity. Sexual freedom, sexual threat and sexual equality were all starting to undermine traditional male-female power dynamics by the time Lee and Kirby launched the X-Men.

So was it pure coincidence that they crippled Scott "Cyclops" Summers and Professor Charles Xavier (the book's principal male characters) in ways that mythologically allude to sexual passivity or dysfunction? By restraining Scott's uncontrollable optic blasts with a blind man's dark glasses and placing the world's most powerful telepath in a wheelchair because of withered legs, Lee and Kirby gave this superhero team two leaders clearly handicapped in competitive functionality with the opposite sex. Little wonder, then, that the Professor's routine mentoring of attractive, adolescent females never strays away from the chaste and avuncular. His very success in helping young mutants fulfill their individual potential may derive from this lack of sexual predation.

Presumably undistracted by sexual tension, the nubile Jean Grey was able to be mentally, spiritually and physically empowered by Professor X because he treated her neither as a sex object nor as emasculating competition on the field of action. Similarly, Scott's instant infatuation with Jean proved only a minor distraction to her personal development because his eye problem kept him shy, questioning his ability to be truly intimate with anyone. For years, their mutual attraction remains somewhat latent, giving them time to develop as friends and peers before complicating their situation with a full-blown romance. In *X-Men* #1, Jean first proved her mettle by playfully tossing her more aggressive male teammates through the air when they flirted with her. By #13, she was complaining about being protectively sidelined during mortal combat against the Juggernaut, asking why the Professor had called upon the Human Torch for extra help when "[o]ur power is as great as his!" So although Marvel Girl started out as the last and most tentative X-Man recruited to the team, she quickly developed confidence as a power player by being guided by a non-predatory male mentor without the distraction of an active sex life or a jealous boyfriend. It may not have been what anarchist Emma Goldman meant when she described a woman's ideal road to perfect freedom and equality, but it was as close as a comic book superheroine could get in the early '60s.

By 1975, the year Claremont inherited the X-Men title, sexual freedom, abortion rights, Title-IX athletic opportunities and EEOC legislation had vividly transformed the lives, aspirations and attitudes of most American women. Claremont incorporated many of those changes into his story arcs, gradually transforming what had been a somewhat obscure, second-string superhero team into America's top-selling mainstream comic book franchise.

Despite interesting art and character development provided throughout the 1960s by various creative hands, sales of *X-Men* weren't generating an increasing fan base fast enough for Marvel. This may have been in part because the publisher's earlier team comic book series, *Fantastic Four*, had a more winning way with similar group dynamics. The Thing's powerful yet brooding loner was more witty and ironic than Cyclops; Invisible Girl was more feisty and proactive than Marvel Girl was initially allowed to be. The brash flashiness of the Human Torch was more fun to watch than Iceman's milder teen enthusiasm, and the incongruous bookishness of the Beast was never as interesting as the aggressive scientific experimentation of Mr. Fantastic. Moreover, some of the earlier X-Men adventures seemed desperately wacky, as when the team ended up in an H. Rider Haggard-meets-Tarzan fantasy set in a vaguely prehistoric island habitat called "the Savage Land." Marvel briefly canceled *X-Men* as a separate title in 1970, letting individual team members be guest stars in other books until they could figure out how to reconfigure the team into something that wouldn't suffer by comparison to the Fantastic Four.

Writers Roy Thomas and Len Wein, and artists Herb Trimpe, John Romita, Sr., and Dave Cockrum, all threw ideas in the pot to add international recruits to the X-Men's original five-member core. By May of 1975, Len Wein and David Cockrum had fleshed out the basic look and feel of the new team for *Giant-Size X-Men* #1. They added an African American (Storm), a Siberian Russian (Colossus), a Canadian (Wolverine), the German circus performer (Nightcrawler) and, as more experimental tryouts, an American Indian (Thunderbird), the Japanese Sunfire and Ireland's Banshee. Since genetic mutation was logically a worldwide phenomenon, and Professor Xavier's intellectual and financial reach was similarly global, an international team made perfect sense.

This firm commitment to multiculturalism, plus the gradual reframing of Xavier's mutant training school as a refuge for insecure teens whose mutant powers are usually triggered by the overactive hormones of adolescence, turned out to be a key factor in differentiating the X-Men from other superhero teams and thereby attracting a larger pool of new readers. And by replicating the original formula of a male majority incorporating one female, the new additions to the team allowed already familiar group dynamics to be reexamined from a darker, more modern perspective. Indeed, the life of constant crisis, struggle and paramilitary violence that comes along with the role of "superhero" would seem a major deterrent to female participation. What kind of woman would voluntarily live in an environment of constant combat? What kinds of personality adjustments might a woman need to make to even survive, much less thrive, under such conditions?

When we first met Storm in the May '75 story line entitled "Second Genesis" (*Giant-Size X-Men* #1), she was living in Kenya as a half-naked sky goddess, bringing rain to worshipful tribespeople. Completely divorced from ordinary human life, Storm was tranquil and happy, fully able to enjoy her supernormal powers more than most mutants ever do. Yet somehow Xavier persuaded her to leave this stress- and conflict-free lifestyle to join the X-Men in their attempts to save the human race from its own worst impulses. Like Jean before her, Storm was processed into the team as a respected equal, but there was one important difference: nobody flirted with Storm. Despite her exotic beauty, her penchant for casual nudity and her youthful vitality, her male comrades reacted to her as somehow beyond their reach, like the intangible goddess she sometimes pretended to be. Unlike Jean Grey's intrepid girl-next-door, the first black X-Man somehow got cast as the mythic earth-mother/matriarch figure critiqued by many black feminists as both unrealistic and racist in its glib projection of inhuman perfection.

Able to fly and manipulate wind, water and lightning as tools or weapons, Storm is considered the most potentially destructive X-Man after Cyclops, a quality that allows her to succeed him as team leader. But because her ability to manipulate weather can be affected by fluctuations in temperament, she must repress extreme or violent feelings...including passion, lust, jealousy, fear and hatred. Naturally, such emotional detachment was easier to maintain in the sparsely populated wilderness of East Africa. But having signed on for the endless cosmopolitan drama of being an X-Man, Storm's biggest developmental challenge has been to find a comfortable middle ground between the woman she was in Kenya and the woman she is forced to become in America. Claremont once said that he was keeping Storm single when his other mutants—even Professor X—were busy finding romance because "nobody was good enough for her." But how much of her enforced isolation can be interpreted as the price unique, independent women must pay for genuine freedom, agency and respect?

As a child of the early '60s, Jean Grey grew up middle class and skillfully mentored, with old-fashioned morals and time to indulge a long, smoldering teenage crush which became the foundation of her reputation for ambitious pragmatism, loyalty and idealistic self-sacrifice. As a child of the turbulent '70s, Storm grew up tragically, orphaned by a terrorist's bomb and surviving on the streets of Cairo as a homeless thief. Once her mutant abilities surfaced, Storm had nothing but instinct and caution to guide her, and intentionally withdrew from modern human society until Professor X convinced her to collaborate with other mutants like herself. Joining the X-Men was easy and natural for Jean; for Storm it was a massive leap of faith.

Team membership made Jean more powerful and confident, further solidifying her sense of self. But for Storm, team membership meant a loss of autonomy and the unavoidable compromise of important personal values, further destabilizing an already fragile self-image. Their respective careers as X-Men provoked profound moments of self-discovery, joy and tragedy by testing each woman to every imagined limit of human endurance. The ways in which they survived (or didn't survive) each test illustrate the many strategies available to beneficiaries of second-wave feminism.

Linking the parallel career trajectories of Jean and Storm and providing perspective on the next generational evolution in mutant womanhood was the thirteen-year-old X-Man-in-training, Kitty Pryde. Introduced to the team in 1980 in *X-Men* #129—the same issue that sets in motion events that culminate in the suicide of Jean Grey—this precocious Jewish Midwesterner immediately embraced Jean and especially Storm as idols and role models. Kitty's romanticized view of what it meant to be a mutant superheroine was pretty quickly shattered as she participated in adventures that transformed her elder "sisters" in ways the naïve adolescent couldn't understand. Full of aggressive '80s attitudes about boys and her own unlimited potential, Kitty's spunky optimism rescued the X-Men and their complicated story arcs from the jaded heaviness of adult concerns.

Although not a major character in Singer's films (to speed plot development he lets the character Rogue assume much of Kitty's pivotal activity as the youngest X-Woman, and references Kitty only briefly in the second film as the "little girl who walks through walls"), Kitty was Claremont's attempt to include a kid's-eye view of increasingly complex issues of identity, morality and friendship within his story lines. The fact that the "kid" was also female only added to the freshness of her point of view. New facets of each X-Man were revealed relative to how they interacted with this hyper-competent adolescent female. With Storm, deprived of romantic distractions and similar forms of emotional intimacy, the bond with Kitty became particularly close, almost that of a child and surrogate mother. This connection became problematic around *Uncanny X-Men* #180, when we discovered that Kitty held some pretty inflexible ideas about how her female idols and surrogate mother figures were allowed to behave!

One of the most interesting things Claremont did with young Kitty was show that even the most progressive postmodern female can still hold other women to unrealistic standards of stereotypical or conformist behavior. After enduring Jean's death and the unexpected pressures of assuming leadership of the team, Storm suffered the first of a series of mini psychotic "breaks" that resulted in significant shifts in her appearance and attitude. Kitty, who remembered how Jean Grey suffered similarly disturbing transformations in her dangerous Dark Phoenix persona, couldn't cope with Storm's new "realness" and confessed as much to her friend Doug:

> KITTY: When we first met I thought [Storm] was the most beautiful person—inside and out—I'd ever seen. Then, last spring in Japan, she cut her hair, changed her clothes—she suddenly got harder, tougher. The gentleness, the serenity, was all gone ... How can you love someone who scares you?

Later in the same issue, Storm abruptly confronted Kitty for her intolerance and unrealistic expectations:

> STORM: So, for your peace of mind, I must force myself to be someone, something—I am not? ... [T]he longer I remained an X-Man the more I came into conflict with what I thought was my fundamental self. Was I Goddess or X-Man? And if an X-Man,

could I find a place for the precepts that defined the Goddess' life? Initially I thought "yes." Then I became team leader and discovered within myself, as Scott Summers had before me— the terrible capacity to, if necessary for a greater good, sacrifice the lives of those I loved.

What Storm and Kitty were learning here (in part from the unfortunate example of Jean Grey's similar struggle with a split personality) is that humans, even superhumans, have a lot of self-help work to do before they can truly claim to control themselves. Further, there can be no true mental health without embracing both the best and worst qualities we contain. *All* our emotional needs must be acknowledged and addressed, even those we may fear or abhor. Like so many women of their respective generations, both Jean and Storm have innate psychological weaknesses based around issues of sexual repression. Storm fears (from experience) that volatile intimate relationships undermine her control of the weather. Since adolescence, she has isolated herself in a mental straightjacket of artificial calm and detachment to avoid zapping innocent bystanders with stray hail or lightning. Jean's years of waiting for timid Scott to admit and fulfill their mutual attraction left a residue of frustrated desire that the evil mutant Mastermind was able to exploit by yoking and addicting her recently enhanced powers to the insatiably selfish lusts of Dark Phoenix. Jean didn't turn amoral and homicidal just because she'd been "possessed" by the seed-energy of the Tree of Life. She was only vulnerable to being destabilized and destroyed by this cosmic Phoenix Force because her normal human psyche was too conflicted, too weak and too structurally immature to control it under her own individual will.

When Professor X realized that Jean returned from her space adventure as the accidental host of the Phoenix Force, he rightly suspected that primitive human psychology would prove unable to safely integrate and use its unlimited elemental power. And yet, it was still Jean's own unstable human emotions—notably her abiding love for Scott Summers and the altruistic mission of the X-Men— that allowed her the brief moment of sanity it took to destroy her own body before the Phoenix entity could derange and claim her completely. But watching how a combination of emotional instability and increasing power slowly corrupted a female teammate long thought beyond the possibility of corruption left a lasting impression on Storm and Kitty. It understandably scared them to realize that either of them could fall prey to the same kind of corruption. Storm—the older and wiser of the two—understood her case was already different than Jean's and struggled to explain that difference to Kitty, who must logically prepare to undergo similar tests of strength and character on her own one day.

> STORM:...I am learning things about myself I do not like. But I must keep learning, striving to find my true self...my place in the scheme of things. I must know who I am. I must live my life as I see fit. If you love me, Kitten, you must let me do so.

With both secondary sex characteristics *and* mutant powers being triggered by adolescence, the new X-Men books contained built-in narrative reasons to examine how uncontrollable sexual urges and uncontrollable deployment of mutant powers might be linked. Learning to control new, shifting or suddenly erratic powers could easily be associated with repressing, sublimating or transferring sexual desire. The known psychosexual connection between strong emotions and erratic reactions allows the behavior of superheroes under pressure to be rendered more recognizably human. Readers gradually learned that hypnotically tampering with the libido of a powerful telepath like Jean Grey could unexpectedly enhance or distort her natural urges. They similarly learned that Storm could only safely manipulate her powers by firmly repressing or neutralizing her stronger feelings and emotions. This physiological limitation was responsible for her movie character—as played by Halle Berry—delivering dialogue under pressure in a somewhat somnolent monotone. But another aspect of psychosexual subtext in *X-Men* is how sexual sublimation is made possible by the exercise of superpowers.

In Storm's, case this was vividly illustrated in #185 of *Uncanny X-Men*, during a vignette wherein Storm allowed the mutant Rogue to steal her powers for a while in order to experience how she did what she did and how differently she perceived "reality." This occurred shortly before the two women were attacked by a government strike force that tried to capture Rogue with a weapon that stripped mutants of all superhuman abilities. Unfortunately, the weapon neutralized Storm, not Rogue, rendering Storm suddenly as powerless as any ordinary mortal. Deprived of her elemental powers as both reason and tool for sexual sublimation, Storm spent the next few issues of a story arc initially entitled "LifeDeath" as neither goddess nor X-Man, and began therefore to discover the power of the kind of romantic love she'd been hitherto denied.

Rescued from government agents by a mysterious inventor named Forge, Storm first felt her crippling loss as if she'd been rendered blind, deaf, lame and dumb. Then, as a sexual attraction blossomed, her depression lifted and Storm manifested new skills and feelings that were not defined or restricted by her former identity as a weather witch. It was as if her aforementioned quest to find her "true self" was being fulfilled in a most unexpected way.

Jean self-destructed in part because she was forced to cope with crisis after crisis under extreme emotional and mental duress while a parasitic alien entity overamped her already formidable powers to a level beyond human comprehension. Had she been stripped of her powers instead and given extended downtime to process the event, its repercussions and her various options, Jean might have survived all her transitional traumas to reach the same higher ground of increased functionality pursued by Storm. As for sexual sublimation—even Scott must have asked himself (around *X-Men* #132—133) if Mastermind could have fooled and seduced Jean so easily if his own love for Jean had been more passionate. Because Mastermind associated love with lust, violence and cruelty, that combination was the decadent cocktail he used to manipulate the Phoenix component of Jean's personality, for which every embodied sensation was an unprecedented and addictive thrill. Little wonder, then, that once it learned to experience all sensory stimulation as sensual pleasure, the Phoenix moved to all but annihilate Jean's microcosmic personality and appropriated her body as the biomechanical means of satisfying its hunger for more peak sensations.

By *X-Men* #135, Dark Phoenix achieved the cosmic version of an orgasm by making Jean devour the raw energy of a star with nary a thought for its inhabited solar system. Even Galactus was never so cavalier about consuming worlds, and by allowing a formerly beloved comic book character to do something so monstrous, Chris Claremont gleefully broke every comfortable cliché in superherodom. So, when challenged to take Storm through a parallel trajectory (exploring the ways in which women sometimes sublimate sexuality to achieve power, sublimate power to achieve sexuality or integrate both into something genuinely transcendent), he started writing stories in which Storm and those around her—from Professor X to Dr. Doom, from Dracula to the denizens of Asgard—become hyperaware of her sex appeal only to realize how secondary it is to her other virtues.

Shifting attitudes toward sex and women became a big part of the book's increasing appeal once Claremont began scripting the X-Men. Between Plato's Retreat, Club Med, the commercial success of porno films like *Deep Throat* and drug-fueled disco hedonism, Claremont knew that people in the 1970s found ethical expectations within their professional and private lives mutating before their very eyes. Social scientists wouldn't quantify the cumulative psychological effect of all these changes until well after the fact, but through the magic of science fiction extrapolation, X-Men story lines (along with similarly edgy pop music and fashion advertising) immediately began exploring this territory.

When Wein turned scripting of the resurrected X-Men title over to Claremont in the mid-'70s, there were no female team leaders in any superhero comic. Despite Golda Meir, Indira Gandhi and ultimately Margaret Thatcher, the decision-makers in mainstream comics didn't seem ready to portray women running the show. Claremont changed all that. First, he increased the abilities and strength of all his female characters. He gave them complex motivations and more "on-screen time" to demonstrate combat proficiency and shrewd situational ethics. Then, and perhaps most uniquely, he imbued his female heroines with traits prototypically associated with ancient goddess traditions.

In truth, by inventing the concept of a "super" hero, seminal comic writers were merely redefining the term "demigod." They imagined a world where instead of praying when scary things happened, people might expect Superman or Spider-Man—in many cases a more accessible, reliable savior—to do things formerly only God could do. That is why the iconic template of "the divine feminine" becomes relevant to the X-Men: whenever superpowered females dominate the action, the Christlike, patriarchal model for Superman and his ilk usually gets replaced by the more visceral and chaotic template of a volcanically volatile Shakti or a violently cyclical earth goddess.

So when you consider that early superhero comics were designed to be read in the trenches by teenaged soldiers to help them dream dreams of godlike indestructibility and strength in the face of possible death by combat, you understand the need to make ordinary humans believe they can become gods. Or at least superheroes. This is nevertheless a somewhat subversive, heretical idea, which evolved because of a deeply felt ontological gap between the modern categories of "god" and "man," which is also why religious metaphors and tropes are constantly interrogated by X-Men story arcs. But what if the X-Men stories exist in part to diminish the conceptual and semantic distance between Humanity and Deity? What if these books were to erase that fragile ontological gap altogether? What if the X-Men mythos seeks to empower its men and women so they can better accept full responsibility for all the heavens and hells of their own making?

After Jean sacrificed herself in her Phoenix persona to save the world and her own endangered humanity, Cyclops, who had been coleading the team with Jean, quit the X-Men. Storm then assumed his leadership position, becoming not only the first female team leader in superherodom, but also the first *black* team leader. Shortly thereafter, Claremont had her defeat Callisto, the female chief of the Morlocks, a subterranean gang of outcast mutants, thereby becoming *their* leader as well. Claremont then showed us how Storm let her mothering instincts compel her to overextend herself as a leader, culminating in a series of misadventures that led first to a gradual derangement, then to a loss of her powers and a concurrent nervous breakdown.

Was there ever any more obvious a tone parallel to what career women were discovering about trying to "have it all"? By letting his female characters have equal work and equal pay, Claremont may have been among the first to illustrate the unique and sometimes dangerous compromises women make to sustain real control over both career and family life. Yet he never showed such unpleasant trade-offs as being exclusively a female burden. Cyclops, Wolverine and Xavier all suffered through tragic love affairs, each losing a beloved as part of the price they paid for allegiance to their "higher" heroic callings. And interestingly enough, each of these alpha males humbly applied to be consorts of women they clearly considered superior to themselves—one an heiress to an ancient line of samurai warriors, another the reigning empress of an interstellar race and the third a self-sacrificing martyr for the Greater Good. If the sex/power dichotomy still challenges women in the X-Men universe, it clearly remains equally challenging for men, even after they've proven willing to share their power and leadership roles. We just never see them whining much about it. Which could be about to change.

One unexpected side benefit of showing females as leaders is how their less impassive demeanor makes it okay for men to show emotional warmth, doubt, vulnerability and other qualities that might otherwise be considered unproductively effeminate. Even berserker characters like Magneto and Wolverine have gradually revealed more humane and redemptive sides of themselves upon prolonged exposure to women like Jean and Storm. Also, the prominence of expressive, estrogen-fueled personalities in these books has normalized the more flamboyant visual signifiers of inner change and conflict than those previously allowed in mainstream comic books. Telegraphing the increasing burden of conflicting obligations, Storm spent much of the 1980s dressed in biker-chick leathers and a punk rocker's Mohawk.

In late 1983, Claremont took his mutants into an alternate universe of evil magic and gothic horror wherein Storm sold her soul to the devil for power and Kitty Pryde prefigured Buffy's supernatural career by slaying demons while clothed in a thigh- and haunch-baring catsuit. That such bizarre sartorial changes mirrored concurrent real-world pop-star imaging was no accident. Madonna's sexual aggression, Annabella Lwin's anarchic innocence and Grace Jones' gender ambivalence were all very much part of the range of feminine expression exalted by the *X-Men* series back then. Women were portrayed not only as superior leaders, but also became the symbolic liberators of various repressed feelings and powers typically demonized by macho chauvinists.

During the early stages of the Dark Phoenix story arc, Jean Grey's personality was fractured to juxtapose her staunchly vanilla passion for Cyclops against a wildly liberating, S/M-flavored involvement with members of the rich and devious Hellfire Club. Under their influence, Jean became a cruel, Victorian libertine dressed in black corsets and fetish footwear, hailed as the Black Queen in the club's nefarious plans for world domination. God knows such extreme depictions evoke stereotypical male fantasies of dominant women as sex objects. That's why skeptics often dismiss the proliferation of kick-ass cheesecake in the X-books as calculated fanboy pandering. But in this case, Jean's outré attire revealed more about the Hellfire Club and the exact brand of corruption Jean was trying to resist than multiple pages of dialogue ever could.

Jean suspected she was being psychically manipulated, but because she also recognized certain core urges as authentically her own, she struggled, albeit unsuccessfully, to restore mental balance on her own. Sex itself didn't derange Jean, only an artificially induced lack of coherent integration of sexual impulses. The unlimited power and freedom granted by the Phoenix power didn't erode Jean's *humanity*, only her inability to integrate that power with the mechanics of relativistic human morality. The lesson of the Dark Phoenix saga was not that women can never have both secular power and sexual agency in equally unlimited amounts. Rather, the moral was that a perfect balance between the two is both desirable and difficult to achieve, as much for women as it is for men.

Erasing outdated stereotypes about male and female capabilities allowed for subtler characterizations and more sophisticated narratives in X-Men titles. Teamwork and collaboration were always emphasized over gender competition, so that although the '90s saw an increase in male-fronted X-Men spin-off books, the testosterone boost offered by Cable, Gambit, X-Man and Mutant X only helped vindicate the gender parity in team comic books like *Generation X* and *X-Force*. Claremont left the series in 1991, after which a host of different talents continued to design the expanding X-universe, using alternate histories, complex genealogies and digital graphics to sustain reader interest. His return to scripting in 2000 was to solidify a legacy of quality innovation upon which few have improved.

Among the many contributions Claremont's more sophisticated plotting devices made to industry-wide shifts in how female action-heroes were written and deployed was his routine depiction of female physical bravery. While I have little doubt that ballsy babes from '70s blaxploitation and chop-socky flicks influenced people like Claremont, his peers on the early alternative comics scene such as Howard Chaykin (*American Flagg!*), Frank Miller (*Martha Washington*) and Alan Moore (*V for Vendetta*) were all comfortable writing women who challenged authority, fought hard and even won against formidable odds. These men wrote comic book women who were allowed to be both violent and sexual with no apologies. But Claremont, by virtue of working inside a corporate machine with the ability to distribute his particular style of storytelling to kids around the globe, mainstreamed the kinds of feisty females who were worthy of respect even before Ripley, Sarah Connor, Xena or Buffy made the scene. Before Cameron's *Dark Angel* or Tarantino's Bride...hell, even before Thelma and Louise, the sisterhood of Marvel mutants were doing it for themselves, often far beneath the radar of real-life working women who might have appreciated such role models.

REFERENCES

Claremont, Chris (w), John Byrne (w, p), and Terry Austin (i). "And Hellfire is Their Name!" *X-Men* No. 132. Marvel Comics, April 1980.

———. "Dark Phoenix." *X-Men* No.135. Marvel Comics, July 1980.

———. "God Spare the Child…" *X-Men* No. 129. Marvel Comics, January 1980.

———. "Wolverine: Alone!" *X-Men* No. 133. Marvel Comics, May 1980.

Claremont, Chris (w), John Romita, Jr. (p), and Dan Green (i). "Public Enemy." *Uncanny X-Men* No. 185. Marvel Comics, September 1984.

Claremont, Chris (w), John Romita, Jr. (p, i), Dan Green, and Bob Wiacek (i). "Whose Life Is It, Anyway?" *Uncanny X-Men* No. 180. Marvel Comics, April 1984.

Claremont, Chris (w), Barry Windsor-Smith (p), and Terry Austin (i). "LifeDeath." *Uncanny X-Men* No. 186. Marvel Comics Group, October 1984.

Lee, Stan (w), and Jack Kirby (p, i). "X-Men." *X-Men* No. 1. Marvel Comics, September 1963.

Lee, Stan (w), Jack Kirby, Jay Gavin (p), and Joe Sinnott (i). "Where Walks the Juggernaut!" *X-Men* No. 13. Marvel Comics, September 1965.

Wein, Len (w), Dave Cockrum (p, i), and Pete Iro (i). "Second Genesis." *Giant-Size X-Men* No. 1. Marvel Comics, May 1975.

Carol Cooper is a New York-based journalist and cultural critic who has been writing professionally about books, music, film, pop trends and social issues for over twenty years. Her work has been published in various national and international publications, including *Essence*, *Elle*, *Latin N.Y.*, *The Face* (England), *Actuel* (France), the *Village Voice*, the *New York Times* and *Rolling Stone*. Her work has been cited in academic journals, and her critical and sociological essays have been included in a number of anthologies, including *Rolling Stone: The '70s* (Little, Brown and Company), *Brooklyn: A State of Mind* (Workman Publishing Company), *Dark Matter 2: Reading the Bones* (Warner Aspect) and *The Rolling Stone Book of Women in Rock* (Random House). She is a member of the national nonprofit comics advocacy group Friends of Lulu and a 1974 graduate of the Clarion Writer's Workshop for Fantasy and Science Fiction. She is widely traveled and holds both B.A. and M.A.L.S. degrees from Wesleyan University in Connecticut.

Dear Magneto

A D A M - T R O Y   C A S T R O

Herewith, in a noble effort to point out the inherent flaws in Erik Lehn-sherr's master plan, the always entertaining Adam-Troy Castro attempts to engage in a little one-sided correspondence with the Mutant Master of Magnetism—only to discover that, when you're trying to reason with Magneto, the postman only rings once... then runs for his life.

24 Aug 2005

Attn: Mr. Erik Lehnsherr
Satellite M
Constant Orbit above Cities of Man
Marvel-Earth, Multiverse

Dear Erik:

First off, I want to thank you for taking time from your busy schedule of fighting superheroes, soliloquizing and plotting the overthrow of human civilization long enough to read these few words by a mere member of baseline humanity. I understand that these words, however pertinent, make demands on your time that you're likely not

able to afford, what with all the other supervillains and megalomani-
acs out there plotting their own assaults on the halls of power. I assure you that I will try to keep this missive brief and to the point.

Secondly, I must extend my best wishes for your health and the
health of your family. I heard about what happened to your daughter, Wanda. I was most sorry to hear it and can only hope that with
therapy, and perhaps a reality-altering crisis or two, she may enjoy a
complete recovery. My best to Pietro, as well. Tell him he's a hard guy
to catch up with. Ha, ha.

Thirdly, I must assure you that I write these words with all possible respect and with no intention of causing you irritation or pain.
Believe me, the last thing I want to do is invite your anger. I know
that most people in your profession, yourself included, have histori-
cally reacted to the interference of mere human beings by "chastis-
ing" them for their "effrontery." I can only beg you not to imprison
me in twisted steel girders until you've heard and considered everything I have to say. As it happens, I've made a long study of your
forty-year crusade to bring mankind under the heel of mutant domination, including your many decades of conflict with the students of
your old friend Charles Xavier, and I believe it possible that I might
be able to offer some insights into your situation that you might have
overlooked.

Let's see if I'm correct about the basics.

You started life as an Eastern European Jew[1] whose family was wiped
out by the Nazis. You barely survived Auschwitz and emerged with the
same "never-again" mindset that drives the state of Israel and such
organizations as the Jewish Defense League. When you manifested
your mutant ability to manipulate the forces of magnetism, you once
again witnessed humanity's irrational hatred for those born different,
and you vowed to protect the new race you dubbed "*Homo superior*"
from the fear and distrust of those who would otherwise seek to exterminate this emerging subspecies of humanity. You further decided
that you could best accomplish this goal by conquering the world and
placing all mankind under a martial dictatorship administered by mutants and ruled by yourself as benevolent dictator.

---

[1] Though, yes, opinion on this varies.

I'm aware that this plan has undergone changes from time to time and that your plans for baseline humanity have included everything from a protected future as second-class citizens to outright extinction at the hands of their mutant rulers, depending on your mood on any given day. (I suppose that, some days, you're more upset with us than others—a position I can heartily agree with, as I read the papers, too.) But the basics remain consistent: mutants in charge, yourself in charge of the mutants.

It's the fundamental, fatal flaw in that plan that I wish to discuss with you today. And I think it has to do with the very nature of the mutant phenomenon, as described in the comic books, novels, motion pictures and cartoons delineating the various ups and downs of your struggle.

You see, I think things would be much easier for you were there some kind of uniformity involved. If every single mutant had the same powerful ability—let's say, the ability to shoot lightning from their fingertips—then everybody within your class would be equal; you'd have a bunch of baseline *Homo sapiens* who need to keep their electric bills paid up and a bunch of crackling *Homo superior* types who don't. There'd be a clear advantage between one group and the other. And in any post-conquest world run by the lightning-types, nobody would have any doubt where they stood. You would either have lightning powers or you wouldn't.

But that's not the way things are, is it?

The mutant gene is all over the place. You have guys who can climb sheer walls.[2] Guys who can teleport.[3] Guys who are merely a little tougher and stronger and faster and meaner than the average.[4] Guys like yourself who can manipulate the fundamental forces of the universe.[5] And, it's been established, guys whose powers are really, really lame. Like one woman we saw in some comic book sometime, and cannot place, whose entire gig was the ability to transform a red rose into a white one. And, my all-time favorite, this guy from Arkansas whose mutant ability makes him the best truck driver ever

---

[2] Nightcrawler.

[3] Also Nightcrawler, come to think of it. And the Vanisher.

[4] You've felt the claws. Need I say the name?

[5] Proteus. Your daughter Wanda. And certain others we'll be mentioning soon.

born to the job.[6] Hell, we even know of one elderly mail carrier in Manhattan who claims superpower status for his ability to, as he puts it, "wiggle (his) ears real good,"[7] and if we concede that the muscular control necessary for pulling off that little trick might be genetically based, then he might actually have a point.[8]

Examine these folks and you establish what the devotees of your adventures figured out long ago: that the power scale in your universe is not a binary issue, separating those who have it from those who don't, but a continuum, where the majority of baseline humanity occupies a single point on the graph that runs all the way from "totally disabled" on the left to "might as well be God" on the right. That decimal point (reflecting, let's say, a human being in his twenties, of average intelligence, health and physical fitness) may be much closer to the "disabled" extreme than it is to your own position within spitting distance of the "might as well be God" end of the graph, but not all mutants can claim such a wide gap between themselves and the human beings you scorn. Most fit the paradigm your colleague Charles Xavier referenced in naming his students the X-Men: human beings, with a little extra.

This would not be a problem in a peaceful world where diversity was celebrated and the weak were never subject to the whims of the strong. I recognize we don't live in such a world, more's the pity.

But neither would the subjects of your proposed mutant paradise.

And that, I'm afraid, is where we would really run into the conceptual problems with your plan.

Let's imagine a future where you've taken over. Baseline human beings are not an issue, for whatever reason. Either they've been exterminated, or the mutant gene has become so dominant that everybody possesses a superpower of some kind, or they're just living underground, working crap jobs like processing sewage, or sweeping the streets, or telemarketing. Whatever. They're irrelevant.

---

[6] Razorback. The single most endearing superhero in Marvel history.

[7] Willie Lumpkin. The Fantastic Four's mailman and one-time paramour of Spider-Man's Aunt May.

[8] Thus leading to the image of a fleet of mutant-hunting Sentinels converging on Willie Lumpkin in the middle of Manhattan, and their leader crying out, "N-no! ABORT MISSION! He's TOO POWERFUL!" Spend enough time thinking about these issues, and you do tend to get a little punch-drunk.

Everybody worth talking about has superpowers.

Further, let's posit a fellow whose superpowers are minimal. He can jump fifteen feet straight up, bench-press about a thousand pounds and, while not quite bulletproof, will not be harmed by most knives. You know the type I'm talking about. In the world you're living in, he wouldn't last thirty seconds against the likes of Spider-Man, but he might be able to give Daredevil or the Punisher a few anxious moments, on a good day. He's clearly a mutant, clearly a guy whose chromosomes buy him a place in this mutant paradise of yours, but not a person who poses any serious threat to the entrenched power structure.

Do you know what the citizens of your mutant paradise would call this man? I mean, aside from his given name?

Human, that's what they'd call him.

Your citizens would inevitably develop a value system similar to that demonstrated by comic book readers, who are known for deriding mutants with less-than-impressive powers as lame. They'd look upon a guy like our bulletproof high-jumper and say, well, he's not really all that. He's practically *normal*. He's almost (shudder) *Batman*.[9] And they'd discriminate against him and anybody on his approximate scale, bullying them, penning them up in ghetto neighborhoods and denying them any meaningful place in the new power structure.

So it turns out that all you've really accomplished, by removing baseline human beings from the graph, is a repositioning of the point that represents your despised minority.

In short, you've done nothing but establish a new baseline.

This shift in your society's paradigm is much like what happened to the X-Man Warren Worthington III, better known as the Angel. At the onset, he was the only member of Xavier's team capable of unassisted flight. This one power, and the visual kick of a dude with wings, was more than enough to earn him an honored position on the team for years and years and years. And why not? It's an impressive thing to be able to do. It's certainly more than any of the readers of the comic book could do.

But a couple of decades later, your world was growing overpopu-

---

[9] Yes, I'm aware he's a DC citizen. I'm just using him as an illustration. Substitute Moon Knight, if you must.

lated with mutants who could not only fly but do other things, like shoot zap beams, or throw devastating punches, or exceed the speed of sound. In such a world, the Angel's really quite remarkable power was perceived as "lame." (This even by readers who grew winded after climbing a flight of stairs.) And so he became the Archangel, with powers that included great strength and the ability to shoot razor-sharp blades from his wings. It unfortunately made him a lot less interesting, but it put a little more space between him and that dreaded baseline. And that was, really, just an editorial judgment. Can you really sit there and say with confidence that a guy with the Angel's capabilities would be immune from societal judgment, as well? That he wouldn't be laughed at, and discriminated against, by guys capable of blowing up entire city blocks with a mean look?

In other words, Erik, your mutant paradise would fail to protect the weak from the strong. It might redefine those qualities, but it would also cement the divisions in place. Before long, your citizens would develop a vocabulary capable of codifying their own places on the power graph and expressing contempt and condescension for those not quite as privileged. Before long, the people in the "might as well be baseline human" category will find that classification enshrined no longer in status but in actual fact. And you'll find yourself living out the axiom proposed by one Thomas Jefferson, who knew what he was talking about. He said that revolutions need to be refought every twenty years. Given the aggressiveness of some of your peers, I'm not even entirely sure I'd give you that long.

That's Point One.

Point Two is that any society where status is determined by accident of birth tends to put a lot of jerks and assholes into positions of power.[10]

You've met some of these jerks. Some of them are called politicians and others are called supervillains. In fact, Erik—and I say this with all possible respect, knowing the heartfelt motivations behind your crusade—there have been times in your life where you've had more in common with them than with the principled freedom fighter you proclaim yourself to be. But in a world where mere power is

---

[10] Again, read the newspapers. Or watch *The Apprentice*.

perceived as superiority, it's inevitable for some of these folks to wind up in positions of wealth and authority, and that's where your real problems will begin.

Let's discuss, for a moment, the kind of personality we're talking about.

I'll employ you as contrast, and assure you I mean this in the best possible way. Your full honorific is Magneto, Master of Magnetism. You are perceived as one of the most powerful mutants in the world, and a lot people think that's just because you command one of the binding forces of the universe. But that's really the least important thing about you. Few people, with the possible exception of Charles Xavier, consider that your abilities do little but define the nature of your potential; it is your drive, your charisma, your leadership and your vision, however misguided, that render you a controversial, influential figure capable of inspiring respect from even your greatest enemies. It's the main reason why the X-Men have been so often tempted by your cause and why you have more than once been tempted by theirs. Wannabe world-conqueror or not, you have *character.*

But you're not the only guy on your world with a command of a binding force of the universe. Two others come to mind right away. They're not generally believed to be mutants, but they are the kind of personalities I'm talking about. And while they may well be as powerful as you and therefore in potential as formidable as you, nobody can say either fellow comes close to being in your class.

First case: Max Dillon, a.k.a. Electro.

I've written four novels touching at least in part on the mental limitations of this particular dickweed, but as you may not have encountered them, and I'm not entirely certain whether you've encountered him, I'll summarize his qualifications. Here's a guy who, thanks to a high-voltage wire accident that fails to make a lick of sense,[11] developed the ability to generate, store and absorb massive amounts of electricity. He can cause citywide blackouts, control lightning, reduce buildings to craters, vaporize large bodies of water and terrorize

---

[11] Hence my own secret theory that he's a mutant, whose abilities were merely activated by that high-wire accident.

entire populations. In short, his sheer potential makes him an individual of genuinely world-shaking import.

Now, what a guy like this could do with such power depends entirely on his ambitions. If he wanted money, he could get a job at the local power company and earn millions of dollars a day driving the turbines. And if he wanted conquest, it wouldn't be difficult for him to work out a campaign of terrorism, resource acquisition and recruitment of allies that could have rendered him as influential, and as widely feared, as yourself. I mean it, Erik. Either way, this guy faces a literally (ha, ha) glowing future.

Now I want to tell you what he does with his powers.

I'm serious, Erik. I hope you're not drinking coffee.

If you are, I advise you to put it down.

Take a deep breath.

Brace yourself.

Max Dillon, a.k.a. Electro, employs his ability to generate unlimited electrical power...by breaking into safes, burglarizing jewelry stores and robbing banks.

Read that sentence again, Erik. I'm not kidding.

He takes a gift that could have earned him enough for a luxurious retirement by his first coffee break and uses it to commit garden-variety felonies. Oh, and beat up on Spider-Man. Who, by the way, always wins.

Now, I know you're not about to underestimate Spider-Man. After all, you fought him once, and he beat the crap out of you, too. Granted, the wall-crawler was by several orders of magnitude more powerful than usual on that particular day, for reasons we don't have the time or space to get into right now, but you nevertheless got a sense of the guy's personality, and you know that he's well used to fighting way out of his weight class. But that shouldn't matter. The fact remains that we're talking about Electro, a possible mutant with the powers of a god, who seems to have all the drive and imagination of a sack of dead cats.

And who would just about have to be one of your society's gifted elite.

Forget the guy who can jump ten feet and lift a thousand pounds, who might actually have a brain on his shoulders and a desire to do the hard work of administering your perfect world.

That guy is marginalized.

Electro, or some other powerful yutz with the brain of a marmoset, winds up as Secretary of Agriculture.

And Electro's a regular Stephen Hawking compared to the other guy I have in mind. Again, I'm not sure whether you've ever run into this particular genius, but it doesn't matter. I'm sure you've heard of him.

His name's Graviton.

He started out life as a mediocre scientist, lonely and despised and harboring an unrequited crush on an attractive young lady who worked in the same facility, but a lab accident blah blah blah blah blah blah blah (you know the drill; something like it happens every Wednesday where you come from), and gave him full command over the powers of gravity. In practice, this gave him powers that superficially resemble your own, albeit in a greater fashion. He could fly, levitate objects the size of Manhattan Island, trap superheroes behind shields of "solid gravity," cause objects to collapse under their own mass and so on, a range of abilities that clearly places him well within the "might as well be God" category. Indeed, any fair overview of his activities cannot avoid the conclusion that his power level probably outstrips your own—as I don't recall you ever doing anything quite as flamboyant as suspending an entire mountain comprising millions of tons of dirt and stone and vegetation over Manhattan Island for hours on end. That would be a bit much even for you. Graviton did it without popping a sweat.

And yet you're a figure known and feared throughout the world, while Graviton is a footnote who shows up now and then to rant about his greatness until somebody knocks him silly.

Why?

Well, let's talk about Graviton's level of ambition.

When he developed his godlike powers and attacked Manhattan, holding the Avengers at bay, his number one ambition was getting that pretty young thing at his laboratory to pay more attention to him.[12]

Really.

---

[12] In short, Graviton is a guy who can crack the Earth in two like an egg, and still can't get laid.

We're talking Brain Trust, here. This guy isn't fit to carry Electro's book bags.

And yet, were he a mutant rather than a yutz lucky enough to get caught in a blah blah blah lab accident, your ideal society would render him part of the powered elite: the kind of guy you would have to trust to contribute to the everyday infrastructure. If you conquer the world and destroy all human opposition, just how long do you think you would enjoy peace before you had to deal with the capricious, me-first whims of people like him? Let alone any of the other people your perennial opponents—not only the X-Men but superheroes throughout your world—have to deal with on a daily basis? People whose motivations are not utopian, as you claim yours to be, but petty, brutal, sociopathic, self-aggrandizing or downright nihilistic? People whose personalities have been so twisted by the acquisition of superhuman power that they cannot live within society's rules? Do you honestly believe that they'll respect your mutant laws any more than they respect the laws of the world you seek to overthrow?

This, Erik, is the entire core of your problem.

Let's make this even clearer by putting it in terms of baseline humanity.

Posit a world-champion heavyweight boxer: a man of tremendous physical strength, impressive endurance and formidable training, whose fists qualify as deadly weapons. This is a man capable of killing another human being with his bare hands. And yet he must obey certain rules. He only fights people within his weight class. He must restrain himself from engaging in practices now prohibited for safety reasons. He cannot attack his opponent until the round begins, must stop when the round ends and, even within rounds, must back off when instructed to back off. For all his power, he knows that failure to fight within these guidelines will lose him the fight, the respect of his fans and quite possibly his career. And when he leaves the ring and returns to everyday life, he cannot just break the jaw of any random civilian he happens to run across on the street. Powerful as he is, successful as he is, wealthy as he is, he must live within a societal context.

Stripped of all legal consequences for misbehavior, many men with this fellow's capabilities would continue to display honor in the ring and respect for the personal space of other human beings outside the ring. Others would not. The threat of legal culpability is what bridges that gap, hammering home the lesson that the mere ability to beat people into bloody pulps is not license to do it at will to any random person who irritates you.

I'm sorry to say this, Erik, but you must know it as well as I do: too many members of your fraternity don't know that.

You must be able to name a thousand people who can knock down walls. Some need fists, others gesture, some shoot force beams through their eyes and still others can just stride through any construct of stone and plaster without even getting their hair mussed. The majority of these folks understand that knocking down walls willy-nilly is just plain rude. It inconveniences people. Which is why they try to avoid it. Still others knock down walls only when they absolutely have to, in part because they don't want to get in trouble. And then there's that third demographic: the guys who knock down walls just because they can and bitterly resent being told, by anybody, that this kind of behavior is not appreciated—guys with the smarts of Electro and the imagination of Graviton, who persist in such obnoxious behavior even when they're beaten up every single time they do it.

Guys like that are already out of hand in your world. They already live with a ridiculous sense of entitlement, when there's no evidence supporting their worldview. Can you imagine how pushy they'll be when you conquer the world and declare them members of the elite? Your streets will be littered with the rubble left behind by the very same people who cover your streets with rubble today: the ones who consider every wall an imposition and every locked door a slap in the face.

So your very first job, as President or King or High Poo-Bah or whatever you choose to call yourself, will be establishing some kind of law-enforcement apparatus: a system capable of responding to superpowered folks, whatever their power level, who step over the line. Ideally, this system will curtail those with insufficient respect for law, imprisoning the ones who cannot be controlled any other way. It might even require you to terminate, i.e., kill, the few who present an ongoing public threat.

And while I can very well imagine you accomplishing such measures, Erik, it amounts to nothing more than replacing the power structure you spent so much effort tearing down with another that differs from it in no significant fashion. You'll still have superheroes and supervillains and huge battles in the city streets, and issues identical to those you've dealt with all your life. Again, all your struggles will have amounted to nothing whatsoever beyond a simple shift of the baseline and a new paradigm separating those with power from those without.

You may find this offensive, Erik, but I say it with all due sadness: given the realities you'd be facing, I wouldn't be all that surprised to find you commissioning a fleet of Sentinels.

Say hello to the New Boss. Same as the Old Boss.

The good news is that the alternative already exists.

Your world was once the home to a great, unknown philosopher, whose one sterling epiphany, spoken in passing to a nephew, was so clear, so primally correct, that its resonance continues to loom large in your life and the lives of just about everybody you know. "With great power," this philosopher said, "comes great responsibility." I would argue that this has been equally valid for every compact from the lowly driver's license to the ability to control the forces of magnetism. Untold suffering in your world and in mine has been brought about solely by the failure to grasp this one simple constant. Your mutant utopia is doomed to failure precisely because it gives those with great power even more power without requiring them to take on the accompanying responsibility.

Alas, the philosopher who spoke those words is dead. A terrible, tragic thing. But he's not the only person in your world who's put his realization into daily practice. And I think we both know the name of one man who has spent his life training other people of great power to take on, and meet, equally awesome responsibility.

And, not coincidentally, he's the one person who hasn't given up on you.

I wish I could trust you to do the most sensible thing.

But, honestly: I think you'd save yourself a lot of trouble if you gave Charles Xavier a call.

Respectfully yours,
Adam-Troy Castro

Adam-Troy Castro's fiction includes the Magneto story "Connect the Dots," from the Marvel anthology *The Ultimate Super-Villains*. His contributions to BenBella anthologies include essays on *Alias*, *King Kong*, Superman, Wonder Woman and Harry Potter. His solo volume about the CBS TV series *The Amazing Race* will see print in late 2006.

Acknowledgments

Many thanks to Christopher Johnson for his assistance throughout the project, and to Dean Clayton of *UXN* (http://www.uncannyx-men.net/) and Tara Devlin of *Legendary*, the X-Men fanlisting (http://www.sirenscall.org/xmen/), for their help reviewing the manuscript.

And particular thanks to Erica Lovett for her invaluable research and copyediting support. Without her, *The Unauthorized X-Men* would be a much lesser book.